An Introduction to
Coaching Skills

Praise for Previous Editions

'Christian again provides both experienced and novice coaches with an art-and-science of coaching gem. In addition to a deceptively thorough and jargon-free history of coaching theory he skilfully describes each step on the pathway to becoming an effective and authentic coach. Each signpost on the journey facilitates a seamless flow of information from basic to more advanced skills, and the content is richly augmented by his characteristic and innovative use of video, activity, stories and applications. This is an excellent resource for both educator and practitioner.' **Sandy Gordon, University of Western Australia**

'Christian van Nieuwerburgh is a world authority in coaching and is leading the intersection between coaching and positive psychology. His book offers the perfect balance of science and practice. The evidence-based tools, strategies and resources will help you excel as a coach so you can help your clients excel in their endeavours.' **Professor Lea Waters, University of Melbourne**

'An inspiring, creative and empowering book about coaching that is as valuable to the novice as it is to the experienced coach. Christian resourcefully draws on and demonstrates coaching skills, connects with the reader and their personal learning journey, and links back, in a stimulating way, to theory, research, coaching culture and the rich connections between coaching, living and what it is to be human.' **Professor Mary Watts, University of London**

'Finally a text that encapsulates theory, application, ethics, supervision, anecdotal examples, visual demonstrations and concepts such as "the way of being" that are often intangible. This text is a must for all students studying in the the area of coaching and counselling – a one stop shop.' **Dr Suzanne Vidler, School of Psychology, Faculty of Health, Deakin University**

'Writing a book on the foundation of coaching is not an easy task. The author needs to strike the right balance between accessibility and the increasing complexity that is emerging from this developing discipline. Only when this is achieved can such a book be suitable for both undergraduate and postgraduate students. A great text to recommend to those entering into coaching.' **Professor Tatiana Bachkirova, Oxford Brookes University**

'Not only did the combination of reading a chapter, followed by watching the video content on it, help to clarify and embed the information, it gave the feeling of being on one of van Nieuwerburgh's sought-after courses, which makes this book great value for money, and a valuable resource, particularly for new coaches.' **Sally Brown, _Coaching Today_**

'Christian van Nieuwerburgh is one of our leaders in the field of coaching. If you're a coach, or simply interested in learning more about coaching, you need this book – packed with tools, strategies, video support and many, many resources that will help all coaches improve their practice.' **Jim Knight, President, Instructional Coaching Group**

'Packed full of ideas, stories and exercises, and backed up by short video clips illustrating key points, this book takes the reader on a journey to learn how to do coaching and – more profoundly – how to be a coach who unlocks the potential in others.' **Bob Thomson, Professor of Practice, Warwick Business School**

'This theoretically-grounded and highly practical book will be of great value – a comprehensive and thorough exposition of vital coaching skills that will guide development and help facilitate constructive reflective practice. Recommended to the novice and advanced coach alike. Enjoy!' **Anthony M. Grant, PhD, University of Sydney**

'This is a wonderfully practical, yet stimulating, inspiring and innovative resource. I just wish Christian had put this together years ago, when I first became a coach! That said, there is heaps of learning to be had here for both the established and the novice coach, accessed via a number of routes, including anecdotes and video clips. I predict this will become one of those resources the coaching profession will wonder how it ever managed without.' **Liz Hall, Editor of _Coaching at Work_ magazine and author of Mindful Coaching**

'Christian van Nieuwerburgh has written an excellent introduction to coaching skills. It really is a practical guide, illustrating skills, tools, techniques and the coaching process. This book may become a classic in its time.' **Professor Stephen Palmer, Centre for Coaching, London**

'_An Introduction to Coaching Skills: A Practical Guide_ is for new and experienced coaches. Christian addresses the complexity of coaching by simplifying it into three key elements – way of being, coaching process and coaching skills. Containing suggested activities, accompanying video clips, this guide will be a much-used resource for every coach.' **Vikki G. Brock, PhD, EMBA, Master Certified Coach, Professional Mentor Coach**

'At last a book on coaching that highlights key coaching skills in visual format that reinforce a time-tested model of effective coaching. Christian has distilled the essential steps in coaching and followed this up with putting techniques into practice using actual coaching sessions. The book follows a simple yet powerful recipe of moving from knowledge to process to a way of being allowing aspiring coaches to get a sense of competence in using coaching skills rapidly and simply. The format of the book is innovative and will be well received by those who appreciate coaching in action.' **Dr Steve Zolezzi, PhD, Head of Positive Education, Knox Grammar School**

'Walking the talk or being authentic is an absolute necessity in this day when so many competing resources are being published on how to be a coach. This book not only walks the talk and helps the reader on the journey to authenticity but does so in a way that brilliantly surrounds the reader with not just words, but practical examples – many drawn from the book author's own experience; succinct video clips that clearly demonstrate skills and perspective, opportunities for studied reflection, and experiential learning activities. The author has truly captured the essence of coaching that distinguishes it from other forms of helping: namely, that coaching is a way of being, of sharing your true self with the world, and assisting both yourself and the people you work with to also become their authentic selves.' **Rey Carr, Editor-in-Chief,** *Peer Bulletin*

'Much more than a book – this practical, comprehensive learning resource makes a significant contribution to the coaching literature. The linked video clips, an innovation not seen elsewhere, will be particularly valued by those beginning to explore coaching, by more experienced coaches seeking to hone core skills as well as those involved in training coaches. A resource for every coach's bookshelf to be referred to again and again.' **John Campbell, Growth Coaching International, Sydney**

'This is the best guide to coaching skills I have come across. It's a must-have handbook for anyone looking to develop their coaching skills. The innovative format of video clips illustrating the written description gives the reader a real understanding of the skills, why they are important and how to apply them in practice.' **Julia Yates, University of East London**

'With the attention of a coach and the care of an educator, Christian van Nieuwerburgh has produced a highly informative and wonderfully easy to read book. He glides between the two roles with remarkable ease to provide the novice coach with a state-of-the art coaching toolkit. The seasoned coach is also bound to benefit, especially from the video material, which is undoubtedly the gem of the book.' **Dr Ioanna Iordanou, Teaching Fellow, Warwick Business School**

Praise for This Edition

'Christian van Nieuwerburgh has once again crafted a masterpiece with this 4th edition of *An Introduction to Coaching Skills: A Practical Guide*. Every word in this book is carefully chosen, woven together like a tapestry that brings coaching to life in the most accessible and impactful way. As a core text in my Essentials of Coaching courses and a first reference in Advanced Coaching studies, I have seen firsthand how it equips new coaches with the confidence and skills to embark on their coaching journey. More than just a book, it immerses the reader in the coaching experience—blending theory, practice, and video demonstrations into an indispensable resource for both novice and seasoned coaches. A must-have for anyone serious about the art and science of coaching!'
Dr Hamed Noori, LLM, Founder and Project Leader of Online Coaching Center, Utrecht University

An Introduction to Coaching Skills

4th edition

Christian van Nieuwerburgh

$ Sage

S Sage

1 Oliver's Yard
55 City Road
London EC1Y 1SP

2455 Teller Road
Thousand Oaks
California 91320

Unit No 323-333, Third Floor, F-Block
International Trade Tower
Nehru Place, New Delhi – 110 019

8 Marina View Suite 43-053
Asia Square Tower 1
Singapore 018960

Editor: Susannah Trefgarne
Editorial assistant: Harry Dixon
Production editor: Sarah Sewell
Copyeditor: Elaine Leek
Proofreader: Martin Noble
Indexer: Elizabeth Ball
Marketing manager: Ruslana Khatagova
Cover design: Jennifer Crisp
Typeset by: C&M Digitals (P) Ltd, Chennai, India
Printed in the UK

Library of Congress Control Number: 2025940845

British Library Cataloguing in Publication data

A catalogue record for this book is available from the British Library

ISBN 978-1-5296-8245-8
ISBN 978-1-5296-8244-1 (pbk)

To Cathia and Christian, with my love and admiration

Contents

Guided Tour of the Book

The aim of this book is to be as helpful as possible to you as you learn to become a coach. With this in mind, I have incorporated a number of practical resources into the text. It is recommended that you engage with these to aid your learning and build confidence in your newly acquired skills and abilities.

This brief tour will cover the following resources that you will find throughout the book:

- A question for you
- Activity
- Find out more
- Reflect on your practice
- Review your practice
- See it in practice
- Snapshot
- Story from practice
- What the professional associations say

A Question for You

Throughout the text, you will notice 'A question for you' boxes. These invite you to reflect on your responses to particular theories or practices. Learning to become a coach is as much about increasing your own self-awareness as it is about studying conversational frameworks, tools and techniques. As with coaching, the intention of these questions is to encourage reflection and provoke new thinking.

Activity

These practical activities will allow you to experience some of the concepts that are covered in this book. Most of the activities should only take a few minutes. Where possible, I would request that you invest some time to engage with them. I think it will lead to a better learning experience for you.

Find Out More

Periodically, I have provided a few references to books or other sources that might be helpful for your learning. The 'Find out more' boxes will provide signposts and allow you to make informed decisions about whether or not to explore some concepts and ideas further.

Reflect on Your Practice

These boxes will provide you with opportunities to reflect on what you are learning. Please start a journal to support your learning and development as a coach. You will regularly be asked to capture ideas or make notes in your learning journal.

Review Your Practice

When it is helpful, these boxes will provide specific guidelines about certain coaching skills. Please use these as checklists to review how you are doing.

See It in Practice

I have provided video clips of real coaching conversations to elucidate certain elements of good coaching practice. The boxes list the clips related to certain chapters and provide short descriptions of each video. As most coaching conversations are confidential, these clips represent a rare opportunity to observe real coaching taking place. They do not aim to demonstrate 'perfect' coaching. Rather, they have been selected to show how the key skills and techniques are used in everyday coaching conversations.

Snapshot

While this book is intentionally focused on the practice of coaching, the text is informed by coaching-related theory and research. The boxes provide snapshots or brief explanations of relevant concepts.

Story from Practice

Many of the skills and frameworks presented in this book are supported by real stories from coaching practice. As you will discover, confidentiality is an essential part of the coaching process. All of the stories presented in this book are taken from my own experiences. For this reason, details have been changed in cases where it may otherwise have been possible for a person or organisation to be identified. While information relating to identifiable factors has been changed, none of the significant coaching-related events have been altered, and therefore these are 'true' stories based on real experiences. I have worked with clients and organisations internationally over many years, and therefore I believe that no clients or organisations will be identifiable. Where I was concerned about issues of confidentiality or anonymity, I shared the case studies with those involved before including them in this book.

What the Professional Associations Say

The professional associations of coaching have an increasingly important role in supporting coaches, providing networking opportunities and ensuring adherence to high standards of professionalism. These boxes show how the content of the chapters align with the competencies of three leading professional associations. This will make it easier for you to pursue accreditation as a coach if that is of interest to you.

Online Resources and List of Videos

Online Resources

An Introduction to Coaching Skills is supported by a suite of video clips that demonstrate key coaching skills in action. As most coaching conversations are confidential, these videos represent a rare opportunity to observe real coaching taking place.

List of Videos

Video 3.1   Noticing a Response
Video 3.2   Noticing a Word
Video 3.3   Being Curious
Video 3.4   Giving Positive Feedback

Video 4.1   Listening Respectfully
Video 4.2   Using Silence
Video 4.3   Saying It Out Loud

Video 5.1   Playing Back Leads to Insight
Video 5.2   Playing Back Leads to Enthusiasm
Video 5.3   Playing Back Words
Video 5.4   Summarising Incorrectly
Video 5.5   Asking the Client to Play Back
Video 5.6   Interjecting for Emphasis

Video 6.1   Asking a Thought-Provoking Question
Video 6.2   Asking about the Future
Video 6.3   Asking about Learning
Video 6.4   Asking a Challenging Question

Video 7.1   A Full Coaching Session
Video 7.2   Starting with Contracting
Video 7.3   Identifying Outcome for the Session
Video 7.4   Highlighting Resources
Video 7.5   Clarifying Next Steps

The videos are available at study.sagepub.com/coachingskills4e

About the Author

Professor Christian van Nieuwerburgh is a highly respected executive coach, an internationally recognised academic, a well-published author, a curious traveller and a sought-after consultant. Christian divides his time across a number of rewarding and meaningful professional roles. His primary academic role is Professor of Coaching and Positive Psychology at the Centre for Positive Health Sciences at RCSI University of Medicine and Health Sciences in Dublin, Ireland, where he is pioneering coaching and positive psychology interventions for health and wellbeing. Christian is a Creative Partner of the Instructional Coaching Group, a US-headquartered global organisation specialising in the professional learning of teachers, coaches and leaders in schools. In this role, he continues to develop and deliver coaching and positive psychology initatives and programmes for educators. In recognition of his contribution to the fields of coaching and positive psychology, Christian is Principal Fellow at the Centre for Wellbeing Science of the University of Melbourne in Australia. Through his own passion project, Coach on a Motorcycle, Christian shares learning and insights from the fields of coaching and positive psychology to a global audience. Regarded as an international authority in the field, Christian regularly speaks at conferences, facilitates training and consults in the US, the UK, Europe, Latin America, the Middle East, Southeast Asia and Australasia. For up-to-date information about Christian, his latest thinking and travel plans, follow him on Instagram (@coachonamotorcycle) or visit his website: www.coachonamotorcycle.com.

About the Author

Preface

Welcome to the fourth edition of *An Introduction to Coaching Skills*. This is a book that I loved writing the first time round. I spend many fruitful days thinking about you, the intended reader of this book, so I'm excited that you are now reading it! Of all the editions so far, this is definitely the best. Every time, I take full advantage of the opportunity to edit the text to take into account latest developments in the field, my most recent professional learning and relevant feedback from readers, clients, students and colleagues. Since the third edition was published in 2020, I have written *Your Essential Guide to Effective Reflective Practice* (Sage, 2025) with David Love and *Radical Listening: The Art of True Connection* (Berrett Koehler, 2025) with Robert Biswas-Diener. The process of co-writing these books has allowed me to rethink and review some of the ideas in this new edition.

In a conversation that took place about 20 years ago, I remember saying to my coach that I wanted to transform my professional life so that I could turn more of my attention and energy towards coaching. That conversation was the beginning of decades of meaningful and fulfilling work coaching others, training people to become coaches, researching coaching and working with organisations all over the world to design and implement coaching and positive psychology initiatives.

I have learned so much through writing, editing and re-editing this book. I am more confident about some of the ideas that underpin effective coaching while I have become less certain about other aspects. Here are the most important things that I have learned through this process.

- Learning about coaching has had positive impacts on my professional life, on important relationships and on how I feel about myself. People who are interested in *becoming* coaches (rather than learning *how* to coach) are more likely to find that the learning is transferable to other areas of their lives.
- I have always been curious about what makes coaching such a powerful intervention. I am becoming more convinced that the 'secret' is the quality of the connection between a coach and her client. Listening in a way that shows people that you hear, value and respect them (I call this 'radical listening') is the quickest and surest way of building that connection.
- Your journey of becoming a coach will be full of meaningful moments, powerful insights and learning opportunities.

Coaching is both complex and simple. Its complexity rests in the nature of the human experience, the richness of relationships and the pace of change in the world we live in.

At the same time, effective coaching is simply a demonstration of the most positive elements of what it is to be human. Those of us who embrace coaching find that it rekindles our curiosity, allows us to be more intentional and deepens our respect for others.

I would like to share a few notes about use of language in this book: After much reflection, I have decided to retain a practice I introduced in the first edition—using 'she' as a generic pronoun. My intention is to highlight that the use of 'he' as a generic pronoun is problematic. Since this is a book about coaching, being aware of the impact of our words is important. Another rationale for choosing 'she' as the generic pronoun is that most readers of this book will be female. I have been teaching coaching for over a decade, and the majority of my students have been women. On the other hand, I have decided to replace the term 'coachee' with 'client'. I have become uncomfortable with the term 'coachee' because it could imply that the person is receiving something from the coach when this book promotes the idea of an equal partnership between the two parties. 'Client' helpfully emphasises the idea that coaching is a service. The act of coaching is always in service of the client and her aspirations. Although neither word is the perfect answer, I hope that explaining my rationale for these choices is helpful to you.

I am passionate about facilitating learning, and this book has one important and constant purpose: to be of service to *you* as you learn to become a coach. To be as supportive as possible in this regard, I have worked closely with my wonderful colleagues at Sage publishers and tapped into the generosity of volunteer clients to give you the resources you will need on your learning journey. We have provided you with newly recorded videos of real coaching practice. Instead of in-person, face-to-face sessions, the new videos are recorded over Zoom – which is now one of the most popular ways of delivering coaching. This text is also peppered with stories from my own coaching practice. Within the bounds of confidentiality and respecting the anonymity of clients, I have included 'stories from practice' which are based on real experiences.

By now, I am fairly confident that learning to become a coach will have a positive impact on many other aspects of your life. As an example, I'd like to share a true story with you:

About 15 years ago, I was working in London for most of the week, driving or taking the train back to my home in the countryside on weekends. On a good day, it was a three-hour drive from the University to our home in Warwickshire. On one of these journeys home in November, I pulled into a service station just off the motorway, about halfway to my destination. It was about 8.00pm, so already dark and bitterly cold. I parked my car, locked it and started walking to the coffee shop for a warm drink. A voice called out, 'Good evening, brother.' Glancing to my left, I saw a man looking out of the window of a small green car. 'Good evening,' I replied. He peered out of his car, looking embarrassed. 'Brother, can I speak to you?' he asked politely. Slightly on my guard, I went over to the car. He told me that he had been having a very bad day. He had driven his brother to Heathrow Airport in the morning. Due to some difficulties with excess baggage and airport security, he ended up having to give his brother all the cash he was carrying. Now, on his way back home, he was out of fuel and had no access to money or a credit card. He had asked the petrol station attendant to call his wife so that she could pay for his fuel over the phone using a credit card, but apparently there was some regulation that meant this was not possible. He asked if I could help him in some way. At that moment, a slight feeling of doubt crept over me. He told me where he worked in his hometown and offered to give me his mobile phone number. I found my personal value of helping people when they are in need was competing with cynical thoughts about the credibility of the situation. However, I decided that I should behave in a way that was in line with my values. I took out the only £20 note in my wallet and gave it to him. 'Here you are,' I said. He thanked me and promised to pay me back as soon as he was paid on the following Tuesday. 'Give me your name and address, and I will post you a cheque on Tuesday,' he promised. Instead of giving him my address, I simply gave him my mobile phone number. I told him not to worry about the cheque for now, but to focus on getting home. 'When you've been paid on Tuesday, just give me a call and I'll let you know how to get the money back to me,' I said. He thanked me for helping a 'brother in need', and drove off. I had decided that if he did call on the following Tuesday, I would tell him that he could keep the £20 as a gift.

Before I learned to become a coach, I would have been much more cynical and less trusting. I probably would not have spoken to this person, and I would almost certainly not have lent him money at a petrol station. However, in the moment, I consciously decided to give the person the benefit of the doubt. Sipping on my takeaway coffee as I drove home, I felt good about having done the 'right' thing. You may already have guessed that I didn't get a call on Tuesday. In fact, I never heard from that person again. But I'd like to think that if a similar thing happened at a motorway services in future, I would, once again, give a stranger in need the benefit of the doubt. Becoming a coach has helped me to be less judgemental and more trusting. I hope you find this book valuable and enjoy becoming a coach as much as I have!

Acknowledgements

I consider myself to be incredibly fortunate to be surrounded by supportive and encouraging people. What a wonderful opportunity to note my gratitude to some of them! I would like to register my appreciation to the learners and students that I have had the pleasure and privilege to work with. I am continually inspired by their commitment, love of learning and desire to support others.

I'm lucky to be able to call on some leading figures in the field of coaching and positive psychology when I need advice or support. I'd like to thank Dr Jim Knight, President of the Instructional Coaching Group; Dr Suzy Green of the Positivity Institute; Professor Peter Hawkins and Professor Jonathan Passmore of Henley Business School of the University of Reading; Professor Ilona Boniwell of Positran; Professor Bob Thomson at the University of Warwick; Professor Michael Steger at Colorado State University; Professor Aneta Tunariu at University College London; Dr Ana Paula Nacif, Dr Kirsty Gardiner, Dr Ayşe Burçin Başkurt and Dr Hannah Kampman at the University of East London; Dr Tim Lomas of the Human Flourishing Programme at Harvard University; Dr Julia Yates at City University, London; Dr Sean O'Connor and Dr Gordon Spence at the University of Sydney; Chris Munro and Claudia Owad of Growth Coaching International; Liz Hall, editor of *Coaching at Work*; James Bridgeman, Co-Editor of *Coaching Perspectives* magazine; Helen Tiffany, Director of the Coach House; Dr Robert Biswas-Diener of Positive Acorn; Michael Bungay-Stanier at MBS Works; Dr Haesun Moon at the University of Toronto; Professor Lindsay Oades at the University of Melbourne; Daniela Blickhan of the Inntal Institut; Professor James Pawelski of the Positive Psychology Center at the University of Pennsylvania; and Professor Stephen Joseph at the University of Nottingham. What an amazing network of passionate, knowledgeable and supportive people! The improvements in this fourth edition have been strongly informed by feedback from readers and the invaluable support of many of the people mentioned above. I am grateful for the many meaningful and thought-provoking conversations that we have had. I am a better author and coach because of them.

Leading the Centre for Positive Health Sciences at RCSI University of Medicine and Health Sciences is a real privilege. I am grateful for the opportunity to undertake research, facilitate learning and co-create with my inspirational academic colleagues – Dr Roger Bretherton, Dr Jolanta Burke, Dr Elaine Byrne, Dr Mary Collins, Dr Pàdraic Dunne and Dr Trudy Meehan. Working with Dr Marina Cans, Miriam Holden and Suzanne Sullivan in our operations team is a joy. I am also grateful to our team of committed doctoral scholars and research assistants who allow us to be a leading global centre for research into Positive Health: Lucy Airs, Jennifer Donnelly, Louise Foott, Aine Garvey, Angel Harper, Branislav Kaleta, Justin Laiti, Croia Loughnane, Ciara Scott, Deirdre

Sheehan and Annette Sweeney. I am grateful for the mentoring and support of Professor Cathal Kelly, Vice Chancellor, Professor Tracy Robson, Deputy Vice Chancellor and Prof. Ciaran O'Boyle, Founding Director of the Centre for Positive Health Sciences. They are role models of positive leadership.

My passion for coaching and the consultancy work that I undertake has allowed me to work with some truly inspiring and generous colleagues. It has been wonderful to work alongside John Campbell and Dr Jim Knight in the field of coaching in education. I have learned so much from collaborating with them. When we first started working together, we agreed that we would continue the collaboration as long as it was fun and it allowed us to do the work we love.

I would not be engaged in this rewarding and enjoyable work today if it weren't for a key group of educators and colleagues who believed in me and supported me. Dr Martin Wiggins, my PhD supervisor, is a model academic and world leader in the study of Elizabethan and Jacobean drama. Sue Herdman, Mary Johnson and Miles Tandy have been valuable colleagues and wonderful teachers, showing me the art of facilitation. David Love, who launched me onto the path of becoming a coach, consistently demonstrates the 'way of being' that I discuss in this book.

I love to work in schools and often ask delegates at conferences or participants at workshops to remember an educator who had a significant positive impact on them. Invariably, when I ask what made the particular educator memorable, participants report that the person 'believed in me'. In my case, a few educators come easily to mind. In the first grade of the American Community School (ACS) in Beirut, the kind and wonderfully positive Nancy Reynolds made me feel safe and valued, even though I could not speak a word of English when I joined her class. In the sixth grade, Donald Corsette discovered a good kid who could be rebellious at times. He transformed my educational experience from that moment onwards. Catherine Bashshur, the consistently patient and kind head teacher of ACS, gave me the benefit of the doubt on more than one occasion. At the American University of Beirut (AUB), Dr Jean-Marie Cook encouraged me to pursue a PhD in Elizabethan Drama. I didn't believe that I would be able to do it. But she did. And I will be forever grateful to Dr George Khairallah who was a natural sage. On the first day of my Shakespeare class at AUB, George stood on one leg, with a set of worry beads as a crown, for the entire lesson. He taught me the power of 'A-ha!' moments.

I was excited about writing this book from the outset. Kate Wharton, the visionary editor who commissioned the book, has been its steadfast and enduring champion. Then I worked with Amy Jarrold, another wonderful editor who has a great way of enthusing and encouraging authors. The extent of her commitment can be evidenced by the fact that she appears in one of the coaching videos for this book! I'm grateful to Susannah Trefgarne and Harry Dixon for their encouragement and support as we worked on this fourth edition. Sincere thanks are due to Elaine Leek for her excellent copyediting skills and Martin Noble for proofreading the text so carefully. Dedicated to education and committed to driving social change, Sage is a wonderful publisher to write for.

I truly appreciate the generosity of those who agreed to be filmed being coached. Their participation has greatly enriched this book by providing glimpses of real coaching conversations. I am grateful to former UEL students Zaydon Alayasa, Jane Ayres, Greg Ette, Karen Foy, Grace Graham, Katie Heath, Ian McIntosh, Michelle Pritchard, Matt Sheerin, Trish Smith, Dionne Spencer, Carol Stewart and Astrid Weinmann. The second and third editions added some new video clips featuring valued colleagues Annette Gray, Claudia Owad, David Love and Denis Sartain. They are inspiring coaches and respected colleagues. I am thankful to the kindness of the people who volunteered to be coached for the new videos that accompany this new edition: Susan Bentley, Hillery Cambre, Mandy Dunn, Deanne Elliott, Julie Fournier, Sharon Garro, Harvey Gratz, Katie R. Hawkins, Yenifer Nahar, Sophie Paterson, Marie Anne Rosario Rajkumar, Dr Nadira Singh and Sandra Tai Chung Wei. Their support has enriched the content of this book.

What makes my executive coaching and consultancy work so rewarding is the opportunity to work with people who are committed to their own development and wish to pursue their dreams and aspirations. I appreciate what a privilege this is. I'd therefore like to thank all the people (adults and young people) that I have had the opportunity to coach.

In 2024, I launched a passion project that I had been daydreaming about for many years – Coach on a Motorcycle Ltd. In that year, I fulfilled a childhood dream by finally riding across Route 66 on a Harley Davidson. Since then, there has been growing interest in the concept of Coach on a Motorcycle. To see my video diary of Route 66 or learn about some positive psychology ideas that I shared along the journey, please check out my YouTube channel: @coachonamotorcycle. The idea is to use this project to share information and insights with the widest possible audience. I am grateful to my wonderful Creative Associate, Brittany Rehal, for believing in the idea. Thanks are also due to Ruth Bates and Melanie Fermín who are supporting me to make Coach on a Motorcycle a sustainable enterprise!

I would like to conclude my acknowledgements by thanking my friends and family. Igor Djordjevic and Jawad Maatouk are childhood friends who have continued to provide encouragement and good times. The Jenainati family has accepted me as one of their own. I am especially thankful to Riad and Hoda, Amin, Suzy, Zeina, Hani, Natalie, Charbel and all of my cousins and nieces for their love and kindness. My father, Arthur John van Nieuwerburgh, lived his life to the full and would have wanted me to do the same. My mother, Tsuyu Tsuchida, was a model of kindness, resilience and generosity. My wife Cathia is the love of my life and the best partner I could ever imagine. My son, Christian Arthur van Nieuwerburgh, is an admirable, caring and thoughtful young man who continually inspires me to be the best that I can be. His partner, Rachel, brings so much laughter and love to our family. I'd like to thank my family for allowing me to flourish by believing in me and giving me the space and time to follow my heart.

Part I
Context

1
First Things First

Welcome

Welcome to the beginning of a thrilling learning journey! This book will be one part of your development as a coach. Like many forms of personal and professional learning, coaching requires determined practice and intentional reflection. On the one hand, by the time you have read this book, watched the video clips and completed the suggested activities, you will be ready to coach others. On the other hand, learning the 'coaching way of being' discussed in this book is a lifetime endeavour. Fortunately, if you have chosen this book for yourself, it will be an enjoyable endeavour. By embarking on your own enriching learning journey, you will inspire others to do the same.

What Is Coaching?

Let's start by agreeing a working definition of the word 'coaching'. It is now a global industry, worth over 5 billion US dollars annually. Despite its worldwide popularity, there is still some confusion about the term. The fact you are reading this suggests that you think that it can be a powerful intervention. What you believe it means is more important than the tentative definition proposed below.

Activity 1.1

One-Sentence Definition

Here is the first activity! Imagine that someone notices that you are reading this book and asks you, 'What is coaching?' Take a few minutes to jot down your own one-sentence definition of coaching. Restrict yourself to just one sentence. Once you have completed this, make a note of your sentence and compare your own definition with those shared below.

At the time of writing, there is no legal definition of coaching. This fact is often cited as a weakness of the 'profession' of coaching. There is little doubt that the fact that anyone can call anything they do 'coaching' can be confusing and potentially unhelpful. At the same time, the lack of a fixed definition allows for a certain freedom for each coach to define her practice in a way that is meaningful to herself and her clients. This flexibility means that the practice of coaching can continually adapt to meet the needs of clients.

Find Out More 1.1

History of Coaching

The most comprehensive outline of the foundations and history of coaching can be found in a seminal book by Dr Vikki Brock entitled *Sourcebook of Coaching History* (2012). A shorter overview can be found in *The Hidden History of Coaching* by Leni Wildflower (2013).

Over the past 25 years, some key definitions have been proposed. A few notable ones are listed below:

'The art of facilitating the performance, learning and development of another.' (Downey, 2003: 21)

This definition stands out because it characterises coaching as an 'art'. This is in contrast with others that propose the existence of a 'science of coaching'. For example, I have taught on a 'coaching psychology' programme within a psychology department at a university, and Psychology has fought hard to establish its credentials as a science. Having said this, I believe that coaching is both an art and a science. In this book, we will consider both angles. The tools, techniques and conversational frameworks may be seen as more *scientific* whereas the 'coaching way of being' can be considered more *artistic*. There has been an increasing amount of credible research into coaching to provide evidence for its effectiveness. This will be brought into the discussion lightly throughout this book.

Downey's definition goes on to suggest that coaching should focus on performance, learning and development. The emphasis on performance is a feature of much of the early literature on coaching, perhaps because of the desire of early adopters to convince potential clients of its suitability in the workplace.

'Unlocking people's potential to maximise their own performance. It is helping them to learn rather than teaching them.' (Whitmore, 2009: 11)

Like Downey, Whitmore highlights the performance-enhancing nature of coaching. This definition captured my imagination and motivated me to become a coach many years ago. The first sentence suggests that every person has the potential within herself, and the wording implies that the client must take responsibility for maximising her own performance. The second sentence is less frequently quoted, perhaps because it could be considered controversial. Whitmore explicitly juxtaposes coaching (helping people to learn) with teaching (telling people what they need to know).

'Coaching is a method of work-related learning that relies primarily on one-to-one conversations.' (de Haan, 2008b: 19)

In a definition that has a clear bias towards executive coaching, de Haan proposes that conversations should focus on work-related learning and development. His use of the phrase 'primarily on one-to-one conversations' alludes to the existence of 'group' or 'team' coaching. This book will focus on coaching as a one-to-one conversation, which is the foundation of powerful relationships. Many of the skills, tools and techniques you develop as you learn to become a coach will be immediately transferable to other aspects of your life. Furthermore, in principle, the skills of coaching are the same, regardless of the context in which they are used (van Nieuwerburgh, 2016). This book will help you to develop your ability to coach in any arena – within organisations, as a life coach, within educational or health settings or as part of a leadership role.

'Coaching is a human development process that involves structured, focused interaction and the use of appropriate strategies, tools and techniques to promote desirable and sustainable change for the benefit of the coachee and potentially for other stakeholders.' (Cox et al., 2023: 1)

This definition is more comprehensive, recognising the important role of coaching as part of a developmental process. Sustainability of the change achieved during coaching is picked out as a significant consideration. There is acknowledgement that there may be benefits to 'other stakeholders' in addition to change for the client. In executive coaching situations, it is hoped that both the client and her organisation will profit from coaching sessions.

Our Definition of Coaching

Considering the quotes above, it is evident that there is some variation in definitions. However, Bresser and Wilson capture the essence of coaching in their description of its core focus as 'empowering people by facilitating self-directed learning, personal growth and improved performance' (2010: 10). Currently, there seems to be broad agreement that coaching:

- is a managed conversation;
- aims to support sustainable change to behaviours;
- focuses on learning, development and growth.

To support you on your journey to become a confident and effective coach, this book will refer to the competencies and ethical codes of the leading professional bodies of coaching: the International Coach Federation (ICF), the European Mentoring and Coaching Council (EMCC) and the Association of Coaching (AC).

> ─────── **What the Professional Associations Say 1.1** ───────
>
> ## Coaching Definitions
>
> The ICF defines coaching as 'partnering with clients in a thought-provoking and creative process that inspires them to maximise their personal and professional potential. The process of coaching often unlocks previously untapped sources of imagination, productivity and leadership.'
>
> According to the EMCC, 'Coaching is an art: that of helping a person or a group to develop and enhance their professional, relational and personal potential in the realisation of their projects and to take their rightful place in the relationship they have with themselves, others and their environment.'
>
> The AC definition is: 'A collaborative solution-focused, results-orientated and systematic process in which the coach facilitates the enhancement of work performance, life experience, self-directed learning and personal growth of the coachee.'

In the box above, you can see the connections to the Whitmore definition which first inspired me to become a coach. Coaching is a facilitated conversation underpinned by a set of easily learned techniques. Many of the skills needed to be a coach, you possess already. They are conversational skills – the ability to listen to others, to ask questions, to play back and to notice. From here onwards, it is simply a case of honing these skills to effectively facilitate thought-provoking conversations with others. Your interest in this topic suggests that you already possess an essential and necessary attribute: a desire to support others to achieve more of their potential. And yet this simplicity does not prevent coaching from being a powerful and rewarding activity. In some cases, it can be life-changing – for you as well as your clients!

Coaching and Mentoring

Many words have been spoken and written in an attempt to tease out the differences between coaching and mentoring. As I hope you will discover, the key skills, many of the approaches and the need for a particular 'way of being' are similar in both activities. To help us distinguish between the two approaches, Passmore (2010) suggests some differentiating factors. First, he proposes that coaching is more formal than mentoring. According to Passmore, mentoring tends to be an informal arrangement between two people. Compared to mentoring, coaching is seen to be a shorter-term engagement. Coaching is considered a more appropriate intervention for skills or performance enhancement whereas mentoring is better suited to career development. It is proposed that the most significant difference between the two approaches is the need for a mentor to have a high level of expertise and knowledge about the topic being discussed. Bresser and Wilson (2010) helpfully highlight two factors that differentiate the approaches:

1   A mentor has 'experience in a particular field and imparts specific knowledge', while a coach does not necessarily have specialist experience in the field and does not impart knowledge (p. 22).
2   A mentor acts as an 'adviser, counsellor, guide, tutor, or teacher', while a coach's role is to 'assist coachees in uncovering their own knowledge and skills' and 'facilitate coachees in becoming their own advisers' (p. 22).

In addition to a shared set of skills, the intentions of coaches and mentors are often closely aligned – supporting others to achieve more of their goals and aspirations. Garvey and his colleagues agree that 'coaching and mentoring are essentially similar in nature' (2009: 27). Further, a piece of research into this question by Willis (2005) found that coaching and mentoring were similar activities, with coaches and mentors sharing the same skills and practices.

I have argued elsewhere (van Nieuwerburgh, 2012) that the terminology is not as important as recognising that both approaches can support people to develop their skills and performance. However, the confusion surrounding this terminology can lead to frustration with, and poor experiences of, both approaches. For our purposes, it may suffice to conclude that both approaches are broadly similar and agree that we will focus on the practice of coaching in this book.

How Will This Book Help?

This book is written to help you in numerous ways. For some readers, it will introduce new ideas and concepts. For others, it will reaffirm existing practices and behaviours. Hopefully, every reader will find the focus on practice helpful. Ultimately, this book will support you to develop the skills needed to be able to coach others while building your confidence to do so effectively. To aid you in the process, this book provides a clear structure (outlined below) that starts with the key skills before focusing on tried and tested conversational frameworks. This is followed by some practical tools that can be used during different stages of the conversation. The section on a 'coaching way of being' captures the 'art' element of coaching, and this is presented once you are familiar with the skills and frameworks involved. You will be supported on your learning journey with learning aids and video clips of real coaching practice which will enhance the practical dimension of this book. Turn back to the Guided Tour of the Book on pages xv–xvii if you would like to remind yourself about the various learning prompts in this book.

Reflect on Your Practice 1.1

Creating Your Learning Journal

Please create an electronic or hard copy learning journal as a companion to this book. At various stages during your reading, journal entries will be suggested. In addition, it may be helpful to capture your own thoughts, reflections and questions as you read.

In the first entry of your new learning journal, please note down your thoughts and feelings about the chapters that are described briefly below. A few bullet points will be sufficient for each chapter.

- What thoughts come to mind when you read the brief description of each chapter?
- What are you curious about as you read the brief descriptions?
- How much are you looking forward to reading each chapter? Perhaps rate this on a scale of 1 (dreading the chapter) to 10 (cannot wait to read the chapter). Please enjoy the process of capturing your reflections. If possible, take your time with note-taking. We can learn so much about ourselves through this kind of 'slow thinking' (Kahneman, 2011).

Chapter Summaries

Every chapter is carefully designed to play an important role in your learning journey. It may be helpful for you to have a sense of where this journey is going to take you. Here is a brief synopsis of every chapter.

1 First Things First

This is the chapter you're reading. It sets the scene by providing an introduction to the book and brief summaries of each chapter.

2 Becoming a Coach

This chapter introduces the three elements of becoming an effective coach: having the necessary skills; being able to use a conversational framework; and adopting an appropriate 'coaching way of being'. Most readers will already have some of the skills of coaching which are defined as 'noticing', 'listening', 'asking powerful questions' and 'playing back'. This book will support readers to strengthen and refine these skills. One of the key responsibilities of the coach is to facilitate the conversation. This can be done by learning and adopting one of many coaching frameworks. These are easy to learn and take practice to master. This book will present some coaching frameworks that can be used straight away. Finally, the best coaches demonstrate a particular 'coaching way of being'. This cannot easily be taught but can be learned over time and with practice.

If you can develop all three elements, you will be able to confidently support others to achieve more of their potential.

3 Noticing

To be as effective as possible, it will be necessary for you to sharpen your ability to notice. Coaches must notice what is happening, what is not happening, signals from their clients and what may be going on within themselves. The better a coach is at noticing, the more likely she will be able to support significant or transformational change in her clients.

4 Listening

Listening is an underrated skill. When used effectively, listening can make people feel valued, respected and resourceful. Different levels of listening will be discussed. Approaches to active listening are explored. The premise of this chapter is that skilful listening can strengthen rapport and encourage others to think more creatively and purposefully.

5 Playing Back

Coaches play back what they hear by paraphrasing and summarising. This chapter considers how best to do this. The importance of playing back as a way of demonstrating care and attention is explained. The chapter provides some useful phrases to use when coaching.

6 Asking Powerful Questions

This chapter highlights the importance of using questions intentionally. Coaches should be able to ask thought-provoking questions. The appropriate use of both open and closed questions will be considered. Four types of questions are proposed. There is a discussion of specific types of questions appropriate to coaching situations.

7 Conversational Frameworks

This chapter begins by introducing a simple coaching framework (GROW). The use of the GROW model (Whitmore, 2009) is discussed in relation to supporting people to change their behaviours. The GROW model is described in detail. Sample questions are provided to help the reader. A few adaptations of the GROW model are presented.

8 Ways of Thinking

Having described some conversational frameworks, the way in which coaches can support the thinking of clients is discussed. While many people seek coaching to change behaviour, sometimes clients may need to change their ways of thinking before sustained change in behaviour can occur. Reference will be made to the concept of the 'inner game' (Gallwey, 1974).

9 Positive Bias

Coaching is essentially a conversation about focusing on the positive and building on existing resources. As a result, the field of positive psychology has much to offer coaches. A brief overview of the field is followed by some positive psychological interventions that may be helpful to coaches and clients.

10 Body Language and Emotional Intelligence

This chapter explores the role of body language and emotional intelligence in coaching conversations. The importance of remaining alert to body language (as additional 'data') is highlighted. Emotional intelligence (Salovey and Mayer, 1990) is also essential for a coach, as she will need to be aware of the emotions of the client as well as her own. By making educated guesses about how the person being coached is feeling, the coach can adapt her own behaviour accordingly.

11 Inspiring Creativity

For novice coaches, the Options stage of the GROW model can be the most challenging. This chapter proposes a range of tools and techniques for increasing the creativity of clients.

12 Being Human

The 'coaching way of being', necessary for the most effective practice, cannot be taught in the traditional sense of the word. Instead, this can only be learned by people for whom it is important. This chapter describes the key attributes of a 'coaching way of being' by outlining the person-centred approach to coaching and discussing a series of 'partnership principles' (Knight, 2022). The chapter concludes by providing some aspirational goals for coaches.

13 Inspiring Others

Coaching is an ideal way of inspiring others to strive towards success. Coaches can do this through their coaching, but also in everyday interactions. In other words, the skills and the 'coaching way of being' are readily transferable into other areas of life. Some ways of doing this are suggested.

14 Coaching in Context

This chapter invites you to consider the contexts in which you will be coaching. It provides an overview of similarities and differences across organisational and professional settings. Two examples ('coaching in education' and 'positive health coaching') are presented. The different purposes of coaching are also considered.

15 Reflecting on Practice

This chapter suggests that the growth and maturity of coaches can be developed through reflective practice. This reflection can take place individually, in peer groups or during coaching supervision. Becoming the best coach you can be is a lifelong endeavour. The importance of ethics in coaching is highlighted and readers are invited to start thinking about their future development as coaches. This chapter will suggest ways of continuing to develop your skills and 'coaching way of being' through practice, formal learning opportunities and supervisory conversations.

Our Focus

My intention has always been to provide a resource that is both research-informed and practical. This is the fourth edition of this book, and each iteration is informed by feedback from readers and recent developments in the fields of coaching and positive psychology. While the focus remains securely on the skills, conversational framework and 'coaching way of being' needed to support others, I am confident that you will benefit personally and professionally from learning to become a coach. Practising coaching will support you to develop the 'way of being' that can be particularly helpful in coaching as well as in everyday life, at work, at school, with friends and with family. As you learn to become a coach, you will find that you start to listen more authentically to others, ask thought-provoking questions and become better at building rapport and meaningful relationships. Whatever else we do, we need to remember that coaching is a human interaction that has as its 'underlying and ever-present goal' the building of others' self-belief 'regardless of the content of the task or issue' (Whitmore, 2009: 19).

2
Becoming a Coach

Let's address a fundamental question at the outset: does a person learn how to coach, or does she become a coach? There are different ways of engaging with this question. Many people learn how to coach in a transactional way, focusing narrowly on the process and thinking about coaching as a pragmatic conversational intervention. For example, I recall hearing some managers, who had recently received coach training, discussing the idea of 'putting on a coaching hat' before starting to coach others. This is an interesting way of thinking about coaching. It is, no doubt, possible to use a coaching intervention without fully adopting the philosophy that underpins the approach. A person can do coaching without being a coach. However, if you are hoping to inspire others and support them to achieve great things for themselves, I believe that you should be working to become a coach. This book will support you to do so.

To become a coach requires three areas of learning, which will be covered in this book: a set of skills; a clear conversational framework; and a 'coaching way of being' (see Figure 2.1). The first two (the skills and the framework) are relatively

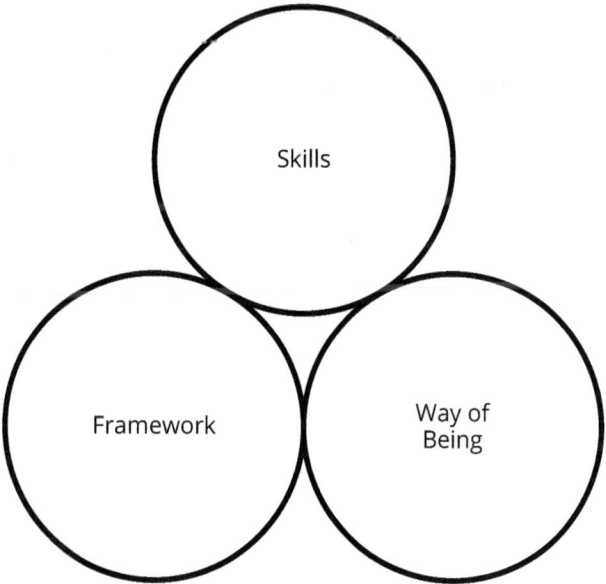

Figure 2.1 The three elements of effective coaching

easy to learn, often forming the basis of short training courses on coaching. I would argue, however, that understanding the skills and following a framework does not guarantee successful outcomes. They allow a person to do coaching. The more I learn and write about coaching, the more I realise that the third element is the most influential. Ironically, I believe that this element, which I refer to as a 'coaching way of being', cannot be taught in the traditional sense of the word. A deep understanding and appreciation of all three elements is necessary for effective coaching practice.

The structure of this book is designed to allow you to develop all three elements. We will start by building on your existing skills. If you are reading this text, you are likely to possess the foundational skills already. It will simply be a case of honing or sharpening these conversational skills so that you can use them for the specific purpose of coaching. Once we have discussed the necessary skills in some detail, we shall move on to considering the conversational framework. We will then look at additional approaches, tools and techniques that can supplement these. Once your skills are honed and the frameworks have been learned, we will explore the fascinating concept of the 'coaching way of being'. Hopefully, you will be able to quickly develop the coaching-related skills and master a conversational framework. Developing a 'coaching way of being' is a lifelong endeavour. The good news is that the best way of developing this 'way of being' is through practising coaching and reflecting on your experiences.

As we start this journey, we should begin by being clear about what we are working towards. There are many different areas in which coaching is flourishing. This introductory book provides a firm foundation for your practice, whichever field you wish to work in:

- Executive coaching: Working in organisations with middle and senior leaders.
- Life coaching: Working with individuals on topics relating to their personal lives.
- Health coaching: Working with patients and health professionals.
- Coaching in education: Working with students, educators and parents.
- Career coaching: Working with professionals about their career development.
- Leadership coaching: Working with leaders in any profession or field.
- Positive psychology coaching: Integrating coaching and positive psychology to enhance performance and wellbeing.

As you work your way through this book, you may wish to start thinking about which arena will be most fruitful. If you are hoping to develop a coaching business, I would recommend focusing on an arena in which you have some credibility already.

Snapshot 2.1

A 'Typical' Coaching Session

Before the Session

Pre-Coaching Discussion (Usually 10–20 Minutes)

This is an opportunity for you to introduce yourself to the client and agree a time for the first session. You and your client may also agree the topic of the coaching session.

During the Session

Coaching sessions tend to last between 30 and 90 minutes. Approximate times below are based on a 30-minute session. The video clips that have been recorded to support your learning were taken from 30-minute coaching conversations.

Small Talk to Build Rapport (2 Minutes)

The coach initiates a discussion which may be unrelated to the coaching topic in order to put the client at ease and start the process of building rapport. In the UK, for example, people like to talk about the weather!

Getting to Know One Another (2 Minutes)

It is helpful for the coach to introduce herself briefly. This is a good time to find out more about what the client does on a day-to-day basis, regardless of whether this relates directly to the coaching conversation. This is also the right time to agree a 'contract' about how the coaching will proceed. The importance of contracting (especially during the first coaching session) is covered in Chapter 7.

Setting Goals (5 Minutes)

In this section, the coach should support the client to identify the topic for the coaching conversation and an overall goal. This will be discussed in detail in Chapter 7.

Talking about What Is Happening Currently (5 Minutes)

This is the part of the conversation in which the client should be doing most of the talking. The coach's role is to listen carefully while the client explains her situation. The coach should ensure that the client focuses on her current situation *in relation to the goal* identified earlier.

(Continued)

Exploring Options (10 Minutes)

Once the client has explained the current state of play in relation to her topic or self-selected goal, the coach supports the client to generate possible ways forward. This is a very important part of the conversation and we will focus on the Options stage in the chapter about conversational frameworks (Chapter 7) and consider creative ways in which we can help the client to generate new ideas in Chapter 11.

Selecting an Option (2 Minutes)

Once some options have been generated, the client should start to evaluate the relative merits of each possibility. She will be encouraged to select at least one option that she would like to pursue.

Committing to Some Actions (2 Minutes)

In this part, the coach should encourage the client to commit to some actions that have emerged from the coaching conversation, based on the option selected earlier. Some clients like to develop an action plan that can be monitored.

Wrapping Up, Discussing How the Coaching Session Went (2 Minutes)

The final stage is a review of the coaching session, with an opportunity for the client to give the coach some feedback. It is helpful at this point to reconfirm arrangements for the next coaching conversation.

Relationship-Related Factors

In an important study about the success factors related to counselling interventions, Grencavage and Norcross (1990) detected four important elements. First, they confirmed the importance of the relationship or 'working alliance' between the counsellor and the client. Second, they found that much of the success of these relationships depended on factors related to the client, such as her level of expectation and the pressure to make changes. Grencavage and Norcross found that the possibility of change (i.e. 'Is the proposed change possible?') also played a significant role. It was recognised that any support available to the client (outside the counselling relationship) could have a significant impact on the outcome. This raises the question 'What does the counsellor have most influence over?'.

It seems to come down to a few key factors. The way the counsellor interacts with her client is important. Grencavage and Norcross (1990) suggest that the warmth, attentiveness and positivity of the counsellor are important. Equally, the counsellor's 'ability to cultivate hope and positive expectancies within the client' is a significant factor (p. 374). In other words, the counsellor should behave and speak in a way that increases the client's optimism or hopefulness about the counselling intervention.

I would suggest that both factors apply to coaching as well. This means that coaches should adopt a warm, attentive and positive approach. We will discuss this further in Chapter 12. A coach should also work to increase the positive expectations of the client (see Activity below).

Activity 2.1

Level of Confidence

Confidence Levels

As we have discussed above, a coach should foster her client's confidence in the coaching process. This is much easier to achieve if the coach is confident about her own abilities.

Take a moment to reflect on your current levels of confidence about coaching. Complete this activity on a new page in your learning journal.

At this moment, how confident are you about your ability to coach? Draw a line with a '1' on one end and a '10' on the other. On this scale, select a number that represents your current level of confidence. Below the line, write down some of your thoughts about why you selected that number. For example, if you have said '6', what makes it a '6' and not a '1'?

What practical things can you do to improve your self-rating? Make a note of a few things that you can do to increase your confidence in your ability to coach.

What Makes the Difference?

More recently, two leading executive coaches suggested that the field of coaching has sometimes overlooked the many years of research that have gone into what makes psychotherapy successful (McKenna and Davis, 2009). According to their analysis of those studies, they conclude that there are some 'ingredients' that lead to successful outcomes in one-to-one relationships:

1 Client Factors (40%)

Interestingly, the most consequential difference between outcomes seemed to be based on factors outside the therapeutic relationship. The character of the client and what is happening in her life (her social network, her professional role, her family) has a significant influence on the likelihood of a positive outcome.

2 The Relationship (30%)

According to McKenna and Davis' analysis of research into this area, 30% of the factors influencing the outcome of therapeutic relationships is the nature of the relationship between the therapist and her client. This means that the single most important factor within the control of the therapist is the strength and nature of the relationship.

3 Placebo or Hope (15%)

Echoing the study by Grencavage and Norcross (1990), McKenna and Davis (2009) note that people on a waiting list for therapy start to improve even before the first session. Simply put, those that expect to benefit from therapy are more likely to do so. My own personal experience confirms that this happens in coaching too (see 'Story from practice' below).

Story from Practice 2.1

What Is Already Better?

In most of my executive coaching assignments, I contact the client prior to our first coaching session for an introductory conversation. I find out a bit more about the client and I say a few words about my own professional background. The conversation usually ends by discussing the broad topic that the client would like to explore. When we meet for our first coaching session, I usually ask how things are in relation to the topic that they mentioned in our very first interaction. Very frequently, the client will report that things are better and that there have been improvements in the situation already.

---

4 Theory and Techniques (15%)

According to McKenna and Davis (2009), hundreds of research papers over many years seem to point towards an uncomfortable reality. Despite the existence of many theories and approaches to psychotherapy, no one approach seems to be more effective than another. In the words of the authors of the study, 'It's not the particular model or tool that makes the difference. Nor is it the brilliant theoretical or experiential insights of the coach. It's how we engage the client to think and act on his own behalf' (p. 256). This reminds us of the importance of 'partnering' with the client. We will discuss this idea further in Chapters 12 and 14.

Therapy is different from coaching. However, both are confidential, one-to-one relationships aimed at improving outcomes. Although the relative importance of each 'ingredient' may be different, it may be helpful to consider how these factors might influence coaching relationships.

McKenna and Davis conclude by proposing some practical suggestions for coaches:

1   First, 'use theory, models, tools, and techniques that you believe in and can deliver
    with competence and confidence' (p. 257). This is why it is important for you to
    build your own confidence in the coaching process.
2   'Draw out and deepen the client's own theory of his situation and how he can
    deal with it most effectively' (p. 257). Rather than impose our theory and therefore
    a solution, it is important that the client understands her situation in a way that
    makes sense to her.
3   'Help the client to identify with precision the strengths she can bring to bear on
    the challenges ahead' (p. 257). In other words, you can support the client by
    helping her to highlight the strengths and resources she already possesses.
4   'Be confident and clear about how the coaching process will work' (p. 257). As a
    coach, your confidence in the process will increase with experience and reflective
    practice. It is important to bear in mind that your familiarity and comfort with a
    conversational framework is likely to have a positive impact on the client's
    expectations.
5   'On a regular basis, ask the client whether she thinks you understand and
    appreciate her view of her situation' (p. 257). In other words, check that you have
    been able to show empathy. This cannot be emphasised enough. Do whatever it
    takes to help the client believe that you appreciate the importance of what is
    being shared.

McKenna and Davis' findings accord with earlier work by Alexander and Renshaw (2005).
According to them, coaches should attend to three areas:

1   Coaches must value their clients, be open and honest in their interactions and be
    able to support and challenge.
2   Coaches must have self-confidence and be self-aware.
3   Coaches must have a clear methodology. They need to have accomplished skills,
    being able to use both a clear framework and a range of effective coaching tools.
    (p. 381)

This book will cover all three areas, discussing the importance of the relationship
in the 'Coaching way of being' section (Chapters 12 and 13), coaching skills in the
'Key skills' section (Chapters 3–6) and conversational frameworks in 'The coaching
process' section (Chapters 7–9). A range of effective techniques that can be used
when coaching will be presented in the 'Tools and techniques' section (Chapters 10
and 11). Your self-confidence and self-awareness should emerge as you read this
book, undertake the exercises, watch the videos, practise coaching and reflect on
your experiences.

We have considered some of the elements that lead to effective outcomes based on research. Before we move on to review the skills related to coaching, it is helpful to get a richer sense of what should be happening in a coaching conversation. I would like to invite you to explore a metaphor that emerges from Whitmore's definition of coaching: 'unlocking people's potential to maximise their own performance' (2009: 11).

Unlocking Potential: Finding the Key

The notion of 'unlocking' in the English language implies the existence of a lock. It follows, therefore, that a 'key' is needed to perform the act of 'unlocking'. This is a rich metaphor for coaching and that is the reason that there is a fingerprint on the cover of this book. Our unique fingerprints are keys that can be used to unlock our devices. There are two fundamental premises that underpin effective coaching practice.

Fundamental Premise 1: Every Client Can Achieve More than She Is Currently Achieving

If a person's potential is locked away, this suggests that it already exists. That is one of the fundamental premises of coaching. Each person has significant potential, and certainly we, as coaches, must start from the belief that every client is able to achieve more than she is currently achieving. This positive belief should be espoused by every coach. As we have seen in the discussion above, the hopefulness of the client can impact on the success of a session. The coach's hopefulness and belief in the client play an important part in increasing and sustaining the positive expectations of the client.

Fundamental Premise 2: The Client Must Discover Her Own Key

The fact that coaching is about 'unlocking' potential means that the process of coaching involves finding a key that will allow the client to maximise her performance. So, we could say that both the coach and client are having a conversation in order to find that key. That is what the relationship is about. However, for coaching to be effective, the client must find the key for herself. The coach's role is to support the thinking and exploration of the client. Indeed, novice coaches often report that the most difficult task is resisting the urge to provide advice. Using this analogy, the challenge arises when the coach thinks that she has discovered the 'key' and proudly hands it to the client saying 'There it is! Now you can use this to unlock your potential.' At best, this is patronising. At worst, you can get in the way of the client discovering her own key. Less obvious – but still unhelpful – is the scenario in which the coach has seen the key and directs the client through leading questions and insinuation to find the key which the coach has already seen. Effective coaches will not look for the key themselves. Rather, they facilitate the client's search for the key. The most important moment in a coaching relationship is the one in which the *client* finds the key. This is often called the 'A-ha!' moment and will be discussed in Chapter 13. When the client discovers her own key, this gives her the positive emotion, the energy and the self-belief to achieve more of her potential.

A Question for You 2.1

What Was It Like?

Think back to a time when you discovered your own 'key' or solution to something. We call these 'A-ha!' moments. Write a paragraph in your learning journal about an 'A-ha!' moment that you have experienced. What was the situation? How did you feel after the 'A-ha!' moment?

Story from Practice 2.2

Extending the Analogy

I enjoy talking to students about coaching and take every opportunity to do so. I was presenting an overview of coaching to a group of students on a Master's in Applied Positive Psychology (MAPP) programme at a university in the UK. As part of the exploration of the term 'coaching', I invited the students to get into groups to talk about the analogy of the key. This type of activity usually generates interesting insights into the nature of coaching relationships. On this occasion, students came up with some wonderful ideas that challenged my own thinking about this topic. One group was curious about whether it was OK for the client to believe that such a key did not exist. Another group wondered if some coaching conversations might be about the existence of multiple keys, with the coach supporting the client to identify the right key. Most interesting was the idea that the coach and the client may sometimes be able to co-create the key needed to unlock the client's potential. These ideas are discussed below.

Co-Creating the Key?

Coaching is a collaborative activity. In other words, both parties are involved in the thinking process. In this regard, it is possible to imagine that two partners (coach and client) actually co-construct the key together. Through conversation, it is possible for the partnership itself to design a key that may unlock the client's potential. This is particularly helpful when the key has been 'lost'.

(Continued)

Too Many Keys?

In some coaching conversations, it may well be the case that the client is overwhelmed by opportunities or choices. She can see keys everywhere and cannot decide which, if any, to choose. In these cases, the conversation can focus on identifying which key might make the most difference, which is best for the client at the moment or which is the easiest to find and use.

No Keys at All?

In other conversations, the client may feel that there is no key to unlock her potential. These conversations can be challenging, because of the centrality of the idea that coaching is about improving performance and enhancing wellbeing. In this case, it may be helpful to clarify the reason that the client has sought coaching. A good coaching conversation could focus on the topic of identifying goals for future sessions. To follow our analogy, the first coaching conversation could focus on a strategy for how to start looking for the key.

Core Competencies

Part of your journey towards becoming an accredited coach will require you to learn and demonstrate some core competencies. By working through this book, you will develop the skills and competencies necessary to become an effective coach. There are references to the guidelines of the three leading professional associations – the International Coach Federation (ICF), the European Mentoring and Coaching Council (EMCC) and the Association for Coaching (AC). Please look out for the boxes called 'What the Professional Associations Say' to see how skills, ideas and concepts in this book align to the competencies of these professional associations.

What the Professional Associations Say 2.1

Core Competencies

Table 2.1 integrates the core competencies of the three associations (ICF, EMCC, AC). In other words, if you are planning to become an accredited coach, you should make sure that you are able to demonstrate these competencies, regardless of which professional association you choose to work with.

Table 2.1 Covering the competencies

Competencies	Description	Relevant chapters
Communicating effectively	You will need to develop your communication skills so that you can be an active listener who asks powerful questions in order to foster client growth	Chapter 3: Noticing Chapter 4: Listening Chapter 5: Playing back Chapter 6: Asking powerful questions
Facilitating learning and development	You should be able to support the learning, growth and goal attainment of clients by facilitating coaching sessions using recognised conversational frameworks	Chapter 2: Becoming a coach Chapter 7: Conversational frameworks Chapter 8: Ways of thinking
Building client-centred relationships	You should be able to establish trust and create collaborative partnerships, adapting to your clients' context and needs	Chapter 9: Positive bias Chapter 12: Being human Chapter 13: Inspiring others Chapter 14: Coaching in context
Practising ethically and professionally	You are expected to work ethically and adopt high standards of professionalism	Chapter 15: Reflecting on practice
Engaging in lifelong learning and self-reflection	You are expected to maintain your own learning and engage in reflective practice	Chapter 15: Reflecting on practice

Conclusion

Having considered some research, explored the metaphor of the key and considered the core competencies of coaching, what can we conclude about 'becoming a coach'? What are the attributes that we should develop if we are to be outstanding coaches who can make a real difference to the performance and wellbeing of others?

Being Interested

To build effective relationships and encourage our clients to explore their thoughts and feelings, we must be able to show that we are genuinely interested in what they are saying. It is not that we must look interested, we must *be* interested in our clients and what they are working through.

Being Genuine

Clients cannot build trusting relationships with people who are putting on a mask. Coaches must be genuine in their interactions. Lying, pretending and faking cannot be part of a coaching conversation. Trusting relationships can only develop between two human beings who are honest and authentic. Coaching will provide you with an opportunity to be honest and genuine in a conversation about the personal and professional development of others.

Liking People

Some people make good money out of coaching. That said, the primary driver for every coach should be to support others to thrive. Coaches must like people. If this statement challenges you, that is OK. Coaching others will increase your appreciation of human beings. If you like people already, you simply have a head start!

Believing in People

Not only should a coach be a 'people person', she must also believe in others. We should give our clients the benefit of the doubt at all times. It is imperative that a coach believes that their clients are essentially good. Again, the practice of coaching can help to bolster this belief.

I hope that you are feeling energised and motivated about becoming a coach! By this point, you should have a clearer idea about what coaching is and a better understanding of its purpose. We will now move on to the skills of coaching.

Part II
Coaching Skills

Part II

Coaching Skills

3
Noticing

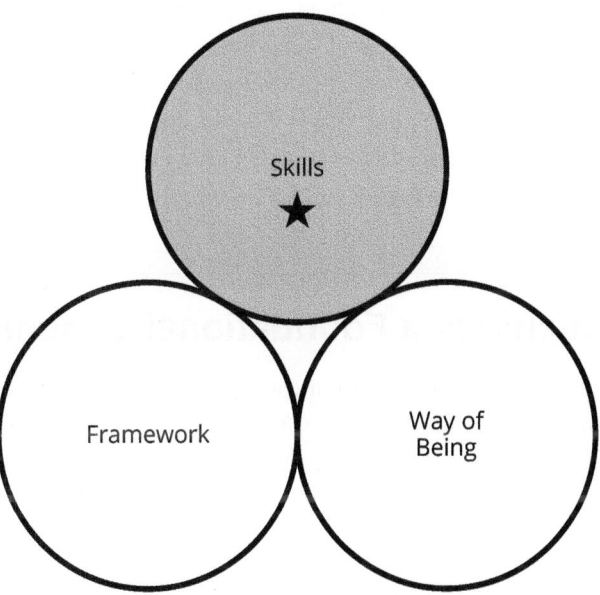

Figure 3.1 The three elements of effective coaching

In this chapter, we will delve into the first of the coaching skills as we prepare to work through all three elements shown in Figure 3.1. The skills chapters are supported by video clips of real coaching conversations. You may wish to read the chapters first, then watch the videos ('See it in practice' boxes). Alternatively, you may prefer to watch the videos before reading the chapter. Choose what works best for you.

Noticing is a subtle yet essential skill of coaching. It is *foundational* because it is necessary to notice what is happening before deciding how to use the other skills. In fact, noticing relates to one of the key purposes of coaching: increasing awareness. By noticing and being alert to what takes place during conversations, coaches make better decisions about how to support their clients. In this chapter, we will define the skill of noticing, reflect on its importance, identify what can be noticed and explore how coaches might improve their ability to notice.

Noticing as a Skill

A dictionary definition of 'notice' is 'to see or become conscious of something or someone' (Online Cambridge dictionary). In the context of coaching, we will refer to noticing as 'becoming conscious of information that may be useful to clients and the coaching process'. To identify noticing as a coaching *skill* raises at least three questions. First, how can we define noticing as a skill if people can do it without effort? For example, a person may notice background music or notice a change in temperature when leaving a building. No conscious effort is required in either situation. However, it is possible for people to *improve* their ability to notice things. Therefore, noticing is presented in this book as a skill. Second, can the skill of noticing be developed? Yes. There would be no purpose in identifying noticing as an essential skill if it could not be improved through practice. Third, how might developing the skill of noticing enhance the effectiveness of coaches? We will address this question below.

Why Noticing Is a Foundational Coaching Skill

Enhancing the skill of noticing is about improving the ability of coaches to become conscious of information that might be helpful to the client and the coaching process. By improving the ability to notice, a coach is enhancing her overall effectiveness as a coach and can therefore be of better service to her clients.

Professional Practice of Coaches

For a coach, improved noticing can lead to better decisions about what to do during coaching conversations. Being better at this skill, a coach will be able to notice details and nuances, increasing the amount of information available to her. For example, if the coach notices a dip in energy during the coaching conversation, she could introduce a creative activity (see Chapter 11). In another scenario, a coach might notice a recurring behaviour or pattern that may seem to be preventing the client from progressing. This pattern can be brought into the conversation and discussed. Even more importantly, being skilled at noticing can influence the stance of the coach. By directing attention to noticing what is happening rather than trying to solve problems, coaches can settle into a facilitative stance that will feel empowering and respectful to the client. This is a significant repositioning of the role of the coach, meaning that she sees herself as the person responsible for being fully attentive and aware of what is happening during the coaching conversation, rather than the one who is primarily involved in thinking about a solution with the client. The responsibility for solving problems or generating new ideas lies with the client. Finally, as part of the coach's ongoing professional development and growth, it is important that she notices which aspects of her practice are effective and which require further refinement. So, in this sense the coach is noticing what works best, and this can lead to even better coaching practice.

Transferability of the Skill of Noticing

For clients, working with a coach who is particularly skilled at noticing can highlight the importance of increased awareness and consciousness. For example, if a coach regularly notices how certain situations motivate or demotivate a client, this may lead the client to become more aware of the effect that certain everyday events can have on her motivation. In other words, the skilled use of noticing by the coach can lead to increased awareness about the value of noticing in the client. Having had positive experiences of noticing during a coaching conversation, a client may, in turn, start noticing things that are important for her own growth and development. In other cases, something that the coach notices may bring to awareness an issue that has been ignored, underplayed or forgotten by the client. So there are numerous ways in which a coach's skill in noticing can encourage her client to develop this ability too.

What Can Be Noticed?

Having discussed how the skill of noticing can be beneficial, let us turn our attention to the kinds of things that coaches can helpfully notice during coaching conversations. In the section below, we will review what a coach can notice about her clients, herself and the quality of the coaching relationship. The client provides a wealth of information during coaching conversations: through her comments, her behaviour, her questions and her body language. There are many things that could be noticed. First, the coach might notice the level of readiness of the client. Has the client spent time preparing for the session? How positive does she seem about the prospect of being coached? Second, it is possible to notice the openness of the client to challenge. Does she invite challenge? Or does she have strategies to avoid uncomfortable situations? Third, the coach can notice the energy levels of the client. Does she seem energised by the coaching conversation? Or is it possible to detect a sense of resignation? Fourth, the coach can notice how the client responds to her. Does the client exude warm, positive intention towards the coach? Or does the client reveal signals that she does not trust the coach? Fifth, the expressiveness of the client can be noticed. Is it possible to read the client's facial expressions? How comfortable is the client when talking about herself? Sixth, the coach can notice the language of the client. What particular words is the client using? Does the client use unusual words or phrases? Finally, a coach should be conscious of the body language of her client. Body language will be explored in more detail in Chapter 10. As you can see from this selective yet extensive list, there are so many things that can be noticed!

Review Your Practice 3.1

Things to Notice in Your Client

Table 3.1   What coaches can notice

• *Readiness of the client*	Enthusiastic, reluctant, disengaged
• *Openness to challenge*	Welcoming, resistant, defensive
• *Level of energy*	High, low, calm, nervous
• *Response to coach*	Warm, friendly, cold, formal
• *Expressiveness*	Reticent, chatty, reserved
• *Body language*	Closed, open, engaged, disinterested

While it is obvious that the client should be a rich source of information for a coach, it is also helpful for her to notice aspects of her own thoughts and behaviours.

The Coach

Even as the coach is attentive and primed to notice emerging information regarding the client, she should also be conscious of what might be happening for her (as the coach). There are some things that a coach might usefully choose to notice about herself: her own behaviours, feelings, thoughts and intuition. For example, what might the coach's body language and behaviours say about what she is feeling? What new behaviours does the coach notice in herself when working with a particular client? Which of these behaviours is uncharacteristic for the coach? What emotions does the coach experience during the coaching conversation? To what extent are these emotions triggered by what the client is doing or saying, and to what extent are the emotions based on the coach's own thoughts and concerns? How does the coach perceive the client? What intuitions emerge during the coaching conversation? How does the coach manage these intuitions? What might these intuitions be suggesting? As becomes obvious when a few of these questions are posed, there is much for a coach to notice about herself. Such noticing can add insight and awareness that can be harnessed in the best interests of the client and the coaching relationship.

Review Your Practice 3.2

Things to Notice about Yourself (as a coach)

How are you feeling about meeting the client?

What unusual behaviours do you notice (in yourself) as you are coaching?

What is your level of energy during the coaching conversation?

What do you think about the client's issue?

Who does the client remind you of?

What else do you notice about yourself?

The Relationship Between Coach and Client

In addition to noticing what is happening for each of the participants of a coaching conversation, the coach can become conscious of certain aspects of the coaching relationship. How warm is it? What is the level of rapport generated? Who takes the lead in the partnership? How is tension managed? Who drives the relationship? Who is taking more responsibility for success? As in the other cases, there are many questions that can be asked. Put together, the data that can be harnessed in support of the client is considerable. Enhancing the skill of noticing is one way of accessing a significant amount of information that can be helpful to the client and the coaching process.

How to Improve the Skill of Noticing

How good are you at noticing already? Some of us are better at noticing than others. You may already be excellent at noticing. If so, you probably enjoy travelling to new places, walking in nature, visiting art galleries and so on. This will be a great advantage when learning to become a coach, and the main area of development will be related to *what* to notice during coaching conversations. On the other hand, you may be someone who prefers focusing on the bigger picture. If so, you may not notice that someone has had a haircut, or that a restaurant has changed its name or that there is an unusual bird in a tree outside your home. In this case, it will be important to start by intentionally honing your skill of noticing. Whether you are skilled at noticing or not, please take some time for the activity below.

--- Activity 3.1 ---

Rediscovery Walk

Allocate 15–20 minutes for a walk. Please select a route that is already familiar to you. For example, you might choose the route to your local supermarket, or a favourite walk in nature or the way you get to work. The purpose of this activity is to intentionally notice things that may have gone unnoticed previously. Take a notebook or use a note-taking

(Continued)

application to list everything that you notice for the first time as you walk along the familiar route. Once you return from the walk, consult your notes and reflect on the following:

- What did you notice for the first time?
- Did you notice anything that had changed?
- What was different about this walk compared to previous occasions?

Hopefully, you will have noticed additional things on your 'rediscovery walk'. If so, this demonstrates that it is possible to increase your ability to notice through intentional practice. Below, we will consider the various ways in which a coach might be able to improve her ability to notice during coaching conversations: applying conscious attention; being 'in the moment'; and cultivating and managing curiosity.

Applying Conscious Attention

To some extent, a coach can notice more things if she applies conscious attention. That means being intentionally observant in the way that you may have been during the 'rediscovery walk' in the activity above. A coach could enter into a coaching conversation with the clear determination to be as attentive as possible to the client and the coaching relationship. Practically speaking, this could be supplemented by having a notebook or note-taking application so that the coach could keep a written record of what is noticed. It is recommended that you practise applying conscious attention during all your conversational interactions so that you continue to develop the skill of noticing.

Being 'in the Moment'

Another way to be better at noticing is to enhance your ability to be 'in the moment'. This term typically means that a person is fully immersed in what is happening to her at any given time. Mindfulness is a popular way of developing this ability. In fact, Liz Hall defines mindfulness as 'deliberately paying attention in the moment' (2013: 13). According to Hall, mindfulness is more than simply the ability to be 'in the moment'; it also requires the person to be non-judgemental about what is happening, bringing a sense of curiosity and compassion to that particular moment. Again, this may come more naturally to some people than others but the surge in popularity of mindfulness meditation suggests that such practices do improve the ability of people to be 'in the moment' in a way that is non-judgemental, curious and compassionate. In her groundbreaking book *Neuroscience for Coaches*, Amy Brann explains that 'mindfulness meditation can be thought of as the practice of attending to present moment experiences and allowing any emotions and thoughts to pass without judgement' (2017: 158). According to Brann, a more recent two-component model of mindfulness 'involves both the regulation of attention on immediate experience and also approaching experiences (regardless of what they are) with a mindset of curiosity, openness and acceptance' (p. 158). For coaches, learning about mindfulness may therefore have multiple benefits from personal growth and calmness through to a heightened, non-judgemental awareness that will improve their ability to notice more during their coaching conversations.

Find Out More 3.1

Mindfulness

As an experienced practitioner who incorporates mindfulness effectively into her own coaching practice, Liz Hall is an excellent source of information. Her book *Mindful Coaching: How Mindfulness Can Transform Coaching Practice* provides helpful and implementable ideas and techniques that allow coaches to integrate mindfulness into their coaching practice.

When reflecting on your own ability to be 'in the moment', it may be helpful to learn more about your individual time perspective. People with a certain balance of time perspectives will find it easier to be 'in the moment' with their clients than others. If you are not already familiar with your own time perspective preferences, you may want to find out more.

Find Out More 3.2

Time Perspectives

Your time perspective preferences will have an influence on how comfortable you are being 'in the moment'. This topic has been studied by Zimbardo and Boyd (1999), who propose that each person has an orientation towards time perspectives. They identify the following time perspectives: past-negative, past-positive, present-fatalistic, present-hedonistic and future. According to Zimbardo and Boyd, it is possible to change our orientation to time perspectives. You can find out more about the concept of time perspectives by visiting www.thetimeparadox.com

---

Cultivating and Managing Curiosity

In addition to applying conscious attention and developing the ability to be 'in the moment', coaches will need to work on cultivating and managing their curiosity. Being inherently curious would seem to be an advantage in coaching. Professor Todd Kashdan

(2010) makes a strong case for the advantages that curiosity can bring to human exist-ence. Indeed, a curious disposition will encourage coaches to be open to new ideas and experiences. This means that they are are less likely to become judgemental when working with their clients. Curious coaches will also be better at asking questions because their wonderment will trigger questions based on what their clients are saying. Most pertinently, a sense of curiosity is likely to lead to the coach noticing more infor-mation during coaching conversations. So there is compelling argument for cultivating a spirit of curiosity and bringing it into the coaching relationship. At the same time, there is a need to manage a coach's curiosity, remembering that every coaching conver-sation must be undertaken with the best interests of the client in mind. This means coaches must bring a spirit of wonderment and *appropriate* curiosity to every coaching conversation. In other words, a coach should be curious and ask questions that pertain to the client and her situation, rather than pursuing avenues that are more related to areas of interest for the coach. To give an example, if a coach becomes curious about the leadership and management structure of the client's organisation because the coach is a leadership development expert, then it would be inappropriate to ask further ques-tions about the structure. However, if the client believes that the leadership and management structures of her organisation might be preventing her from reaching her goals, then questions about these structures would be helpful. Throughout any coaching interaction, the key driver should always be the best interests of the client. This is no different when it comes to curiosity, and effective coaches will cultivate a sense of curi-osity and bring it to coaching conversations intentionally and in service of the client.

Activity 3.2

Practising Noticing

Whenever there is a 'See it in practice' box, you will have an opportunity to practise your noticing. One way of sharpening this skill is to try noticing in different ways. What happens if you watch the video with the sound off? What if you just listen to the audio? What if you focus on the body language? What if you pay attention only to the client? Or only the coach? Please use the video clips as a way of experimenting with different ways of notic-ing and capture your insights in your learning journal.

By developing the ability to notice as you have experienced above, coaches can be more alert in coaching conversations, thereby gathering data and information that will be of use to both the coach and the client. In some cases, the information that the coach gains in this way may be of value to the client. In these circumstances, it is recommended that the coach provides this feedback directly to the client.

What Type of Feedback Should Coaches Provide?

How much helpful feedback a coach can provide will depend on how well the coach knows the client. Even if the coach and the client do not know one another at all, the coach can provide feedback about two important factors. First, it may be helpful to the client to know how you, as a coach, experience her as a person. If you experience the client in a particular way, it is possible that other people may experience her that way too. Second, any impressions and thoughts formed through what is noticed during interactions with the client can be a rich source of additional data. While others may have similar interactions with the client, they may not be willing or able to share their views.

Snapshot 3.1

Sharing Feedback

There are many opportunities to share what you are noticing during a coaching conversation. Here is an example: 'As we have been talking, I have noticed that you are not very expressive. You haven't used any hand gestures and your tone of voice has not changed during our conversation. Even when we were talking about a future aspiration which you said you were excited about, it was not evident through your facial expressions.'

The feedback shown in the Snapshot above could be helpful to a client. If presented positively within a strong coaching relationship, feedback can raise self-awareness and provide the client with valuable information about how others might perceive her. At times, it can be a challenging task to give a client accurate feedback.

Providing Helpful Feedback

It may be beneficial at this point to remind ourselves what coaching is all about. The coach's role is to partner with the client to support her to achieve her goals and unlock more of her potential. Often, clients feel stuck or unable to achieve their goals, but they are not exactly sure what is stopping them. Coaching can be helpful in providing clients with more information about their strengths and areas for development as they work towards their goals. By being attentive and noticing better, coaches can pick up valuable additional information. One of the responsibilities of the coach is to be honest with the client. Morally this is the right thing to do, but it is also a way of building and maintaining a strong relationship with the client. Part of this honesty includes providing accurate and timely feedback if this will help the client to achieve her goals.

How Can We Tell that Feedback Would Be Helpful?

There are some indications that additional information could be helpful for the client. In each of the cases presented in Table 3.2, it is possible that the coach may notice something during her interactions with the client that could shed more light on the situation.

Table 3.2   Indications that feedback might be helpful

Situation	Example	Implication
The client does not understand why something is happening	'I don't know why I never get selected for interviews for senior leadership positions.'	The surprise or lack of understanding suggests that the client is missing some information, either about herself or about her context.
The client notices that the same situation keeps recurring	'It's the same with every manager I have had. They always take advantage of my good nature.'	If a client finds herself caught in a cycle or pattern, there is a possibility that she is not aware of her part in the situation.
The client makes numerous assumptions about what others think	'I think she assumes that I am intimidated because I have only been in the business for less than a year.'	Basing actions or responses on untested assumptions is risky.

What Other Sources of Feedback May Be Helpful?

While we may agree that feedback is helpful for clients, the coach is not always the best source of feedback. In fact, it is often more appropriate for the client to seek feedback from other sources. Sometimes it is simply a case of asking people. For example, a good coaching question to ask a client who is uncertain about what others think of her presentations is 'How can you find out?'. Sometimes the client will need encouragement to do this.

Snapshot 3.2

Sources of Feedback

- Asking colleagues, friends and family.
- 360° assessment tools.
- Psychometric questionnaires.
- Performance review meetings.
- Being observed.
- Video recording.

How Can a Client Collect Feedback?

When it emerges that additional feedback would be helpful for clients, there may be various sources of information available to them.

Asking Colleagues, Friends and Family

The simplest way of getting feedback is to ask someone for it. Work colleagues can be useful sources of information. For example, if a manager feels that team meetings are not valued by members of her team, it makes sense to ask them directly. Some will prefer to go to people they trust or have an existing relationship with. Others will be comfortable to talk to anyone. Often, clients will resist this approach, saying that they will not get truthful feedback. First, this is an assumption. Second, dubious feedback is better than no feedback at all. And finally, seeking feedback shows that a person is committed to learning and improvement.

360° Assessment Tool

A generally accepted way of collecting work-related feedback is the 360° assessment tool. These are usually externally administered questionnaires, which are completed by colleagues in an organisation. A questionnaire is sent to the person's line manager, peers and those who report to her. Recipients are asked questions about the person's competencies and behaviours. The assessment tool generates a report that collates all the responses, providing some quantitative data and some qualitative data. The 360° assessment tool can be helpful because it provides an external view of the person based on multiple responses. From a coaching perspective, the report provides a very good starting point for discussion.

Psychometric Questionnaires

Clients can be asked to complete psychometric questionnaires. Most are available online and measure a whole range of attributes, skills and strengths. In all self-report questionnaires, the feedback is based on the information provided by the client. The reports produced by psychometric questionnaires also provide a starting point for coaching discussions. Any results that are surprising to the client may be a focus for further exploration.

Find Out More 3.3

Psychometrics

The best resource about the use of psychometric and psychological tools for coaches is *Psychometrics in Coaching* (Passmore, 2012). This edited book includes chapters on the use of coaching alongside many of the most relevant psychometric tests.

Performance Review Meetings

The notes of performance review meetings between the client and her line manager can contain useful feedback. Clients can take advantage of performance review meetings to solicit clear and explicit feedback that can inform future coaching sessions.

Being Observed

Some executive coaches offer to observe their clients in the workplace. This can create a link between the coaching space and the place of work. However, even with the attendance of a coach, the feedback is still being generated by someone else and it is not as powerful as allowing the client to see herself in her professional role.

Video Recording

Video recording oneself is a particularly powerful way of getting feedback. As there is no external interpretation, it is difficult for a client to reject the information that she is seeing with her own eyes. Often, we do not know what it looks like when we do what we do. When using video with clients, it is recommended that they are given time to watch the clip by themselves first. This gives them a chance to get used to seeing themselves on a screen so that they will be able to focus on the changes they want to make when they meet with a coach.

———— What the Professional Associations Say 3.1 ————

The Skill of Noticing

The skill of noticing is an important foundational skill that will allow you to develop some of the key competencies required by most professional associations.

Specifically, the skill of noticing is required to demonstrate three of the ICF's core competencies. By noticing the quality of the relationship and gathering information about the client's level of comfort, coaches will **cultivate trust and safety**. By noticing nuances and subtle cues during a conversation, coaches will be able to **listen actively**. For example, the coach might notice that the client avoids talking about their own emotions and bring this topic into the conversation. Noticing is also needed to **facilitate client growth**. Being alert to new ideas during a conversation allows coaches to raise awareness of insights that emerge. The coach's role is to follow up with questions about how such insights can be put into action to support the client to learn, grow and develop.

Noticing is also a cornerstone skill that supports the competencies of the EMCC and the AC. It supports the EMCC's competencies of **building the relationship, understanding self** and **enabling insight and learning** and the AC's competencies of **establishing a trust-based relationship with the client, raising awareness and insight** and **communicating effectively**.

Conclusion

In this chapter, we have considered the central role that the skill of noticing can play during coaching conversations. We have seen that noticing supports the coach as they manage a coaching session, and that it can increase the amount of information available to the client. Increasing the ability of coaches to notice will support relationship building with clients because it demonstrates interest in them and their topics. And by being better at noticing relevant factors when coaching, coaches will be able to focus their mental energy on being fully present, rather than formulating solutions or generating advice.

See It in Practice 3.1

The Skill of Noticing

Video 3.1 Noticing a Response

When you watch this clip, what do you notice about the client's response when they are thinking about how to manage 'squeaky wheels'? The client clicks and unclicks their pen before responding. How can this information be helpful to you as a coach?

Video 3.2 Noticing a Word

This clip shows the importance of noticing words that are important for the client. In this case, the word is 'freedom'. When the word is noticed and played back to the client, they have the opportunity of reflecting how this is important for their sense of identity.

Video 3.3 Being Curious

In this clip, the coach demonstrates appropriate curiosity by asking about what notes the client has taken. This gives the client the opportunity to share an important insight about what they need to remember as they move forward.

Video 3.4 Giving Positive Feedback

This clip shows the coach sharing what they have noticed about the client. As you watch, notice the effect the positive feedback has on the client.

4
Listening

In this chapter, we will consider the second of the coaching skills as we continue to work through all three elements shown in Figure 4.1. This chapter is also supported by video clips of these skills being demonstrated by the author. They will give you a sneak peek into what happens during real coaching conversations. Please refer to them as you read this chapter.

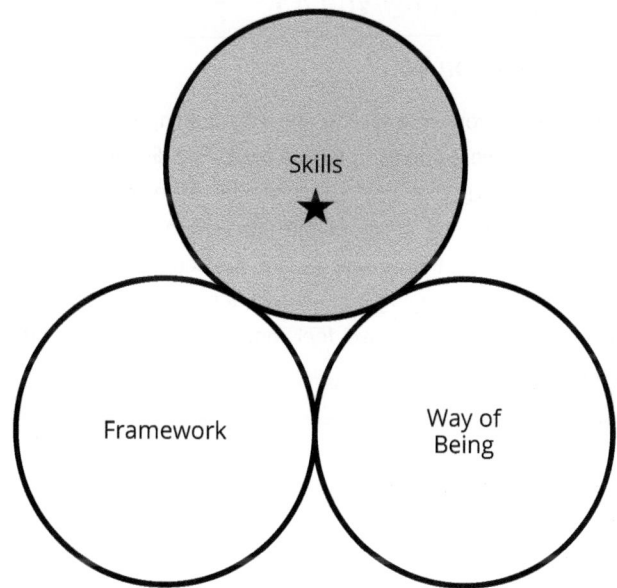

Figure 4.1   The three elements of effective coaching

Why Listening Is an Important Skill

Most of us listen every day of our lives. We listen to what is happening all around us. We listen to the news. We listen to what people are saying to us. What is different about listening for the purposes of coaching? We normally use our skills of conversational listening to *understand* what others are saying. In coaching, we listen with a different purpose: to connect with the client and demonstrate interest. When listened to in this way, the client will enjoy speaking to the coach; they are able to think *better*, and they will feel that they have been heard. Listening effectively to someone is a guaranteed way of showing that we care.

Find Out More 4.1

Radical Listening

For an in-depth exploration of the power of listening, I would recommend a book that I co-authored with one of the world's leading positive psychologists, Dr Robert Biswas-Diener. *Radical Listening* (van Nieuwerburgh and Biswas-Diener, 2025) uncovers how the skill of listening can be used to make stronger connections and build better relationships with people.

A Question for You 4.1

What Was the Impact on You?

Think back to a time when you were talking about something that was of genuine interest to you but the person you were speaking to was obviously distracted or not listening. How did that impact on what you were saying? It can be a demoralizing experience. Poor-quality listening can diminish the ability of the speaker to think clearly and convey her message. If it seems to us that the person we are speaking to is uninterested, we start to doubt the value of what we are saying. Fortunately, the opposite is also true. If people listen to us genuinely and attentively, we feel more confident about our topic and can discuss it more fluently.

Story from Practice 4.1

Power of Listening

When I deliver training on coaching skills, I like to run a short activity on the power of listening. Participants are asked to work in pairs. One person is asked to think about a hobby or topic of interest and the other person is given a 'listening card'. The card instructs the participant to listen in a certain way. There are four different cards: 'radical listening', 'attentive listening', 'half listening' and 'not listening'. The 'radical listening' card asks the participant to use her best listening skills, using positive affirmations, nodding and appropriate body language. The 'not listening' card instructs the participant to doodle on a piece of paper, interrupt the other person by asking seemingly irrelevant questions, jump in with her own experiences (e.g. 'That happened to me, too! In my case ...') and look out of the window or otherwise seem distracted.

I am uncomfortable when I facilitate this activity because it can feel very disempowering and demotivating for the person who is paired with someone with the 'not listening' card. The reason I continue to use this activity is because it can show so powerfully the difference between 'radical listening' and 'not listening' for the person being listened to. Invariably, those who were listened to will feel positive and enthusiastic about their topic and will have enjoyed the chance to talk about it. On the other hand, those who experienced talking to someone with the 'not listening' card will have had a negative experience. Many participants report literally 'losing their voice' or feeling that their topic is 'boring' or 'silly'. The difference between the experiences is extreme. Coaching is all about listening in a way that makes a client feel as if she has been heard, that she is intelligent and that her topic is interesting.

What Can We Do to Improve the Quality of Our Listening?

There are three ways in which a person can enhance her listening skills: by being more intentional about demonstrating that she is listening; by becoming familiar with the concept of 'levels of listening'; and by embracing curiosity. In this chapter, we will consider strategies for being a more intentional listener and levels of listening. At surface level, coaches need to ensure that they *look* like they are listening to their clients. You may already be familiar with such techniques. They are useful in many aspects of everyday life. This chapter will present a few ways to demonstrate that you are listening. If you use these techniques already, that is great – please continue to do so. If not, think about the value of adopting a few of the ideas presented below. As with any new skills, it will be necessary to practise these techniques.

Staying Quiet

The most important difference about listening for the purposes of coaching is that the coach should stay quiet. For a variety of reasons, our society affords people little opportunity to be genuinely listened to. Often, a conversation can seem like a battle for 'airtime'. It may be an exaggeration to say that we spend most of our time in conversations 'waiting for our turn to speak', but it can sometimes feel that way. If we start to plan how to respond to what the speaker is saying *while she is still talking*, this means that we have diverted a big chunk of our attention away from listening. In our increasingly busy lives, this is something that we might be doing without even realising it!

In coaching conversations, there are also things that we should *stop* doing.

Completing Sentences

When coaching, we must allow the client time to complete her thoughts and sentences. If the client is starting to think differently or see things from another perspective, it is normal that she will pause as she is talking, even in the middle of sentences. As coaches, we must control our (usually well-intentioned) impulses to finish the sentences of others. For example, a half-finished sentence such as 'I don't know … there are times that this work gets so difficult, and there's just so little reward, I wonder whether to just …' can be completed in so many ways! Coaches should avoid the trap of attempting to demonstrate empathy by finishing such sentences for the client (e.g. 'retire early?'). As you can imagine, there are many reasons this could be unhelpful. First, there are often benefits for the client to struggle to find the right words for herself. If the idea of early retirement has been problematic in the past, the client saying it herself is crucial so that she can experience what it feels like to say it out loud. Second, you will have necessarily made an assumption about what the client was going to say. We can offend the client by making a derogatory assumption (as in the example noted here, especially if the client did not consider herself to be of retirement age). On the other hand, the client may not feel able to contradict the coach, and therefore an element of confusion is introduced. It can also be considered disrespectful to interrupt in many cultures and social contexts. Finally, we may be missing out on some insightful comments or realisations from the client.

Guessing at Difficult Words

Another behaviour that is perfectly acceptable in everyday conversation is to provide suggestions for words that speakers seem to find difficult. This is particularly unhelpful in coaching and should be avoided. The temptation to help a speaker to find exactly the right word is perfectly natural. But in coaching, the choice of words is critical. That is why we should encourage the client to come up with those words for herself. This applies even when the client asks 'What's the word?' or you are speaking to someone for whom English is an additional language. The choice of word, especially when it requires hard thinking, is particularly important. As a coach, it is desirable to wait until the word has been chosen. Usually, it is worth unpicking why a particular word was chosen, and this can often be quite interesting for the client. If the coach simply says, for example, 'The word you're looking for is "paradox"', many coaching opportunities are lost and the client may not feel fully listened to. Doing this also suggests impatience, when the coach should be demonstrating the opposite. The client should feel that she can have as much time as she needs to explore her topic.

Comparing Ourselves

Again, this happens frequently in everyday conversations. This is the 'it happened to me' scenario. In a back-and-forth dialogue, this can have the positive effect of keeping the conversation flowing between both parties. In coaching, it is unwelcome because it takes the focus of the discussion off the client and onto the coach. The purpose of the coaching session is to give the *client* thinking and speaking time. For example, if a client says 'It was three weeks before I met my line manager', it might be very tempting for you to reply with 'Yes, I know how that works. It was the same for me. Mind you, I wasn't too bothered …' and so on. This may seem to be an effective way of demonstrating empathy, but what in fact happens is that the conversation turns to focus on you, the coach, instead of the client, where the focus must always remain. When you are *being* coached, take advantage of this situation! When you *are* the coach, note any thoughts like this but do not compare yourself. If it is necessary or helpful to inform the client that you have been in a similar situation, keep it very brief. Using the example above, 'I had a similar experience. How did that make you feel?' is sufficient. In other words, share the fact that you have had a similar experience *if you think that this information will be helpful to the client*, and then turn the focus back on the client's experience of the situation.

Competing with the Client

This is probably unhelpful in any conversation. This refers to comments that are intended to show that you are better, or that you have had an even more noteworthy experience, than the speaker. Refer back to the example above: 'Three weeks? I don't think I met my manager for well over a year!' Such comments minimise the experience of the other person and therefore have no place in a coaching conversation.

Doodling

While some people (including me) would argue that they are able to listen better when they doodle, it is not conducive to good listening in coaching conversations. This allows us to consider a very important point of principle when it comes to coaching. While it is necessary that you listen attentively to your client, it is even more important to *demonstrate* that you are doing so. Both must be happening. So, even if a coach may feel that she *does* listen better when she doodles, there is a risk that it may not be perceived that way by the client.

Story from Practice 4.2

Talk to me

At one point in my professional life I had a manager who used to ask me to talk to her while she was typing emails: 'Talk to me. I can listen to you while I respond to this email.' Even if she did have this amazing multi-tasking ability to type and listen at the same time, my perception was that she was not interested in what I had to say. In turn, this meant that I was less able to express myself. I also felt less valued as an employee and a person.

Looking at Other Things

As we will discuss later, the use of eye contact is significant in coaching. Therefore, looking over the client's shoulder to see what is going on behind them, or noticing an unusual bird through the window, is unhelpful. However discreetly you do this, there is a risk that the client will notice. Avoid being distracted by other visual cues. Looking at your phone, inspecting your fingernails or being interested in a pet will get in the way of good listening.

Story from Practice 4.3

Minimising Distractions

When coaching on Zoom or Microsoft Teams, I make sure to turn off all notifications so that I am not distracted by email or calendar notifications. Checking that my laptop is fully-charged or connected to a power supply is part of my preparation. Knowing that I am a naturally curious person, I place the laptop or computer in front of a wall, rather than a window or door. This is to ensure that my attention is not drawn towards things that might be happening outside.

Fidgeting

Become aware of any unintentional fidgeting that you may do. The best way to discover this is to watch a recording of your coaching practice. Most people do not really know what it looks like when they are listening to others. Minor behaviours, such as drumming fingers, clicking pens or twiddling thumbs can be distracting and may also suggest to the client that the coach is bored or impatient.

Being Self-Conscious

For some of us, seeing our own face during a coaching conversation over Zoom or Microsoft Teams can be an unnecessary distraction. Experiment with the various settings and see what works best for you – to see both faces on the screen, side-by-side; to have just the client's face on the screen; to make the client's face bigger and yours smaller etc. The same applies to the client. It may be helpful to mention the various options to her at the start of the first session.

As you can see, there are many ways of being more intentional about how you listen during coaching conversations. It is not sufficient simply to listen – you must demonstrate that you are doing so. Below is a checklist you can use as you hone this ability.

———— Review Your Practice 4.1 ————

Quality of Listening

I stayed as quiet as possible as the other person was speaking.   ☐

I avoided thinking about my response while the other person was speaking.   ☐

Even when the speaker hesitated, I did not attempt to complete her sentence.   ☐

Even when the speaker struggled to find a word, I did not intervene.   ☐

I resisted any temptation to compare myself to the speaker.   ☐

I did not say anything that would suggest that I was competing with the speaker.   ☐

I did not doodle or make excessive notes.   ☐

I provided eye contact throughout the session.   ☐

I did not fidget, drum my fingers or twiddle my thumbs.   ☐

———— Activity 4.1 ————

Coffee Break

Visit a local coffee shop on your own. While enjoying your drink, observe others. Who is truly listening? How can you tell? Can you notice mirroring of body language? For example, are both people leaning towards each other? Is one person obviously listening to the other? What can you tell about the relationship just by noticing body language? Are there people there on video calls? How attentive do they seem? How about the barista? Do they make eye contact with you? Does the barista have a headset on to take drive-through orders even though they are at the till taking your order? How valued do the staff make you feel through the way that they listen to you? Make notes in your learning journal.

Coaching should have a different dynamic to everyday conversations. Where we may be used to the flowing, back-and-forth nature of social interactions, coaching should feel more like one person talking and the other person listening. It will look and sound more like an interview of a sportsperson or a movie star. Coaches recommend a ratio of 80:20 or even 90:10 of the coach listening. It is natural for this to feel unfamiliar at first because social conversations tend to work best at 50:50 or 40:60.

Snapshot 4.1

Listening as a Coach

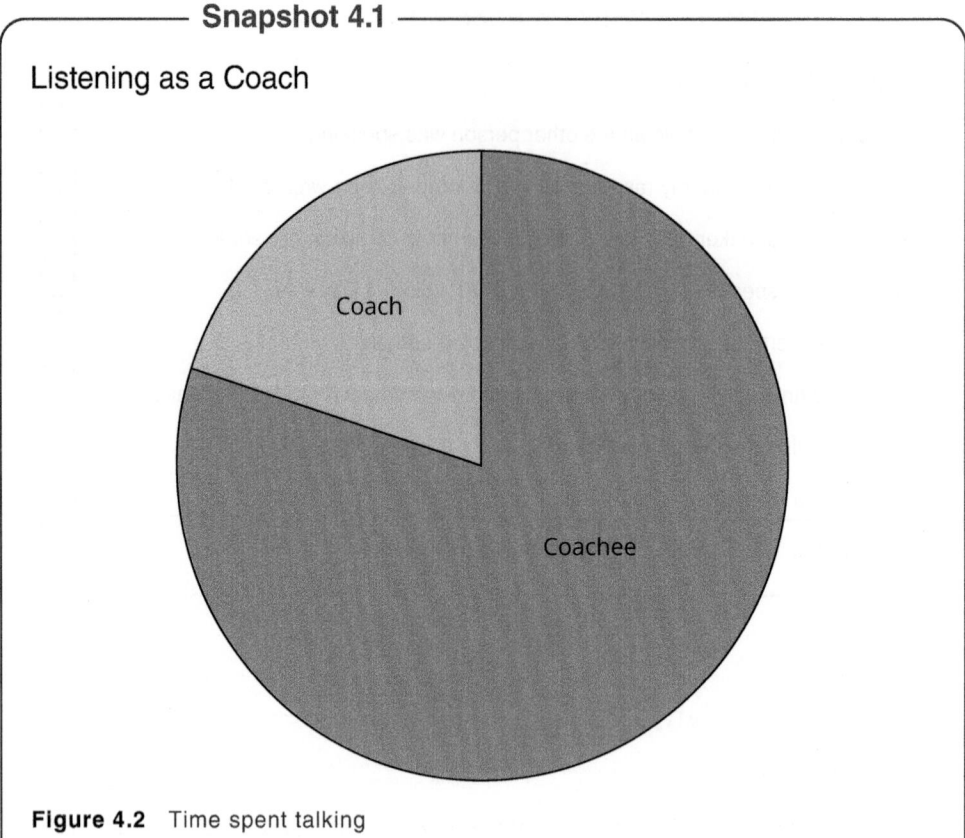

Figure 4.2 Time spent talking

Activity 4.2

Twenty Words

Practise limiting the amount of time you speak. Find a person who will appreciate being listened to – on the phone, over a video call or in person. Start by telling her that you are curious about something that she has done. Make this activity challenging by allocating yourself only 20 words in the conversational interaction. If you only allow yourself 20 words in a conversation, you will have to be very careful about how you use them! See what impact this has on the person who is speaking. After completing this exercise, note your reflections and any feedback from your conversational partner in your learning journal.

Purposeful Listening

When coaching, we listen with purpose. We want to allow the client an opportunity to speak freely. Our intention is to give our client a voice. Coaches should focus on listening *for meaning*. The purpose is to respectfully understand the situation or experience of the client. Being respectful entails being interested and open to a person's experiences. Especially important is the idea of not 'knowing' the other person's experiences or 'what it's like'. Understanding the situation is not the coach's primary purpose. As discussed above, the aim is to enhance the client's ability to think well and deeply about the topic that she has brought to a coaching session.

Maintaining Eye Contact

It is important to show a keen interest in what the client is saying by maintaining appropriate eye contact. Commonly, it's something we do without much planning. Once you start to intentionally manage your eye contact, you may find that this is more complex than you initially imagined. This is because different cultures and social contexts have different expectations regarding eye contact. Coaches need to become familiar with cultural and social norms in order to ensure that they are providing sufficient eye contact to communicate respect and interest in what their clients are saying.

Keeping Open Body Language

Your body posture can also transmit subtle messages about how open you are to what another person is saying to you. Clients may start the early coaching sessions with closed body language, as they may be slightly nervous. Body language will be discussed in more detail in Chapter 10. For now, it is helpful to note that open body language invites the client to share more of what she is thinking.

A Question for You 4.2

How Expressive Are You?

How do you sit when you are most comfortable? Even if you are comfortable in that position, how might others interpret it? To what extent do your facial expressions communicate what you are thinking or feeling? Do people say that you are too expressive? Or maybe they think that you are not expressive enough?

Matching and Mismatching Levels of Energy

Coaches need to manage their energy levels in relation to the client. For example, if a client is very excitable and drawn in many directions, it may be helpful for the coach to be less excited, perhaps conveying a sense of calm. On the other hand, if the client is very sedate and quiet when trying to generate new ideas, it may be helpful for the coach to be a bit more energetic. Usually, in the first part of the coaching conversation, it is helpful to match the client's level of energy because it is a proven method for building rapport. In the latter part of the coaching conversation, the coach may want to counter-balance the client's level of energy. How loudly a client speaks may give an indication of her levels of energy. This also applies to the coach.

A Question for You 4.3

How Loud Are You?

How loudly do you speak in most situations? If you consistently speak loudly or very softly, be aware of the implications of this in a coaching session. A very softly spoken coach will bring a sense of calm and relaxation to a coaching session. A coach who is boisterous will bring excitement and energy. A good coach needs to be able to vary this based on the best interests of the client. It is good practice to aim to end the coaching conversation on a positive, upbeat and high-energy note.

Setting Up for Video Coaching

When coaching people over Zoom or Microsoft Teams, it is important to build rapport through conveying a sense of connection and equality. Where possible, it is helpful to match the client's approach to using technology. For example, if the client is using a headset and has a blurred background, the ideal scenario is for the coach to have a similar arrangement. Equally, if the client is very casual and just chatting into a tablet from their garden, it can create barriers if the coach looks like they are in a recording studio with special lighting, audio equipment and a headset that makes them look like an airforce pilot. Of course, we must be pragmatic, and it may not be possible to completely match the client's attitude to the call. However, the important point is that the coach should, whenever possible, aim to build connection with their client.

Seating Arrangements for In-Person Coaching

This may seem like a detail but the arrangement and choice of seating can imply more than first meets the eye. How people sit during a coaching conversation can influence how the relationship develops and conversation progresses. Ideally, there should be no physical obstacles between coach and client. At the same time, it is important to ensure that each person has enough 'personal space' for herself. As a matter of principle, coaches and clients should consider themselves to be equal. For this reason, coach and client should be sitting on the same type of chair or sofa. When one person sits on a grand leather office chair and the other person is sitting on a wooden stool, there can be no equality. If you would like to introduce any activities (see Chapter 11), it may be helpful to have a table nearby.

Story from Practice 4.4

Personal Space

When delivering an in-person training session for coaches, two colleagues from a multinational communications organisation came to me to share their concerns. We had been talking about the need to respect 'personal space'. While both people worked for the same organisation, one was based in Northern Europe and the other in South East Asia. The question related to the ideal distance between coach and client. The two colleagues had very different views about the importance of 'personal space' and they were wondering how to manage this. This has left me curious, and I am wondering whether the very concept of 'personal space' is culturally specific. However, when in doubt, it is always best practice in coaching to align with the preference of the client. While we do not wish to completely ignore the preferences of the coach, the needs of the client should always be given priority.

Minimal Encouragers

Encouraging noises and words like 'uh-huh', 'go on', 'oh, I see' (or other, culturally-appropriate phrases) show the client that you are listening and interested in what she has to say. When used in the natural gaps in a person's speech, it can reinforce the fact that you have no intention of interrupting – allowing the other person to take her time explaining something or exploring an idea.

How to Manage Silences

Silences are an underrated but important feature of good coaching conversations. Often, silences precede important realisations by the client. However, this can be at odds with social norms. Social etiquette in many cultures may imply that it is polite to keep conversations going by filling silences. A gap in a conversation can seem awkward and uncomfortable, and even though we may not be aware of it, many of us have techniques and strategies for filling these silences.

In coaching, silences are desirable. They create a conducive atmosphere for considered reflection. First, they can create 'thinking time' for the client. Second, allowing a client protected moments to reflect quietly without interruption can demonstrate respect. Finally, silences encourage a deeper and more meaningful conversation. Silences build serenity into a conversation. They can also demonstrate your respect for the other person by showing that 'silences are OK'. You are, in effect, communicating your intention to view the client positively regardless of whether she has anything to say.

Step 1: Notice When Silences Occur

Normally, our socially conditioned 'alarm system' kicks in. In normal, day-to-day situations, silences are perceived as 'awkward' or 'uncomfortable'. (The only exception seems to be when we are in elevators when such silences are expected!) Many of us are always on the alert for potential silences in conversations. In the first instance, do your best to notice when these silences occur, accepting that they may be a normal part of a coaching conversation.

Step 2: Do Not Implement the Emergency Procedure

Once a silence descends, it is tempting for a novice coach to blurt out a follow-up question to relieve the perceived tension. However, silence following a question may indicate that the client has been encouraged to think carefully. Remember, we are listening to encourage new thinking. So, in a sense, silence following a question is likely to be an indication that you have asked a very good, thought-provoking question. Stated differently, if the client answers a question immediately, this may suggest that she did not need to think deeply before answering.

We will discuss the skill of 'asking powerful questions' in Chapter 6. Sometimes a client's question can pose a dilemma for the coach. Clients often ask, 'Do you know what I mean?' or 'Can you see where I'm coming from?' When a coach is actively listening to a client, this question can be challenging to answer. On the one hand, we know that it is important to build rapport with the client. From that point of view, it would make sense to say 'Yes, I know *exactly* what you mean.' However, although most of us would feel encouraged by such a response, it also negates the need for the client to explain further. Our main intention is to get the client to speak as much as possible.

Story from Practice 4.5

Saying it Out Loud

In my own experience, clients have often realised something significant only when they have spoken it out loud. For example, one client said 'I didn't realise why I was so annoyed about this relationship until just now.' So, on the one hand it is important for us to maintain rapport, but it is also important not to assume that we 'get' what the client is saying before they have described the situation fully.

As mentioned above, it is tricky if the client asks 'Do you know what I mean?' or a similar question. Below are a few answers that I have given:

'What you've said so far makes sense. Please carry on.'

'I think I'm getting a picture of what it's like. Tell me more.'

'It's becoming clearer …' [followed by a summary of what the client has said so far].

Here is an example conversation:

Client:	I don't know if I've explained that very well …
Coach:	Take your time.
Client:	I'm not making any sense, am I?
Coach:	I think it's worth exploring.
Client:	I can't explain how I feel about this.
Coach:	Could you try?
Client:	It feels like a muddle. I'm in a maze. Do you know what I mean?
Coach:	It's becoming a bit clearer. So, it feels like a muddle to you?
Client:	Yes, that's the right word. It's a bit of a muddle. On the one hand, I feel that I should be grateful for the opportunity. But on the other, I feel that this work should be recognised by the organisation. That's probably the real issue.

In all cases, silences from the coach will show that it is OK for the client not to be able to articulate what she is thinking straight away. We are aiming for increased self-awareness and the ability of the client to see her situation from a different perspective.

Review Your Practice 4.2

The Skill of Listening

I focused on listening for meaning, rather than listening to solve a problem. ☐

I maintained appropriate eye contact throughout the conversation. ☐

I was aware of my body language and remained conscious of the need
to seem open. ☐

(Continued)

I noticed and matched the level of energy of the speaker at the start of the conversation. ☐

I set up the coaching session so that it was equitable. ☐

I used minimal encouragers throughout the conversation. ☐

I was aware of silences and allowed the speaker time to think. ☐

Levels of Listening

In an influential book about coaching and mentoring, Hawkins and Smith (2013) identify four levels of listening which are helpful to consider here.

1   *Attending*: At this level, the coach would give the client her 'full and undivided' attention (p. 252). This includes focusing on the client and giving the appropriate non-verbal signals that the coach is interested in what the client has to say.
2   *Accurate listening*: To listen accurately, the coach must not only be fully attentive but also be able to play back the content of what the client has said, either directly or by paraphrasing. Matching the language or sensory modes used (e.g. 'I feel' or 'I see') can demonstrate accurate listening to the client.
3   *Empathic listening*: This type of listening builds on the previous two levels. According to Hawkins and Smith, 'this involves listening not only to the words being spoken, but also to the feelings being conveyed' (p. 253). Listening in this way means that the coach is able to acknowledge the feelings of the client and reflect these back to her.
4   *Pure listening*: This is the highest level of listening identified by Hawkins and Smith. At this level, the coach is 'able to play back the thoughts and feelings that are at "the edge" of the awareness' of the client (p. 254). In some cases, the coach can pick up a sense, a feeling or thought that the client may not be fully aware of herself.

A Question for You 4.4

How Are You Listened to?

Take a moment to reflect on how you are listened to on most days. What level of listening is most common in your everyday life? When are you listened to at level 3 or level 4? What does it feel like when you are listened to in that way?

When you are listening to others, what is the level of listening that you most often use? Are there certain situations when level 1 listening is helpful? Write a few lines in your learning journal about how you currently listen to others.

To be an effective coach, it is necessary to be able to work at the first three levels identified by Hawkins and Smith (2013). Level 1 listening (being fully attentive) and level 2 listening (hearing what the client has said and being able to reflect this back accurately) are essential for every coaching session. At these levels, the client will feel that you have listened to her and that you have been able to understand what she has said. Often level 3 listening (empathic listening) can be a powerful experience for the client. Not only has the coach been attentive and heard what the client has said but she has also picked up the emotions and non-verbal communications of the client. As novice coaches, developing and practising level 3 listening is an important part of your development.

Level 4 listening (pure listening) is a more challenging concept. This requires much more intuition and can be risky. At level 4, the coach senses feelings and thoughts that are just on the edge of a person's awareness. Coaches who listen at this level report that they get a 'gut feeling' or a 'sense' that there is something that is not being said. For experienced coaches, it is sometimes worth the risk of sharing this feeling or sense with the client to see whether this resonates with her. However, this level of listening is not essential for effective coaching, and it is not recommended for novice coaches.

Find Out More 4.2

Advanced Practice

Once you have become more experienced, you may wish to find out more about 'advanced coaching practice'. This is explored in detail in a book called *Advanced Coaching Practice: Inspiring Change in Others* that I have co-written with my good colleague David Love.

What the Professional Associations Say 4.1

The Skill of Listening

The professional associations are unanimous and unequivocal: Being a good listener is essential if you are interested in becoming a qualified coach. The ICF has a competency about **listening actively**. They define this as focusing on 'what the client is and is not saying to fully understand what is being communicated' and supporting 'client self-expression'. The EMCC and the AC consider listening as an essential communication skill. The skill of listening underpins the ability of coaches to meet many of the other competencies (e.g. **managing self and maintaining coaching presence (AC), raising awareness and insights (AC), building the relationship (EMCC), enabling insight and learning (EMCC), maintaining presence (ICF)** and **evoking awareness (ICF)**.

Conclusion

In this chapter, we have considered the precious skill of listening. Hopefully, you now have an enhanced appreciation of the importance of listening when coaching. It is not sufficient to *look* as if you are listening. You must *be* interested in what the client is saying. Excellent listening is at the heart of effective coaching. Practice is the best way of developing this skill.

─── **See It in Practice 4.1** ───

The Skill of Listening

Video 4.1 Listening Respectfully

Notice how the coach gives full attention to the client. The coach nods, uses facial expressions and remains quiet as the client reflects. As a result of this opportunity to think, the client gains an important insight.

Video 4.2 Using Silence

In this clip, the coach asks a question and then allows time for the client to think before responding. Watch for clues that the client appreciates having time to reflect.

Video 4.3 Saying It Out Loud

Watch this clip to see how the client becomes energised when given the opportunity to voice what she is thinking. These opportunities emerge when you listen in a way that encourages your clients to think.

5
Playing Back

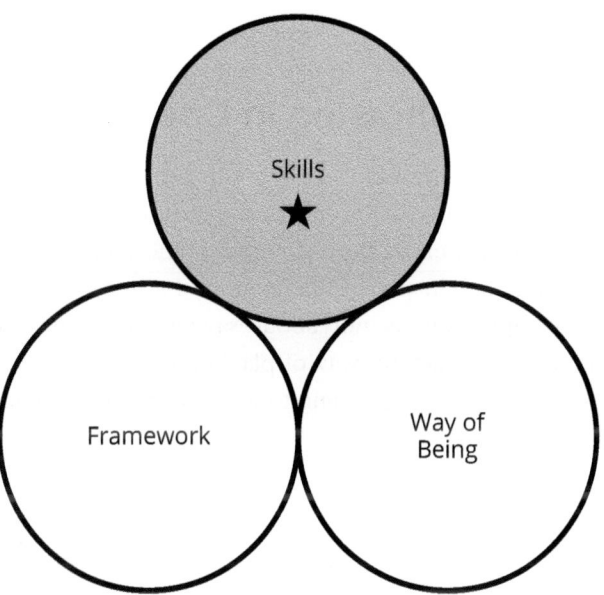

Figure 5.1 The three elements of effective coaching

In addition to noticing and listening, effective coaches 'play back' words, phrases and thoughts to their clients. Compared to noticing and listening, playing back requires the coach to intervene in the conversation. Although almost all coaching skills courses emphasise the importance of listening and asking questions, playing back can sometimes be overlooked. In fact, playing back is just as vital to good coaching conversations. This includes repeating words, paraphrasing and summarising. This chapter will explain why playing back is an essential skill and make a case for the necessity of interjections as a way of managing coaching conversations.

The most common forms of playing back during coaching conversations are summarising and paraphrasing. It is reasonable to wonder whether there is any significant difference between the two. The words are often used interchangeably and sometimes treated as synonyms. When the words are discussed in the context of academic writing, there *is* a clear distinction. 'Paraphrasing' relates to the act of presenting existing written information using a different form of words. When paraphrasing, writers are conveying the same meaning using their own choice of words. Usually, the purpose is to elucidate meaning. As a result, both the original piece of writing and the new text will have roughly the same number of words. Summarising is different. In the same context, writers summarise when they reiterate the meaning of the original text using fewer words. A summary is, by definition, a shorter version of the original. When we talk about academic writing, the distinction seems obvious but not particularly significant. In coaching, each should be used intentionally, depending on the purpose of playing back.

Paraphrasing in Coaching

In coaching, the intention of paraphrasing is not to provide a condensed account, but to play information back to the client to check the meaning of what has just been said. One reason for doing this is to raise the awareness of the client. The other is to confirm that both the coach and the client are talking about the same thing. In coaching, as in academic writing, paraphrasing is not about saying something with fewer words. Paraphrasing is a particularly helpful way of playing back when the client is exploring her understanding of a situation or coming to terms with a dilemma.

Snapshot 5.1

Paraphrasing

Client: 'I don't know … Sometimes it feels like people want me to be more decisive but when I do make a decision, nobody is prepared to support me personally.'

Coach: 'It sounds like you're not certain about what people want. It feels to you like others want you to be more decisive, but when you behave that way, you don't get the support you're expecting.'

Sometimes, hearing back what was said in the voice of another person can provide a new perspective or insight for the client. There have been many times in my own practice as a coach when I have played back, almost word for word, something the client has said. Often, the response is 'I've never thought of it like that'! It can be surprising to see how some clients react to their own stories being played back to them. For many, it can seem like it is the first time they have heard an idea – even though the coach is only playing back what the client may have just said. Apparently, it can be quite powerful to have someone else vocalise the challenges and situations that are of concern to us.

Summarising in Coaching

At its core, the skill of summarising is about listening attentively to what a client says and then playing back the essence of what has been stated using fewer words. The key purpose of summarising is to interpret what the client has said and present it back 'in a nutshell'. As with paraphrasing, summarising can demonstrate that the coach is listening. More importantly, summaries can be used strategically to highlight aspects of the client's narrative or to reframe the client's interpretation of their situations.

Summarising is useful during coaching conversations for the following reasons:

- It demonstrates that the coach is listening.
- It allows the coach to check her understanding of what has been said.
- It can refocus the attention of a conversation.
- It can be used to reframe the client's perception of a situation.

Snapshot 5.2

Summarising

Client: 'I'm not as confident at work as I used to be. There are a million reasons for this.'

Coach: 'A million reasons?'

Client: 'Well, maybe not a million, but quite a few. First, there are three of us who started here together, in 2012. Both of the others are now in senior management positions. They've both been promoted *twice*, and I'm still in the same role. In addition, I've missed some of my performance management targets recently. It may be because of this, or for other reasons, but my line manager has not been very positive about the targets that I do achieve. I don't think the work I do is being valued. And even more worryingly, some of my colleagues, who used to do great work, have been made redundant in the latest round of cuts. I guess that all of this overshadows the fact that I do work hard and put in the hours. I don't know. It just feels different, and I'm starting to doubt my own abilities.'

Coach: 'So it sounds like you've recently started to question your own abilities because of a few things that have been happening at work. You're worried that this doubt is starting to overshadow the good work that you are continuing to deliver. Have I understood this correctly?'

The Benefits of Playing Back

In the section below, we will consider the benefits of playing back. As you will see, there are benefits to the client, the coach and the professional relationship.

Demonstrating that You Have Been Listening

A recurring theme of this book is that it is the coach's responsibility to *demonstrate* that she is interested in her clients and what they have to say. One way of demonstrating that a coach is truly listening is to accurately and empathically play back what the client has been saying. A good summary proves beyond reasonable doubt that a coach is listening. Paraphrasing works in the same way. Some people are good at *looking* like they are listening. The right noises ('uh-huh'), nodding at the right moments, tilting the head sideways – these are useful techniques, but, on their own, they do not prove that the coach is genuinely listening. One of the reasons coaches play back is to show, beyond reasonable doubt, that they are fully invested in the conversation.

Checking Shared Understanding

An accurate summary of the client's narrative is a good way of minimising the chance of misunderstandings or confusion. This applies to both parties. Sometimes, the coach will not have fully grasped the meaning behind a client's explanation. In this situation, a summary is a good way of checking understanding and can give the client an opportunity to clarify what was meant. At other times, a summary can highlight inconsistencies in the client's understanding of a situation. In this case, the client could reassess her own interpretation of what is happening.

─── Story from Practice 5.1 ───

Being on Track

This example comes from a coaching assignment for a large financial services organisation. The contract was for six coaching sessions of 90 minutes in length. In a pre-coaching meeting with the client and his line manager, it became clear that both the client and the organisation were hoping that the coaching sessions would lead to a clearer understanding of the client's future career plan.

As a result, the first coaching session centred on the client's professional history, his current role and future plans. As we discussed his current role, he said that it felt like he was on 'train tracks'. We then explored how well he felt he was performing within the organisation. Before moving on to explore options, I thought it would be useful to play back what the client had been saying. 'So, you were recruited straight into this organisation from university on a graduate programme about five years ago. You've been performing exceptionally well by your own assessment, that of your line manager and peers. You feel that you're on track with your career, and now you are starting to ask questions about what might come next. Is that a fair summary of where you are?' There was an embarrassed silence before the client said kindly that it was 'mostly right'. When he mentioned train tracks, he did not mean that he was 'on track' in the way that I had understood. It felt to him like his career was like a train that could only run on one set of tracks. In other words, he felt very restricted, and he wanted coaching so that he could explore whether there might be other directions for him to pursue. Having initially misunderstood the analogy, we were then able to use it correctly, and we talked about the next stations if he were to stay 'on the tracks' and whether there were any junctions that would allow the train to get onto different tracks.

Since one of the intentions of playing back is to invite corrections, adaptations or elaborations from the client, it is important that a coach plays back in the most tentative way possible. Summaries should not be presented as 'fixed' or certain. For example, 'Right. So that's fairly clear. You only have two options, you've tried one of them already, and you're not prepared to have a go at the other', is less likely to encourage a response than, 'OK. If I've understood correctly, you've identified two options. You've tried one of these, and you're not inclined to try the other. Is that about right?' The tentative nature of the summarising may encourage the client to engage more constructively with what has been said. Coaches should also think about their style of delivery. Gentle delivery and a tentative tone of voice can enhance the value of playing back.

A Question for You 5.1

How Forcefully Do You Present Your Views?

Do you naturally tend towards being quite categorical when you present your views? Or do you prefer to be more tentative when sharing your thoughts? Whichever your preference, experiment with the other. Observe how it feels. Are there times when the unfamiliar approach may be helpful? Add a section in your learning journal entitled 'Being tentative' and jot down some phrases that you can use when playing back.

Refocusing on the Client's Goal

Playing back can be used as a way of managing a conversation and focusing attention on aspects of what is being discussed. For example, if a client decided to talk about her desire to return to college to study art but spent much of her time complaining about how funding for the arts was being cut, summarising might be a helpful way of bringing the conversation back to its original purpose. For example, the coach could say: 'OK. So you started by talking about wanting to go back to college to study art. You've also shared your disappointment about government policy in this area. Despite this, you seem to be committed to signing up for an art course in September. Have I understood you correctly?'

Reframing What the Client Has Said

Summaries are helpful when reframing something that a client has said for the purposes of highlighting a particular aspect. For example, if a client has been talking in general about her career history without recognising the importance of her own successes, the coach could highlight these in the summary: 'So it sounds like you've had a rich career history, achieving some notable early successes including being elected "young entrepreneur of the year" and then becoming the youngest senior manager within the region.' In many ways, coaching is a reframing exercise in itself. Often, new insights, learning and motivation emerge from the client seeing their situation in a new frame.

Slowing Things Down

Another reason for playing back is to slow things down. In the increasingly busy world we find ourselves in, the pace of life can sometimes get in the way of the quality reflection needed to make important decisions and evaluate our lives. Paraphrasing and summarising allow you to slow down the pace of the conversation, inviting your client to think more deeply about her topic.

——— Snapshot 5.3 ———

Playing Back Without Words

We have focused in this chapter on summarising and paraphrasing as the main ways of playing back during coaching conversations. In practice, coaches can play back in non-verbal ways too. A puzzled look, a shrug, furrowed brows and holding one's breath are all ways of playing back what you are picking up from the client. Like the other forms of playing back, you are showing the client that you are trying to understand what things are like for them. In your next conversation, experiment with non-verbal ways of playing back. You will know that it's working when your conversational partner says 'Exactly!' or 'You get it!'.

Snapshot 5.4

Look Who's Playing Back

Often, it is the coach who is carefully playing back her reflections to the client. It may be helpful, on occasion, to pass this task onto the client. For example, if the client has been discussing a particularly complex topic or a large number of potential opportunities it may be interesting to ask her 'Would this be a good point to stop and reflect on what we've covered so far?' or 'Now that we've talked through the current situation, how would you summarise the situation in one or two sentences?' In this case, you are asking the client to do the playing back.

In Summary

Playing back is a key skill that allows coaches to demonstrate that they are listening. While both paraphrasing and summarising can be used to check understanding, summarising is particularly suited to supporting a client to refocus attention and reframe her perceptions. Paraphrasing, on the other hand, can helpfully slow down the pace of a coaching session. In addition, there are non-verbal ways of playing back what you are picking up. Many clients report that they value the 'quality thinking time' that coaching provides. If they feel overwhelmed in the office or pressured by a busy workplace, a less-harried coaching conversation can create the ideal environment for meaningful reflection.

Review Your Practice 5.1

Paraphrasing

I listened attentively to the client. ☐

I selected and played back statements or thoughts that seemed to have significance to the speaker. ☐

I played back entire phrases or complete sentences. ☐

I played back through non-verbal communication. ☐

I was tentative when playing back. ☐

When paraphrasing what I had heard, I did not include my own interpretations. ☐

Review Your Practice 5.2

Summarising

I provided summaries that were clear and brief.   ☐

I included any unusual words or phrases that the speaker used.   ☐

I included words or phrases that the speaker had emphasised.   ☐

I let the speaker know that I would be summarising.   ☐

I made sure that my summaries were tentative.   ☐

If the speaker corrected my summary, I welcomed this.   ☐

Snapshot 5.5

Useful Phrases for Playing Back

'I wonder if it would be helpful to summarise what you've said …'

'I'd like to play back what I have heard …'

'What I've understood so far is …'

'What I think I've heard you say is …'

'Would it be OK to check my understanding of the situation?'

'Would I be right in saying that …'

'I may be wrong, but …'

'So it seems that there are a few key issues …'

'It would be helpful for me if you could summarise the main points …'

Snapshot 5.6

Tentative Concluding Questions

'Did that sound about right?'

'Would you say that was a fair summary?'

'Have I missed anything?'

'Was that an accurate representation of what you said?'

'How would you phrase it in your own words?'

Appropriate Interjections

This is where it gets a bit complicated. Playing back requires the coach to intervene in the coaching conversation. This raises the question 'should coaches interrupt their clients?'. The answer is a definite 'no'. However, as we have seen in this chapter, there are sometimes good reasons for the coach to intervene. As a matter of principle, we should never interrupt the client because it can seem disrespectful. Obviously, this raises some challenges for coaches. As we will discuss later (Chapter 7), the responsibility for managing the conversational framework rests with the coach. Ensuring that best use is made of the time available is primarily the coach's responsibility. So, what is the way forward? I propose three different types of interjections that are acceptable during coaching conversations, while continuing to insist that, as a matter of principle, we should never interrupt the client. This is not a case of semantics or playing around with words. An interruption is when you stop the flow of what someone is saying. It risks derailing the conversation. On the other hand, an interjection is more like jumping in and jumping out of a conversation. It adds something to the conversation without disrupting it.

1 Procedural Interjection

The first type relates to interjections that help to manage the conversation. Timekeeping is the responsibility of the coach and therefore it will sometimes be necessary to intervene to ensure that the conversation comes to an appropriate conclusion within the time available. For example, if there are 10 minutes remaining in the coaching conversation and the client starts to revisit information that was already covered earlier, a procedural interjection may be appropriate. For example, 'I'm sorry to intervene but I have noticed that we have 10 minutes remaining for our coaching conversation.' Procedural interjections are used to ensure that the client is broadly following a selected conversational framework (this will be discussed in Chapter 7).

2 Emphatic Interjection

This phrase refers to the purpose of the interjection (emphasis) rather than the way the coach intervenes. Often, clients will say something of significance as part of a longer exploration of their current situation or preferred future. In some instances, the coach may think it helpful to emphasise these points. There will be times when it may be better to wait until the client comes to a natural conclusion. There will also be occasions when it is helpful to highlight the point straight away. For example, if the client has been speaking for a good amount of time and says 'Anyway, what I think about this is not important' and carries on talking, the coach may want to highlight that assertion in order to explore the origin of that view: 'Sorry to intervene, but I noticed that you said that what you think is not important. I wonder if it might be helpful to explore what made you say that.'

Other occasions for emphatic interjections are when the client overlooks or underplays her strengths, talents or resourcefulness. For example, if, as part of a longer explanation about her role in an organisation, a client says 'Because I led on our successful bid to gain Investors in People recognition, I never had a chance to be involved in … ', it may be helpful for the coach to use an emphatic interjection: 'Wow. You led that project? What an amazing result!' This is helpful because it highlights one of the client's achievements. Talking about such successes is often motivational and can build energy into a conversation.

3 Minimal Encouragers

These are very brief noises or comments that are intended to encourage the client to continue speaking. When used skilfully, they can blend into the conversation. For example, 'really?', 'how fascinating!', 'wow!', 'I can't wait to hear this!' and 'I see' are minimal interjections that can enhance the conversation and strengthen the relationship between you and your client.

—— What the Professional Associations Say 5.1 ——

Playing Back

The professional associations have not yet explicitly embraced 'playing back' as a coaching skill. However, this skill underpins some core competencies of the ICF, the EMCC and the AC. As we discussed in this chapter, playing back will demonstrate to clients that the coach has been **listening actively** (ICF). It is also an effective way of **evoking awareness** (ICF). The EMCC highlights the importance **building the relationship** and **enabling insight and learning**. The AC promotes the idea of **communicating effectively** and **raising awareness and insight**.

Conclusion

In this chapter, we have considered the skill of 'playing back'. It is a way of demonstrating that the coach is listening attentively. Paraphrasing is simply repeating back what you have heard, using your own words (or sometimes using the client's words). Summarising involves understanding what the client has said and playing it back to her in a condensed way. Both are good ways to check understanding. Clients should feel comfortable correcting the coach if they think that what has been played back does not accurately capture their meaning. Finally, we briefly considered situations in which it is helpful to interject: when the coach is managing the conversation to get the most benefit from it, when it is important to immediately highlight something that the client has said and when there is an opportunity to be encouraging.

See It in Practice 5.1

The Skill of Playing Back

Video 5.1 Playing Back Leads to Insight

In this clip, the coach plays back to the client. Hearing the summary leads to positive emotions and an insight for the client.

Video 5.2 Playing Back Leads to Enthusiasm

Notice how the coach's summary leads to the client becoming more enthusiastic. The client takes notes as the coach plays back what they have heard.

Video 5.3 Playing Back Words

Take time to notice the subtle playing back of a short phrase by the coach. Repeating back exact words or phrases can have a positive effect on rapport.

Video 5.4 Summarising Incorrectly

In this clip, the coach gets the summary wrong. This is the reason that it is good to be tentative when playing back. The client corrects the summary, leading to greater shared understanding.

Video 5.5 Asking the Client to Play Back

Watch how the coach asks the client to play back. Notice the energy and positive emotions that are generated in the client as they review what has been discussed.

Video 5.6 Interjecting for Emphasis

Watch this clip for an example of when it can be helpful to interject in coaching conversations. The coach intervenes to emphasise admirable qualities in the client.

6
Asking Powerful Questions

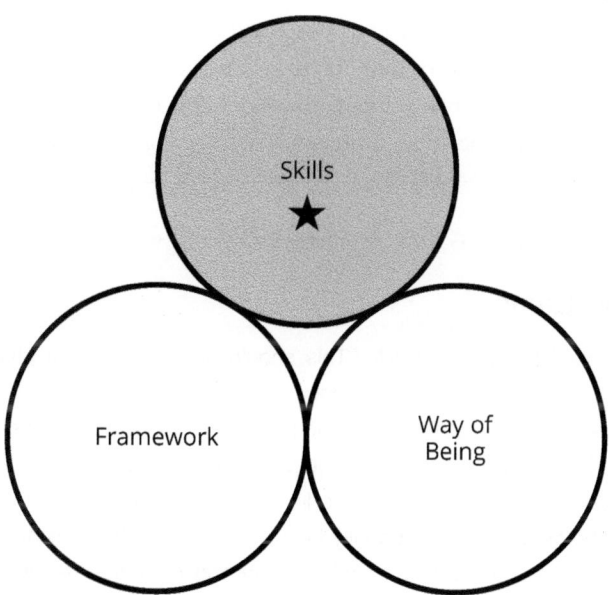

Figure 6.1   The three elements of effective coaching

Asking questions is one of the most dynamic skills of coaching. Like listening, one could argue that asking questions is a standard conversational skill. This chapter considers the skill of asking thought-provoking questions for the purposes of coaching. As we will discuss in this chapter, the use of questions in coaching will be different from their use in everyday conversations. In coaching, questions are deployed intentionally. They are used to clarify, provoke new thoughts, challenge the client and elicit relevant information. That makes it necessary for the coach to determine what type of question will be most helpful in different situations. When we consider the conversational framework (Part III), it will become apparent that some types of questions are more appropriate at certain stages.

Types of Questions

Four types of questions are of interest to coaches: closed, open, leading and multiple.

- *Closed question*: A closed question is one that can be answered with a single word (e.g. 'Yes' or 'No') or a short phrase. Generally speaking, closed questions are straightforward to answer and can provide the questioner with specific information, facts and numerical data. For example, 'How often do you exercise in a week?' or 'Do you speak Arabic?' are closed questions.
- *Open question*: An open question is the opposite of a closed question. It invites longer, more thoughtful answers. For example, 'How would you describe your attitude to work?' or 'What encouraged you to become a coach?' are open questions. If we think back to the 80:20 ratio of listening (coaches should be listening for about 80% of the time and clients should be listening for about 20% of the time), it becomes apparent that open questions are a necessary part of coaching conversations.

Activity 6.1

The 'Yes–No' Game

Find someone playful to practise with. This should be enjoyed as a game and can be played at home, online, in the car or at work.

One person takes the role of 'Questioner' and it is her role to ask open questions. The other person, 'Speaker', chooses a topic that is of interest to her (e.g. Korean food). The Questioner's intention is to ask as many open questions in a row as possible. After every question, the Speaker should be given ample opportunity to answer. The Speaker's intention is to catch the Questioner asking a closed question, so will be attempting to answer 'Yes' or 'No' at any opportunity provided. The Questioner wins if the conversation lasts for 5 minutes without being caught out. The Speaker wins if they can legitimately answer 'Yes' or 'No' to any question asked. This includes sub-questions such as 'isn't it?' Give it a go. It's more difficult than it sounds!

Activity 6.2

Increasing the Use of Open Questions

Without telling others what you are doing, simply try increasing the proportion of open questions that you ask. Observe the change in dynamic of your conversations. When you have tried this, make notes in your learning journal about how it changes the nature of the interaction.

- *Leading question*: A leading question is one that manipulates the listener to think in a particular way. Some leading questions even contain the preferred answer within them. For example, 'Would it be a good idea if you spoke to your colleagues about how you feel?' is a leading question. Although framed as a question, there is a clear suggestion ('speak to your colleagues about how you feel') embedded in the sentence. Leading questions are manipulative and should not be used in coaching.

- *Multiple questions*: These are a series of questions posed one after the other without an opportunity for the other person to respond. For example, 'What is the best way of managing an inexperienced team? I mean, is it better to simply tell them what to do? And anyway, what is the point of consulting with people when the decision has already been made?' are three questions presented in quick succession. While they may feature in everyday conversations, multiple questions can be particularly unhelpful in coaching. They can disorient the client and it is likely that the client will only answer the last question, ignoring or forgetting the earlier ones.

Using Questions with Intent

So to return to the idea of *intention*, closed questions are ideal if the coach is trying to clarify some aspect of what the client has said ('Do you work in the same office as your manager?'), ascertain numerical data ('How many people are in your marketing team?') or extract a clear 'yes' or 'no' answer ('So you're *disappointed* with the latest developments?'). Closed questions are easier for the client to answer, so can be used at the beginning of the conversation to get it started ('Are you based in Amsterdam?'; 'Do you commute to work?'; 'Would you like a cup of coffee?').

On the other hand, if the intention is to provide the client with an opportunity to think freely, open questions will be more helpful. Bearing in mind the 80:20 ratio of listening to speaking, closed questions are unhelpful. Almost certainly, the closed question takes longer to ask than for the listener to answer.

Good open questions start with 'how' or 'what'. For example, 'What are the main reasons for your change of heart?' or 'How would you go about reclaiming your authority?'. Fulfilling the same function as an open question is any statement that invites the client to speak: 'Tell me more about ...' or 'Please describe how ...' or 'I'd love to hear your thoughts about ...'.

Snapshot 6.1

Thought-Provoking Questions and Statements

How could you ...

How would you describe ...

How might this situation ...

(Continued)

What would you …

What other options …

What makes this situation …

How else might you …

Tell me more about …

Please describe …

Perhaps you could share your thoughts about …

I would like to hear your perspective on …

I'm curious to know more about …

Asking leading questions is an easy trap for novice coaches. Conventional wisdom implies that the best way of helping someone is to give her advice about what to do. As a result, it happens frequently, meaning that many people have become very good at giving advice. What is positive about this situation is that there is a good intention behind advice-giving: to help others. Coaching expert Jim Knight addresses this challenge when he writes about the 'complexity of helping': 'To bring about the improvements we hope to see, we need to recognize – in fact, honor – the complexity of providing support within professional relationships' (2011: 20). Knight proposes that there are five factors that should be considered by coaches.

1   *Change*: Many people are unaware of the need to change or improve. They cannot see how others perceive them.
2   *Status*: Coaches must ensure that they do not present themselves as being of higher status than their clients. According to Knight, 'Skilful coaches use a variety of subtle communication strategies to create equality' between themselves and their clients (p. 22).
3   *Identity*: The way we see ourselves, our identity, is often connected to our professional roles. 'Our understanding of how good and competent we are is frequently tied to our success or failure in our work' (p. 23). Coaches need to be sensitive to this.
4   *Thinking*: It is important that the person we are coaching is involved in the thinking process. Most often, people are not looking for others to do the thinking for them. The client must feel that she is the lead thinker in the relationship.

5   *Motivation*: What the client is working on must matter to her. If the topic does not matter to the client, there is little incentive for her to make any changes to her thinking or behaviour.

Reflect on Your Practice 6.1

Your Tendency to Give Advice

As you start to coach others, be aware of your tendency to give advice or provide suggestions. It is normal for novice coaches to fall into such traps in the early stages. During coaching sessions, simply make a mental note every time you find yourself giving advice. When the session is over, reflect on how often this happened, and what led you to provide advice. Take notes in your learning journal and jot down some ideas about how to manage similar situations in future.

Perhaps the real paradox is that most of us are better at giving advice than being gracious when receiving it! In any case, coaching is about allowing others to find their own ways forward – not telling people what to do or pointing out the 'obvious' solutions. Hopefully, the analogy of keys presented in Chapter 2 was helpful in this regard. The power of coaching comes from the fact that the coach supports the client to find the key for herself. The experience of discovering the key is what inspires and motivates the client to invest energy into the change effort. When the client makes progress, this will build her self-esteem and confidence.

As novice coaches become aware of a tendency to give advice or provide solutions, they will start to withhold such comments. However, the intention to solve other people's problems can sometimes become apparent when a coach replaces advice with a leading question. For example, if the coach thinks that the client should not respond to work-related emails over the weekend, she may ask a question like this: 'Is there any way of switching your mobile phone off over the weekend?' It looks like a simple closed question. But is there more to it?

While acceptable in everyday conversations, multiple questions are counterproductive in coaching. Multiple questions are more likely when the coach or client is in an excited or anxious state, or when a conversation is rushed. They occur most often when the coach attempts to 'correct' a question which she has just asked, providing a second, 'better' question. Even if, as the coach, you feel that you have thought of a more incisive question, it is good practice to allow the client to answer your initial query. Clients can be trusted to let you know if your question is obscure or difficult to answer. That can be your cue for rewording a question, if necessary.

Review Your Practice 6.1

Asking Better Questions

1 Notice Advice-Giving

Notice when you have given advice or provided a solution to the client.
Reflect on your intention. What was driving you to give advice or provide a solution?
What can you do the next time you are tempted to give advice?

2 Notice When You Have Withheld Advice

Be alert for situations in which you were tempted to give advice but managed to stop yourself. How did it feel to withhold advice? What was the outcome?

3 Make a Note of Any Leading Questions

Reflect on your questions. Were there any leading questions? What strategies can you put in place to avoid leading questions in the future?

4 Check for Multiple Questions

Note any occasions when you asked a second question before the client had answered the first. What was the reason for the second question? What made you want to ask it? What strategies can you use to minimise the chances of this happening in future?

Beyond Asking Questions to Get Answers

Apart from the functional aspects of questions that we have discussed above, they play a significant role in building the relationship between coach and client. Questions can be pivotal in creating the right environment for effective coaching conversations. Used intentionally, questions demonstrate curiosity, which is a necessary part of the 'coaching way of being' (this is discussed further in Chapters 12 and 13). By asking questions, the coach shows that she is interested in the client and her topic. Showing an interest in someone is often the best way of building meaningful relationships.

Perhaps even more importantly, certain types of questions can create thoughtful and reflective environments. For example, 'And what is it about this situation that makes you feel uneasy?' is likely to lead to a meaningful response. The question 'So what is your level of motivation in relation to this change programme?' is much more likely to encourage reflection than 'What's your view about this change programme?'. Well-crafted questions invite deeper reflection. Thought-provoking questions do not have to be 'clever' questions. In fact, they can be relatively short. For example, 'How important is this?' or 'How did that make you feel?' can be thought-provoking questions. There are two obvious ways to find out if your questions are thought-provoking. First, a silence from the client before she answers the question is a good sign. That is why coaches need to be comfortable with silences. Those silences represent the time that the client is starting to engage in new thinking. Second, ask the client about the quality of your questions. Any responses suggesting that the questions 'made me think' can be considered an endorsement of your coaching practice.

This is one of the most valuable contributions of coaching: it creates environments for quality thinking. Coaches should ask thought-provoking questions so that clients get into a more reflective state of mind than when they are busy doing what they always do. For example, in most social situations, the question 'How are you?' is not meant as a genuine invitation for a comprehensive answer. Ironically, some social conventions *minimise* the possibility for meaningful conversations. It is expected that others will say something bland such as 'Fine' or 'Not too bad'. On the other hand, if you can create reflective spaces that encourage meaningful conversations, asking 'How are you today?' to a client may elicit a much more thoughtful response. The key difference is that coaches demonstrate that they are genuinely interested in the answer.

Powerful questions can also inspire creativity and new thinking. One of the roles of a coach is to support the client to see things differently. For example, a question like 'If everyone on the leadership team resigned tomorrow, and you were given full control of the strategic direction of this organisation, what would you propose?' might help a client to see things from a different perspective. The thought-provoking question 'If you knew that you could not fail, what would you do in this situation?' can unlock creative ideas.

Story from Practice 6.1

It's Good to Be the King

Having heard the phrase 'If I were king for a day' at a conference in the US,[1] I asked this question during a coaching conversation: 'If you were king for a day, how would you change what's happening in your organisation at the moment?' Having grappled with the issue of 'lack of communication' within the client's department for two coaching sessions with limited success, this question allowed the client to see the situation completely differently. 'If I were king for a day, I would decree that everyone should share important information with others, when they think it's relevant for others.' I asked how that decree could be implemented, wondering, 'What would have to happen within the organisation?' In discussing how the royal decree would be implemented, the client realised that the issue of 'relevance' was more complicated than he had originally thought. 'I guess that it is going to be a balance of sharing the information with the right people,' he said. Finally, he concluded that there should be a mix of ways in which interested people could access

(Continued)

information. For key stakeholders, the information would be sent in a variety of formats. However, it would not be sent to everyone. Others who were not directly involved in the project would be given the opportunity to join an email list. Finally, all the correspondence would be posted online for anyone who was interested in finding out more. Being 'king' for 20 minutes allowed the client to see the situation from a completely different perspective, and this led to a helpful insight for the client. And this was triggered by one thought-provoking question.

[1]With thanks to Bob Marzano.

Questions are also a powerful tool for for seeking commitment. Often, closed questions can be helpful here: 'Are you confident that you will be able to follow through with this?' or 'What is the percentage chance of success if you do what you've just suggested?'.

So asking *thought-provoking* questions is a key skill for you to develop. As coaches, we must move away from questions that help *us* to understand a situation or provide a solution. This can be a liberating experience, allowing us to focus more intently on helping the client to increase her own awareness of the situation.

Using Questions to Elicit Precision

It can be helpful, at times, to invite the client to be more precise in her descriptions. Such questions can uncover any assumptions or significance in what has been shared. For example, 'People don't seem to appreciate it when I share my personal opinion' could be challenged with the question 'When you say "people", who are you referring to?'.

Snapshot 6.2

Questions to Elicit Precision

Client:	'I used to enjoy my work, but now I don't.'
Coach:	'There is nothing you enjoy in relation to your work?'
Client:	'I guess there are some things that I might have done differently.'
Coach:	'What kind of things?'
Client:	'People don't like it when I'm very honest about what I think.'
Coach:	'When you say "people", who are you referring to?'

Using Questions to Manage the Conversation

Questions can also be used to move a conversation along by focusing on a future state ('So how will doing this help you achieve your goal?') or by bringing the client back to the original topic ('How does this relate to your objective?'). As we study conversational frameworks (in Chapter 7), you will see how questions can be used to move clients from one stage to the next.

Asking Questions Without Knowing the Answers

As coaches we need to develop our courage to ask questions that neither we, nor our clients, have answers to. The fact that there are no quick answers necessitates new thinking. This can be unsettling at first, especially if the client looks to the coach for an answer. However, the shared sense of 'not knowing' and working in partnership to find an answer lies at the very heart of coaching practice. The famous Greek philosopher Socrates is remembered for the way in which he asked people a series of open-ended questions to help them think things through for themselves. Socrates' intention was to promote reflection, encouraging others to find their own answers. It has been convincingly argued that this type of Socratic questioning is an essential part of effective coaching (Neenan, 2009).

Questions, and the way they are used in some of our educational systems, create a strange situation where clients may think that the coach must know the answer before asking the question. The same line of thinking assumes that there might be one, 'right', answer, and that the coach is waiting for the client to provide it. Therefore, it is important for the coach to create a climate that is more open and exploratory (see Snapshot below).

— Snapshot 6.3 —

Creating Open and Exploratory Learning Spaces

Demonstrate that you do not necessarily know the answer to a question that you have asked. This can be done explicitly by saying, 'I don't know the answer to this question, but …'.

Show that there is no 'right' answer to your questions. This can be done by being non-judgemental about a client's answers, accepting each as a possible and equally valued response. Asking, 'How many different ways could you answer that question?' will also make the point that there are many possible responses.

Ensure that the client's answers are based on what she thinks, rather than what she assumes the coach wants to hear. An indication that a client is providing an answer that meets the approval of the coach is that the statement ends with an implied question mark.

(Continued)

Coach:　'How else could you improve your chances at interview?'

Client:　'I guess I should probably spend more time planning for it?'

or

Coach:　'What opportunities does this situation present to you?'

Client:　'A chance to show what I'm capable of?'

In both examples, it is likely that the client is seeking approval from the coach. It is helpful to explicitly reject the invitation to become an adviser by asking 'What do *you* think? Does that sound like a good option to you?'.

Reflect on Your Practice 6.2

Not Having the Answer

Think of the most recent time that you asked a question that you did not know the answer to. What was the context? Are there situations in which you avoid asking questions that you do not know the answer to? Please think carefully about this question.

Favourite Questions

As we will be considering conversational frameworks in the next chapter, you are invited to start collecting 'favourite' questions for the various stages. As a coach, you will find your own questions which are consistently helpful at different points in the conversation. Very often, however, the most helpful question will emerge from a client's response if the coach is listening intently.

A Question for You 6.1

What Is One Thing You Can Do?

What one thing can you do from now on to greatly increase the effectiveness of the questions that you ask?

Broadening your array of questions will improve your coaching practice. It will also be helpful in many other situations, including the questions you ask yourself. The craft of asking thought-provoking questions is, however, only part of what is required. Coaches must also be curious. It seems that we are born with an insatiable curiosity. You only need to watch 1- or 2-year-old children to notice that they are naturally inquisitive. As coaches, we must find a way to tap into that natural (and sometimes latent) sense of curiosity.

If we are able to attend fully to the client and bring with us a natural sense of curiosity about the client and her situation, this will greatly enhance the likelihood of a positive outcome for the client. Curiosity will provide us, as coaches, with appropriate questions and prevent us from falling into the trap of generating solutions for our clients.

Activity 6.3

Being Curious

As with all the other activities in this book, it is up to you whether you undertake this. However, this is a particularly important activity, so please consider ways of finding the time for it.

Although we are born inquisitive, the level of our curiosity can decrease over time. Perhaps as we have more experiences, we learn more and therefore feel that we have less to be curious about. However, for coaching it is important to rekindle this spirit of curiosity, which will enhance our presence, our listening and our questioning.

For this activity, please identify an experience in which your natural curiosity will be aroused. Find some time just for yourself (between one hour and one weekend) when you can indulge yourself by going somewhere to find out more about something of interest. This could be a visit to a motor museum, an aquarium, a zoo, a place of worship, a small village you have heard about, an underground bunker, a submarine, a hallowed sporting ground or anything that sparks your imagination. The indulgence relates to the time that you invest in the activity. If, for example, you have always been interested in meerkats, allow yourself a couple of hours at the zoo, just watching them. If there's a town or village that you have never been to, but is of interest to you, perhaps spend the whole afternoon walking around it. If you've always wanted to ride a motorcycle, fly a plane or learn to ski, spend some time in a place that will give you more information about the activity. Allow yourself time to be curious. That is all. You need to be interested and make sure that you are there for no other purpose than 'finding out'. Take your learning journal with you and write down every question that comes to your mind during your experience. When you have concluded your experience, write down your thoughts about how it felt.

What the Professional Associations Say 6.1

Asking Questions

By asking powerful questions, coaches show engagement, manage the flow of the conversation, clarify understanding, elicit insights and provide supportive challenge. Due to its dynamic nature and its multiple purposes, this skill is connected to numerous competencies.

For the ICF, asking appropriate questions allows the coach to be focused and responsive to the client (**maintaining presence**). Additionally, powerful questions are important when **facilitating client growth** by inquiring about how the learning from the coaching conversation

(Continued)

will be put into action. The EMCC links powerful questions to **enabling insight and learning**. They see questions as a way of encouraging an **outcome and action orientation**. The AC considers the skill of asking questions as part of **communicating effectively**. For them, asking powerful questions is necessary for **raising awareness and insight**.

Conclusion

Hopefully you have not skipped over the 'being curious' activity. If you were able to make time for it, I hope you found it to be an engaging and thought-provoking experience. If you have not done it yet, with apologies for my persistence, I would highly recommend doing so. Reconnecting with your natural sense of curiosity will bring many benefits to your coaching practice.

Now that we have covered the key coaching skills, we will turn our attention to the necessity of having a conversational framework to underpin our coaching sessions.

——— See It in Practice 6.1 ———

Asking Powerful Questions

Video 6.1 Asking a Thought-Provoking Question

Notice how the client takes some time to think before answering the question. Usually, this is a sign that the coach has asked a thought-provoking question.

Video 6.2 Asking about the Future

This clip shows the coach asking a question that requires the client to imagine what they might be doing in the future. This type of question can remind clients of what is most important to them.

Video 6.3 Asking about Learning

Watch this clip to consider the value of asking the client about what they are taking away from the session. In this case, articulating the learning seems to motivate and energise the client.

Video 6.4 Asking a Challenging Question

Watch how the client responds to a challenging question. Notice the pause before responding. The client seems to grow in confidence as they answer the question.

Part III
The Coaching Process

7
Conversational Frameworks

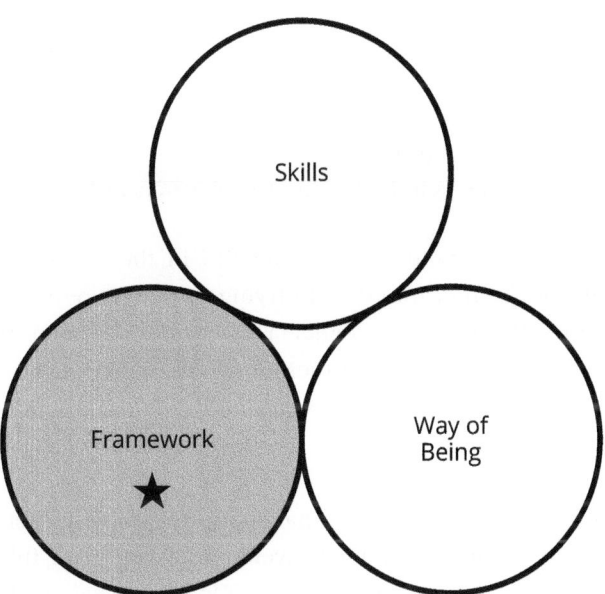

Figure 7.1   The three elements of effective coaching

Having covered the key skills, let us turn our attention to the conversation that is at the heart of coaching. In 1992, Sir John Whitmore popularised a conversational framework which was to transform the professional lives of millions of people. Simple, but not simplistic, the GROW model presented in this book is a framework that can underpin your coaching practice. It is important to emphasise that the GROW model is *one* conversational framework out of many that are now available for coaches. Some adaptations of the GROW model are presented later in this chapter.

GROW is an acronym derived from the four words representing the stages of the conversational framework: Goal, Reality, Options and Will (Whitmore, 1992). The strength of the model is that using the GROW framework increases the likelihood of conversations that will lead to change. It was originally devised as a behavioural coaching model. This means that the framework was created to support conversations about behavioural change – helping clients to *do* something differently. However, the GROW framework lends itself to cognitive-behavioural approaches as well. In other words, it can help people to change their cognitions as well as their behaviour – helping people to *think* differently so that they can *act* differently. The cognitive-behavioural aspect of coaching will be discussed in Chapter 8. The GROW framework has been heavily imitated, with many authors proposing alternative sets of letters and finding new words to describe each of the stages. In one way, these can be considered endorsements of the original concept.

While you have the choice to select a preferred conversational framework, or even create your own, there are two key points that should be addressed before we proceed:

- Coaching is a facilitated conversation.
- The purpose of coaching is to bring about positive change.

Over decades of research, writers and academics in the fields of counselling and coaching have invested significant effort in trying to determine whether one particular approach is more effective than another. This has not yet been proven, so we can tentatively work on the assumption that there is no one conversational framework that is the 'right' one. However, it has been suggested that a coach's belief in her chosen framework has a significant impact on the perceived success of the coaching partnership (de Haan, 2008b).

At its core, coaching is an interaction that supports people to get better results. In a sense, the desire to achieve something, overcome a barrier or fulfil an ambition is what brings people to coaching in the first place. One of the leading figures in the field of coaching psychology, the late Professor Anthony Grant, was emphatic: 'all coaching conversations are either explicitly or implicitly goal-focused' (2012: 149).

If you remember, it was suggested in the introduction that novice coaches should develop three elements of coaching as part of their learning journeys. The first element is a set of skills. We have already discussed the skills of noticing, listening, playing back and asking powerful questions. In this section, we will be considering the second necessary element: a conversational framework.

Most coaching conversations last between 30 and 90 minutes. When you use the GROW framework, there are certain stages that should be followed. Each of these is listed below, with questions that give an indication of the primary focus of each stage:

Goal: What would the client like to achieve?

Reality: What is the current situation (in relation to what the client has identified as a goal)?

Options: What options can the client think of (that will help her to move closer to her goal)?

Will: What will the client do as a result of the coaching conversation?

Snapshot 7.1

The GROW Framework

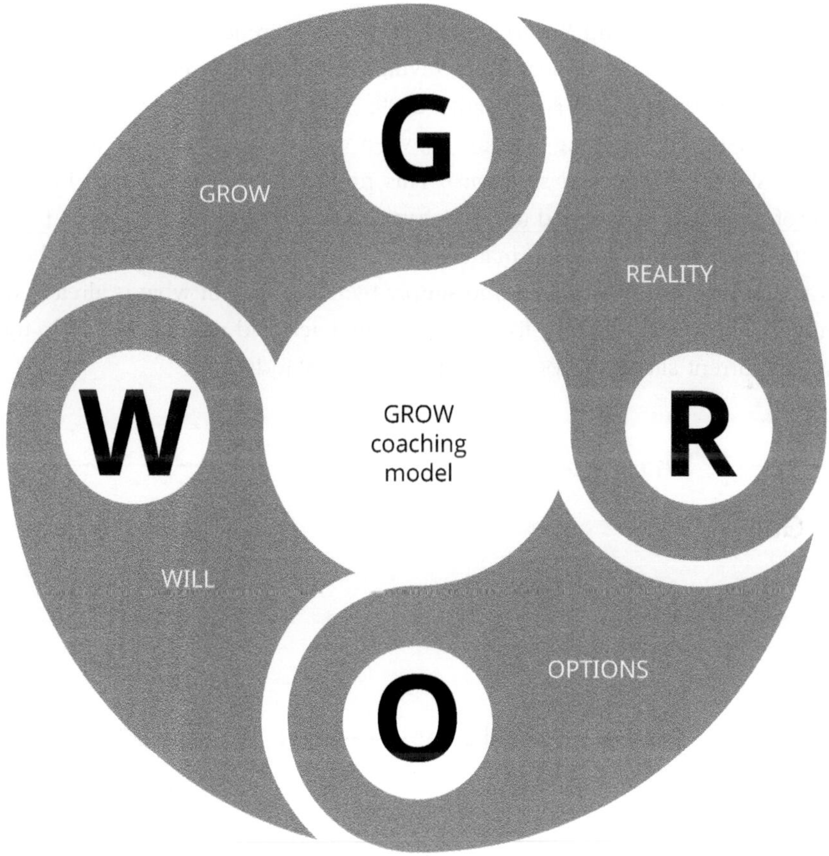

Figure 7.2 The GROW framework

(*Source*: based on the GROW model, Whitmore, 2009)

According to Whitmore (2009), coaching has two primary intentions: to raise awareness and to develop a sense of personal responsibility. He proposes that coaching should raise the *client's* awareness about her situation and should instil a sense of personal responsibility. In other words, a client should be supported to view her situation differently so that she realises that she is able to progress towards her goals.

Awareness

The purpose of the *Goal* and *Reality* stages is to raise awareness. According to Whitmore, 'awareness' is 'gathering and clearly perceiving the relevant facts and information, and the ability to determine what is relevant' (2009: 34). The client's awareness is raised in three ways. First, by identifying the gap between where she would like to be (her goal) and where she is (her current situation). This provides the client with a better understanding of what may be needed to move forward. Second, the Reality stage focuses the client's attention on relevant information about the present (in relation to the desired goal). Usually, new insights can emerge simply by talking about what is already happening. Third, the coach's questions, listening, playing back and noticing can help the client to view the current situation from a more 'objective' standpoint.

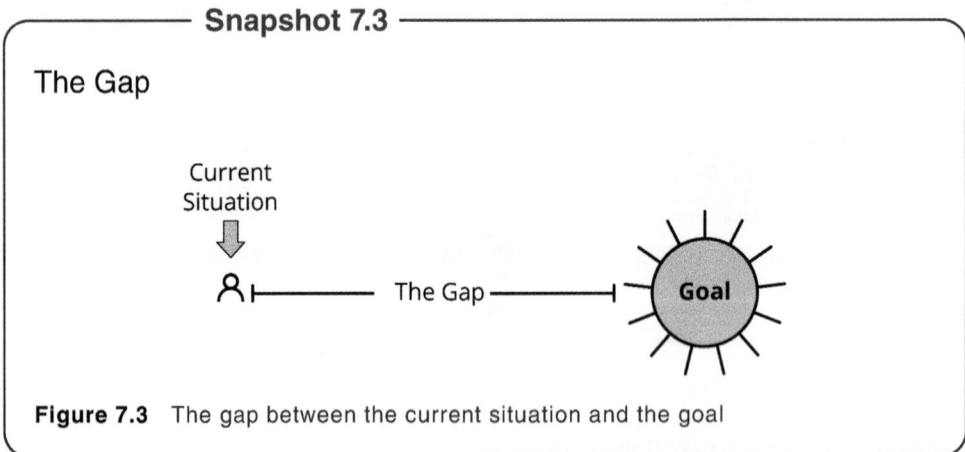
Personal Responsibility

In the two latter stages, *Options* and *Will*, the client is encouraged to take personal responsibility for working towards her goals. Whitmore points out that responsibility is necessary for high achievement: 'When we truly accept, choose, or take responsibility for our thoughts and our actions, our commitment to them rises and so does our performance' (2009: 37). This is one of the reasons that it is crucial for the *client* to identify possible options before she selects a specific way forward. The client should also commit to a self-selected action to implement. As we will explore later when we discuss the 'coaching way of being', one strategy for encouraging the client to take personal responsibility is for the coach *not* to take responsibility for finding solutions or generating new ideas.

Coach and Client Responsibilities

Coaching is a shared enterprise between coach and client. In this partnership, each has responsibilities. The client is entirely responsible for the 'content' of the coaching conversation. This means that she should select the topic for the conversation and identify her own goals with the timeframes in which she would like to achieve these. In the meantime, the coach is responsible for facilitating the 'process' of the coaching conversation (in this case, by following the GROW framework). It is the coach's role to manage the time allocated for the conversation, help the client to stay focused on her goal and show an interest in progress. Let us consider the GROW model now, as a conversational framework, looking briefly at each stage.

Stages of the GROW Framework

This section will outline and detail the stages of the GROW framework.

Goal

The first stage facilitates the selection and discussion of the client's goals. The coach is interested in finding out what the client seeks to achieve through coaching. What has motivated the client to seek coaching, and what does she want as an outcome of the conversation?

Reality

The second stage provides the client with an opportunity to explain the current situation. At the same time, this offers the coach a chance to build rapport and demonstrate empathy by listening attentively and respectfully. The gap between the 'current situation' and the client's self-selected goals can be explored during this stage.

Options

This stage moves the process from a focus on 'raising awareness' to a conversation which encourages the client to take 'personal responsibility' by thinking of ways to move forward. The main outcome of this stage is a range of options generated by the client.

Will

The final stage, crucial for the success of a coaching conversation, requires the client to commit to a next step. Coach and client work together to identify what the client will *do* as a result of the conversation.

Let us now consider each of the stages in more detail.

Goal Stage

According to Grant (2012), coaching is a goal-centred intervention. As a result, he proposed that coaches should be familiar with evidence-based theories of goal-setting and attainment. First, it is a good idea to set *short-term* (proximal) and *long-term* (distal) goals to aid performance over time. Second, Locke and Latham (2002) found that goals that are *stretching* and *achievable* can lead to better performance. If a goal is too easy, it is no longer motivating. If it seems impossible, there is little incentive to pursue it. Third, it is helpful if the client's goals are measurable so that she can tell when they have been achieved (*outcome* goals) (Locke, 1996). Finally, and perhaps most significantly for coaches, goals should be *self-selected*. Deci and Ryan (2002) have shown that people are more committed to goals which they have chosen to pursue (rather than goals which are imposed by others). It is the coach's role to facilitate the Goal stage so that the client can select relevant and meaningful goals.

The implication of the discussion above is that different types of goals should be discussed and agreed during the Goal stage. The first is the 'overall goal' or aspiration that has brought the client to the conversation. In other words, what does the client hope to achieve by being coached? Usually, it is this goal that provides motivation. Sometimes, by asking what the client is passionate about, it is possible to identify this aspiration. The second goal, which is the topic of the coaching conversation, should focus on what the client would like to do to move closer to the aspiration. Whitmore terms this a 'performance goal' (2009: 59). This should be perceived as something that the client is able to achieve (or is at least within her control). Finally, it is important for coaches to clarify what the client would like to achieve by the end of the coaching conversation. It may be helpful to distinguish this goal by calling it an 'outcome' of the coaching conversation. This should be very specific. The coach has an interest in ensuring that this outcome is achievable within the given time constraints.

Snapshot 7.4

Sample Questions (Goal)

Identifying Aspirations

- What are you building towards?
- What has brought you to coaching?
- What are your aspirations?

Identifying Goals

- What is it you would like to achieve?
- What do you hope will be different because of these coaching conversations?
- What are your goals?

Identifying Outcomes for the Session

- What would be the best use of our time together?
- What is your desired outcome of this conversation?
- What would you like to achieve during this coaching conversation?

Reality Stage

The Reality stage allows the client to explore the current situation and creates an opportunity for the coach to strengthen her relationship with the client by listening with interest and demonstrating empathy. As a novice coach, it may be helpful to focus your attention on *listening* to the client rather than trying to understand the situation so that you can offer a solution. This is a common trap as many of us are trained to listen for 'problems' in order to try to identify 'solutions'. In fact, many novice coaches report that 'having the answer' can get in the way of genuine listening.

To keep your mind busy during this stage, it may be helpful to focus on the skill of noticing. Effective and experienced coaches may seem to be 'just listening' during the Reality stage, but they are doing much more in the background.

A Question for You 7.1

What Is Reality?

The word 'reality' can be confusing in this context. There are many different viewpoints and interpretations. For the purposes of coaching, it is helpful to be aware that

(Continued)

---

reality is not always fixed. It is shaped by our perceptions and experiences, making it subjective. This idea is known as the phenomenological approach – human beings experience reality through their perceptions and interpretations. From this perspective, reality is subjective for each client. Each person is making sense of what is happening around her, based on her individual circumstances and through a particular lens that is informed by her world view. In the Reality phase, clients are supported to uncover and understand *their* reality. In addition to being interested in 'what is *really* happening at the moment', a coach supports her client to explore the following question: 'What is it like for you at the moment?'.

Demonstrating that You Are Listening

The skill of listening has been covered in Chapter 4. It is in the Reality stage that it can make the most significant impact. Instead of listening to 'come up with an answer', the experienced coach will listen to create a 'thoughtful' space for the client. Even more important than listening in this way is to *demonstrate* that you are listening attentively through your attitude and behaviours. A good question to ask yourself when reflecting on your practice is not 'How well did I listen?' but 'What evidence did I provide that I was listening?'. This kind of respectful listening has the added and powerful effect of allowing the client to feel valued and appreciated.

Asking Open Questions

The Reality stage is primarily an opportunity for the client to share her experiences. This is the stage where the coach should do the least talking. Having said that, an experienced coach will ensure that most interventions are presented as open questions, because these encourage further reflection and exploration. A good question to ask yourself when evaluating your own practice is, 'How did my questions help the client to do her best thinking?'.

Avoiding Leading Questions

Leading questions have no place in effective coaching conversations. Inevitably, these questions are manipulative, insinuating how the coach believes the client should behave. A good coach will first notice that she has offered a leading question, then avoid asking any more during the conversation. With time and with the appropriate 'coaching way of being' (which will be discussed in Chapters 12 and 13), the desire to make suggestions or advise through leading questions will diminish. Two good questions to ask yourself when reflecting on your practice are, 'Did I ask any leading questions?' and 'What do I have to change so that I am not seeking to find solutions for the client?'. Remember that you are likely to be disempowering clients if you tell them what they should do.

Being Aware of the Process

As explained earlier, the GROW model is one framework of many. However, a coach should keep a conversational framework in mind while coaching. While it is presented in a linear fashion, the GROW framework is cyclical and flexible. Often, clients will want to return to the Goal stage to refine their goals. At other times, it is the coach who feels the need to return to the Goal stage to renegotiate the focus of the conversation with the client. At all times, the experienced coach will be aware of where the conversation is in relation to a conversational framework. Facilitating the conversation is the coach's responsibility. So, depending on the length of the session, the coach should be thinking about how much time will be spent on each stage. A good question to ask yourself when reflecting on your practice is 'What interventions did I make to ensure that our conversation followed a recognised conversational framework?'

Ensuring an Appropriate Focus on the Goal

The Reality stage is the client's opportunity to 'offload' or 'paint a picture' of what things are like for her. The coach's role is to listen attentively and ensure that there is a link between the context that is described and the goal that has been selected. A good way of doing this is to ask the client about the relevance of what she has been talking about. For example: 'How does this relate to your goal of achieving a better work–life balance?' Often there is a relationship, and it is helpful for the client to verbalise this. At other times, the client may realise that she has pursued an avenue of thinking that does not relate directly to the selected goal. At this point, it is helpful for the coach to play back to the client that there is a 'disconnect' between what is being discussed and her stated goal. The client can either refocus on the original goal or select a different goal as the topic for the coaching conversation. In these situations, it is important to explicitly renegotiate this with the client. For example: 'It sounds like you have identified a different goal. Shall we set the original goal aside and spend our time talking about this goal instead?' A good question to ask yourself when reflecting on your practice is: 'What interventions did I make to ensure that the conversation focused on the client's stated goal?'.

Listening for 'Facts'

During the Reality stage, a coach should remain alert for statements that are presented as 'facts'. For our purposes, we will define a fact 'as a statement or observation that is independently verifiable'. For example, these could be facts: 'I was born in 1982';

'My company employs 240 people'; 'There are only three other people involved in the applications process.' This type of information can (theoretically) be verified by checking with other sources of data. However, other statements may be presented as facts when they are not: 'No one in my team will ever support that initiative'; 'In my organisation, you will not get promoted unless you are one of the boss's favourites'; 'People here are motivated by self-interest.' Each of these can be presented as 'facts' when they are beliefs or assumptions. This becomes a problem when the so-called 'fact' limits the client or gets in the way of what she wants to achieve.

Noticing Emotions

During the coaching conversation, the coach has an opportunity to listen carefully to gather information about emotions that the client may be experiencing. This can be done by making a mental note of references to emotions during the conversation, but also by noticing the client's posture, body language and mood. The Reality stage is an ideal setting for the client to reflect on the situation that she is in – and often a chance to talk about how she is feeling about this. If the client does not mention emotions at all, the coach could ask 'How do you feel about this situation?'. Helping the client identify the relationship between her goal and current situation in relation to that goal, *and* how she feels about the gap between the two can provide profound insights during the Reality stage.

Observing Body Language

Noticing the client's body language is another way of keeping our minds busy (so that we do not spend our mental energy trying to 'solve' things for the client). Much has been written about body language (this topic will be discussed in more detail in Chapter 10). In coaching, we can use our understanding of body language as one source of information to supplement what we learn about the client. Of course, it is necessary to be tentative about any data derived in this way. If a client crosses her arms, it may be that she is feeling defensive. But it could also suggest that it is cold where she is, that the client is angry about an earlier conversation or that she feels comfortable with her arms folded in that way. Often, the most helpful way to use observations about body language is to play them back to the client: 'I noticed that you were very animated when you talked about the possibility of leading the finance team. You were sitting up straight and using your hands when describing your ideas.' This is an important way of using the skill of noticing. Demonstrating that you are being attentive may support the client to raise her levels of self-awareness.

While it is good practice to notice the body language of a client, the coach may also benefit from being mindful about her own non-verbal communications. Nodding is helpful but overdoing it can have a negative effect. Excessive nodding can make the client feel rushed – or even as if she is talking to someone who is trying to 'sell' her something. Leaning backward in a chair may help the coach's posture but may also imply a lack of interest in what the client is saying. In most cultural contexts, adopting an open, relaxed body posture is most appropriate.

Snapshot 7.5

Sample Questions (Reality)

- What is happening at the moment?
- How do others perceive this situation?
- What are the benefits of this situation?
- What is getting in the way of resolving this issue?
- How similar is this to situations you have faced before?
- What feedback have you had about the current situation?
- What do you do really well?
- What have you already achieved?

Options Stage

The Options stage is the one that should be led mostly by the client. Paradoxically, it is also the time when coaches will have to work the hardest. By now, the client's goals should be clear and the current situation will have been discussed. Normally, there is a gap between what the client hopes to achieve and where she perceives herself to be at present.

Generating Options

At this point, the client should be encouraged to think about ways of moving closer to her goal by generating as many options as possible. Tools and techniques for helping the client to think creatively are explored in Chapter 11. It is important for the coach to push the client to identify as many options as possible. It has been suggested that the 'quantity of options is more important at this stage than the quality and feasibility of each one' (Whitmore, 2009: 79). In some cases, a client can change her self-perception from victim ('I have no control') to actor ('I can choose my own destiny') simply by realising that she has some options. Seeing how clients can surprise themselves with the options that they generate is one of the most satisfying aspects of being a coach.

Evaluating Options

Once options have been identified, the coach should work with the client to evaluate them. While having choices can be empowering, too many choices can be counter-productive (Iyengar, 2010; Schwartz, 2004). The evaluation criteria should be selected by the client. In other words, the client should decide how she will choose the best option to pursue. Sometimes this can be done by asking the client which option is the easiest to implement, the most likely to result in a positive outcome or the most desirable. At other times, it may be more helpful to go down the list of options, assessing the pros and cons of each. There will also be occasions when a more structured process feels appropriate. In this case, the client can create a grid identifying some criteria to apply to each option. For example, a client might want to think about her future career options with reference to 'job security', 'work–life balance', 'level of fun', 'remuneration' and 'status'. In this case, the career options could be entered along the first column and the criteria across the top of the grid. The client could then rate each criterion on a scale of 1–10. This would allow for a 'mathematical' calculation of the desirability of each option.

Snapshot 7.6

Sample Questions (Options)

- What are your options?
- What could you do?
- What else could you do?
- If you could do anything, what would it be?
- If you were to advise a friend who faced the same situation, what would you suggest?
- What would really unlock this situation for you?
- How would someone you really admire deal with this situation?
- What is your heart telling you?
- What is your head telling you?

Will Stage

The Will stage is the last one of the GROW framework. Now that the client has selected the options she wishes to pursue, it is time to check for levels of commitment and agree an action plan. At this stage, the client should be encouraged to commit to her next steps. The coach's role is to seek precision in this stage: Exactly what will the client do? When will she do this by? How will she know she has accomplished it? How likely is she to achieve this?

Assessing Intention to Act

If we accept that behavioural coaching is about supporting a person to change how she acts so that she can achieve her goals, then being able to assess her 'intention to act' is a necessary skill for coaches. By noticing the language a client uses, the emotions she expresses, and information gathered from her body language, the experienced coach is able to make informed judgements about how likely she is to proceed with an action that she has identified. For example, if a client looks engaged throughout a session, sits forward when deciding what needs to happen and is avidly writing down notes about her next steps, her 'intention to act' may be perceived as high. On the other hand, if the client looks despondent throughout, has her arms crossed, refuses to write anything and spends most of her time looking down at the floor, it is not likely that she will proceed with any action. Ultimately, it is impossible for the coach to know whether a client will undertake the actions that she has identified, but a subjective assessment of 'intention to act' allows the coach to check a client's level of commitment. If there is a discrepancy between the level of commitment and the proposed task, the coach can either work with the client to raise the level of commitment or select a less challenging task. It is important that the client leaves the coaching conversation motivated and hopeful that she will be able to achieve the task that she has set herself.

Assessing Readiness

Throughout the conversation, and especially during the Will stage, coaches should be considering the 'readiness' of their clients. In other words, using all the information that has been collected through the skill of noticing (e.g. body language, mood, what is said, punctuality) the coach should consider how open the client is to addressing the topic or issue that is under discussion. For example, if a client has been directed to receive coaching, there is a good chance that she may not be 'ready' to be coached. Equally, if a client has a migraine or is otherwise unwell, she is less likely to benefit from the discussion.

Snapshot 7.7

Sample Questions (Will)

- What will you do?
- What is the first step that you need to take?
- How will you know that you have succeeded?
- What will happen if you achieve this objective?
- What will not happen if you achieve this objective?
- How committed are you to the actions that you have identified, on a scale of 1–10?

Activity 7.1

Coaching Practice

There is only one way of becoming a coach: that is by coaching. To use the analogy of learning to drive, the only way to pass your test is to practise! And, just like learning how to drive, the GROW framework may seem a bit uncomfortable at first. However, we have all been through the initial stages of learning the coaching skills and conversational framework. So, let's get straight into it and start coaching others! While you are learning to coach:

- adhere to the GROW framework, ensuring that you are able to facilitate a conversation from start to finish;
- avoid the temptation to give advice or propose solutions;
- be clear with your client that you are learning how to coach;
- if you have the good fortune to be learning coaching with someone else, coach each other;
- if you are courageous enough, record yourself coaching so that you can reflect on your practice.

Just like driving, once you have mastered the basics, the process will feel smoother. You will then be able to adapt the framework, add your own techniques and make decisions about when and how to share your own experiences. Until then, please follow the GROW framework as closely as possible.

Adaptations of the GROW Framework

The GROW model is one of the best-known conversational frameworks in the field. As a result, a few adaptations have been developed. Three are presented below.

(T)GROW

Proposed by Miles Downey (2003), the letter 'T' is added to the conversational framework. This encourages coaches and clients to start by discussing the overall 'topic' for coaching. By discussing the topic first, there is less pressure to dive straight into talking about the goal. It can be particularly helpful when the additional stage allows the client to talk about her values and aspirations. This would support the client to identify goals that are congruent. Such self-concordant goals that are 'in alignment with the client's core personal values or developing interests are more likely to be engaging and elicit greater effort' (Grant, 2012: 152).

(RE)GROW

To emphasise the iterative process required for successful coaching, some practitioners add Review ('R') and Evaluation ('E') to the beginning of the framework. The 'R' and the 'E' are used from the second session onwards. This allows for the modification of goals during a series of coaching sessions. The process of reviewing, evaluating and modifying goals can lead to a cycle of self-regulation that can enhance the chances of successful behavioural change (Grant, 2003).

GROW(TH)

A leading global coach training provider for the education sector, Growth Coaching International, has developed the GROW framework for use in educational settings. Their model is called 'GROWTH' (Campbell, 2016) (see Figure 7.4). It emphasises the critical importance of the relationship at the outset. Then the framework moves into the Goal stage and the Reality stage, as in the traditional GROW model. In this process, however, 'R' also refers to 'Resources'. Coaches are invited to pay attention to the existing skills, experiences and practices of their clients during this stage. Doing this will build clients' sense of resourcefulness and optimism. The Options and Will stages are the same as in the GROW framework. Two new stages (Tactics and Habits) are added to ensure that new practices are embedded. In the 'Tactics' stage the client is asked to consider how and when she will undertake the tasks that she has identified. The 'Habits' stage is designed to help the client consider how she will maintain the new behaviour and mould it into a habit. The GROWTH framework concludes with a stage called 'Celebrating the results' so that both the coach and the client can explicitly and intentionally celebrate progress towards the client's goals.

The Four Curiosities

For those of you who do not like acronyms or rigid frameworks, I have reimagined the GROW framework as a series of 'curiosities'. When you start the coaching conversation, the first curiosity is 'what does the client want?'. This includes what the client wants overall, what she hopes to accomplish through coaching and what she believes that she can achieve during the coaching conversation. The second curiosity is 'where is the client now?'. This addresses the question of where the client believes she is in relation to where she would like to be. The third curiosity is 'what ideas does the client have about ways of moving forward?'. At this stage, the coach supports the client to explore various pathways towards what is wanted. The fourth and final curiosity is 'what will the client do?'. This allows the client to be explicit about what she will do as a result of the coaching session. The Four Curiosities mirror the GROW framework very closely. For some

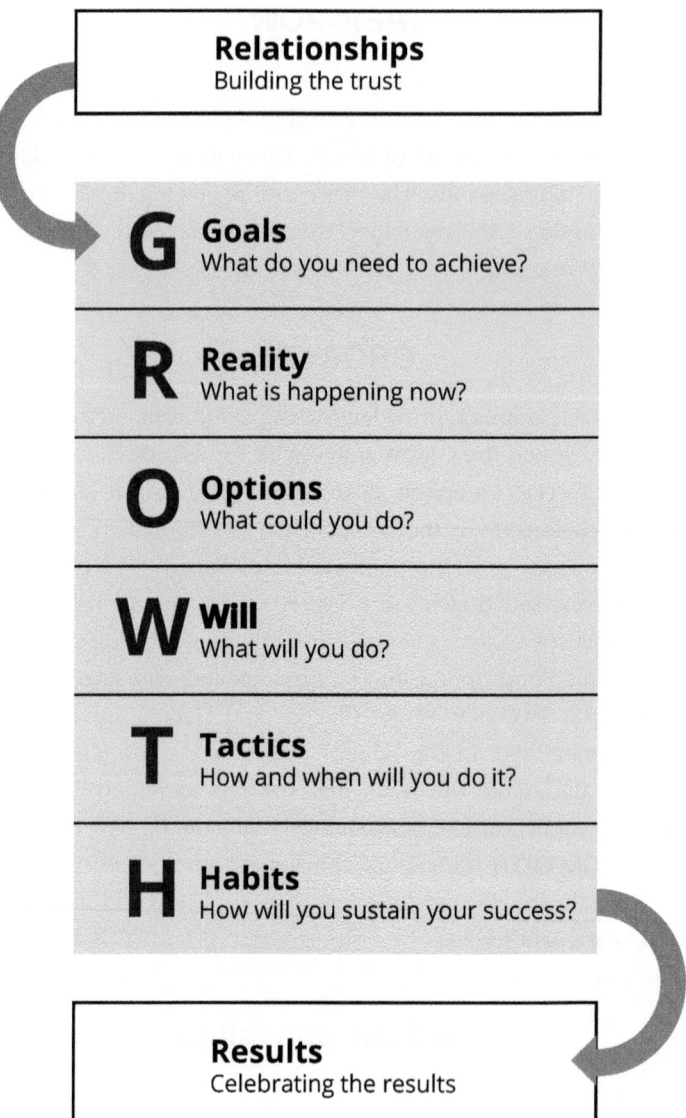

Figure 7.4   The GROWTH framework

(Source: Campbell, J. (2016) 'Framework for practitioners 2: The GROWTH model', in C. van Nieuwerburgh (ed.), *Coaching in Professional Contexts*. London: Sage. pp. 235–9.)

coaches this could be a more engaging way of keeping in mind the broad arc of the conversational framework whilst also emphasising the importance of maintaining a curious stance throughout.

As we can see from this review of some adaptations, the GROW framework can be redesigned to suit different circumstances. It is a well-known and robust model that has stood the test of time.

What the Professional Associations Say 7.1

Conversational Framework

To become an accredited coach, you will need to learn and master a conversational framework. According to the ICF, being familiar with a framework will allow you to deliver a coaching conversation with flexibility and confidence. It is the skilful use of a conversational framework that **facilitates client growth**. By facilitating the process and the time available, the coach creates the ideal environment for the client to do their best thinking. The EMCC highlights the importance of coaches **using models and techniques** to bring about insights and learning for clients. The use of a conversational framework supports an **outcome and action orientation**. For the AC, being able to follow a framework will allow the client to **design strategies and action** and **maintain forward momentum.**

Activity 7.2

Observing a Coaching Session

Please refer to Video 7.1 for this activity. In this full-length coaching conversation, the author coaches a professional on the topic of networking strategies. This is a real coaching conversation that was not scripted or staged. Hopefully, it will give you a good sense of how a conversational framework underpins effective coaching conversations.

Watch the clip, paying special attention to the way the coach facilitates the conversation.

Are you able to pick up the various stages of the GROW framework?

What strategies does the coach use to facilitate the session?

Which of the coaching skills do you notice?

Capture your notes in your learning journal.

Coaching Contract

Before embarking on any coaching, it is important for you, as a coach, to establish a coaching contract. The coaching contract should set out how the coach and the client will work together. This should be undertaken before starting on the GROW conversational framework. Remember, even if the topic is of a personal nature, coaching is a professional conversation. The coaching contract is a recognised way of establishing the professional parameters of the conversation.

Some coaches have written contracts that they ask their clients to sign. Others simply discuss the contract verbally with the client at the beginning of the coaching relationship. It is good practice to refer back briefly to the coaching contract at every session.

──────── Snapshot 7.8 ────────

What Should Be Included in a Coaching Contract?

Table 7.1   Topics to include in a coaching contract

Topic	Specific examples	Importance
Operational issues	• Number of coaching sessions • Length of time per session • Location of meetings (online or in person) • Date of meetings	Recommended
Shared understanding of 'coaching'	• Check that you and the client are expecting the same kind of interaction • Clarify the difference between coaching and mentoring • Clarify the difference between coaching and counselling	Recommended
Financial arrangements	• Agree fees for coaching (per session or for the entire contract) • Explain when payment is due • Explain how payments will be made	Essential (if charging for coaching)
Agreement about withdrawal	• Agree how each party might be able to pull out of the coaching arrangement • Indicate whether reasons should be given	Recommended
Ethical conduct	• Explain which code of ethics will apply • Declare which professional association the coach is a member of	Essential
Confidentiality	• Be specific about the rules of confidentiality • Explain when confidentiality may be broken (usually, this includes situations when the coach believes that the client or others are at risk of harm or when the client divulges an illegal activity)	Essential
Competence	• Be explicit about your level of experience • Be clear about your boundaries (in relation to counselling)	Recommended
Permissions	• Seek permission for taking notes (and explain what they are for) • Seek permission to interject • Seek permission to challenge (if you will be doing so)	Personal preference
Personal style	• Share with the client how you work as a coach (e.g. 'non-directive', 'challenging')	Personal preference

---

Activity 7.3

Drafting Your Own Coaching Contract

At this stage it is sufficient to draft your coaching contract. What would you like to agree on before starting the coaching? What is important for the client to know? Make some notes in your learning journal under the heading 'My coaching contract'.

What the Professional Associations Say 7.2

Contracting

According to the ICF, the coaching contract is a central component of **demonstrating ethical practice**. In fact, the contract will require you to be explicit about the code of ethics that you follow. Being competent at contracting conveys that you are good at **establishing and maintaining agreements**. The existence of a clearly articulated contract will **cultivate trust and safety** for both coach and client. The EMCC has an explicit competency called **managing the contract**, highlighting the importance of establishing and maintaining expectations and boundaries. From the perspective of the AC, contracting is necessary to **meet ethical, legal and professional guidelines** and in order to **establish the coaching agreement and outcomes**. The contract is the basis for **establishing a trust-based relationship with the client**.

Conclusion

In this chapter, we have considered a few conversational frameworks. We discussed each step of the GROW framework and sample questions were provided. While you have a choice of frameworks, it is essential to recognise that coaching is a conversational process that is facilitated by the coach. We also highlighted the importance of agreeing a contract before any coaching conversation.

See It in Practice 7.1

The Conversational Framework

Video 7.1 A Full Coaching Session

This is a recording of a complete coaching conversation. As you watch this clip, see if you notice how the coach facilitates the conversation from identifying a goal through to supporting the client to commit to actions.

(Continued)

Video 7.2 Starting with Contracting

Watch this clip to see the coach contracting at the start of the conversation. This is a necessary part of every formal coaching session.

Video 7.3 Identifying Outcome for the Session

In this short clip, the coach follows up a conversation about the client's goal with a specific question about what they would like as an outcome of the coaching session.

Video 7.4 Highlighting Resources

As you watch this clip, notice how the coach invites the client to reflect on the fact that they have experience that is relevant to the challenge being discussed. Notice how the client starts to recognise the value of what she already knows.

Video 7.5 Clarifying Next Steps

In this clip, the coach turns attention to the practical implications of the coaching session. It is your role as a coach to manage the transitions between the various phases of a conversational framework.

Video 7.6 Checking Outcome Was Met

In this segment, close to the end of the coaching conversation, the client is asked to reflect on whether the outcome of the session has been met. It is helpful for coaches to ask this type of question to highlight that progress has been made.

Video 7.7 Asking about Important Insights

Notice how thoughtful the client is when asked about how helpful the session was. This is a good way of capturing the learning from coaching conversations.

Video 7.8 Asking for Feedback

Watch the client reflecting on the value of the coaching conversation. When coaches ask for feedback, there are opportunities for both the coach and the client to learn.

8
Ways of Thinking

There are times when it will be necessary to move beyond simply talking about behaviours during coaching conversations. The GROW framework discussed in the previous chapter was first popularised by Whitmore in *Coaching for Performance* (1992). Whitmore brought welcome attention to the relationship between coaching and performance in a way that made coaching attractive to the world of business. Based on Whitmore's book, it seemed that coaching held the promise of improved performance of employees, which would, in turn, lead to greater profitability.

Initially, there was an understandable assumption in organisations that staff performance would be enhanced by focusing on behavioural change. Much of the support and evidence for this view derived from the work of behavioural psychologists (see Snapshot 8.1) and this approach has been dubbed 'behavioural coaching'. Some argue that the GROW framework is best suited for behavioural coaching (e.g. Alexander, 2010; Passmore, 2007), and it is true that the final stage of the GROW framework ('What will you *do* differently?') focuses on a behavioural outcome.

Snapshot 8.1

Behavioural Psychology

Behavioural psychology is a branch of psychology committed to studying observable human behaviours. Famous behaviourists such as John B. Watson, Ivan Pavlov and B.F. Skinner argued for a *scientific* approach to studying psychology. They concluded that the scientific study of 'consciousness' was not possible, advocating instead that psychologists should study behavioural adaptation and the relationship between stimuli and responses (Banyard et al., 2019). Despite waning in popularity, theories that emerged from behavioural psychology continue to inform how institutions, organisations and governments try to get people to act in certain ways. For example, 'nudge theory' (Thaler and Sustein, 2008) is rooted in behavioural psychology. According to this theory, small changes that people make can lead to longer-term behavioural changes. If you have been to a cafeteria that places healthier food options at eye-level and the less healthy choices lower down, you have been nudged to make better dietary decisions!

In Chapter 1, we discussed definitions. One of these needs to be updated. We initially said that coaching 'aims to support sustainable change to behaviours'. We should amend that to 'aims to support sustainable change to behaviours *or ways of thinking*'. The reason to add 'ways of thinking' is because sometimes people need to change the way they think before they can alter what they do, especially if they are trying to make sustainable changes to their behaviour. There has been a long-running, interesting and still unresolved debate about the best way of bringing about sustainable change in human behaviour. The view that both behaviour *and* thinking should be addressed is called the 'cognitive-behavioural approach'.

An intriguing question emerges: 'Should clients change their behaviours *first*, which would bring about a change in the way they think, or does it work better if clients start by changing the way they think, which will then lead to changes in how they behave?' There is no need to resolve this question here. In my own experience as a coach, I have seen beneficial and sustainable change being embraced by clients using both approaches.

Find Out More 8.1

Understanding Psychology

Essential Psychology (Banyard et al., 2019) is an accessible and clearly written introduction to the field. It offers an overview of six areas of psychology that are covered in most university courses. The short, readable chapters provide a foundational understanding, allowing readers to make informed decisions about the topics that they would like to investigate further.

Relationship Between Thoughts and Behaviours

An understanding of psychological theories and approaches is beneficial for a coach as it will allow her to address topics which may require a change in thinking before a sustainable change in behaviour can be achieved. However, using technical language or psychological jargon is hardly ever conducive to a good coaching conversation! There are alternative approaches to helping clients reflect on the relationship between their thoughts and their behaviours. In the following section, we will consider some helpful ways of discussing this: the concept of the 'inner game' (Gallwey, 1974); a quote by a Greek philosopher; a thought-provoking series of statements; a Shakespearean passage; and a list of 'thinking errors'.

The 'Inner Game'

Gallwey's notion of the 'inner game' was originally introduced in 1974. As a tennis player, and then a tennis coach, Gallwey was interested in the relationship between what happened in the mind of a player and what happened (physically) on the court.

In a concept that quickly extended beyond the tennis context, Gallwey proposed that 'every game is composed of two parts, an outer game and an inner game' (p. 11). The outer game is the one that is played on the tennis court, between two players. The inner game 'takes place within the mind of the player and it is played against such obstacles as lapses in concentration, nervousness, self-doubt and self-condemnation. In short, it is played to overcome all habits of mind which inhibit excellence in performance' (p. 11). Gallwey argued that for people to 'maximise their own potential' they must win both the 'outer game' (what happens in the 'real' or external world around us) as well as the 'inner game' (the world of our mind).

A Question for You 8.1

What Do You Say to Yourself?

Many of us experience Gallwey's concept of the 'inner game' regularly when we engage in what is called 'self-talk'. Self-talk describes the 'inner voice' that operates in our mind in certain situations. It is the dialogue that we have with ourselves. For example, in job interview situations, many people experience negative self-talk. This may include thoughts such as, 'I am really bad at interviews', 'I haven't got enough experience compared to the other candidates' or, 'Why did I ever think I would get this job?'. In this scenario, performance at the job interview is the 'outer game', visible to the interviewers. At the same time, there is another game going on. The second game involves the negative self-talk that the applicant is engaging in. This, obviously, is not directly visible to the interviewers. Gallwey's point, however, is that the 'inner game' influences the 'outer game', and therefore it is important for people to become aware of their 'inner game'.

Can you think of any negative self-talk that you have engaged in recently? What impact is it having on your 'outer game'? Make some notes in your learning journal under the heading 'My inner game'.

Although Gallwey's contribution in 1974 was to significantly impact the coaching profession, the thoughts that underpin the concept of the 'inner game' can be traced back to classical times.

Greek Philosopher

In the first century of the Common Era, the Greek philosopher Epictetus (55–c.135 CE) is reported by one of his students to have said that people 'are disturbed, not by the things that happen, but by their opinion of the things that happen'. This view suggests two different factors: things that happen (the 'outer game') and a person's opinion of those things (the 'inner game'). In coaching, there is an opportunity to work with people on their opinions about the 'things that happen'.

Thought-Provoking Kantian Koan

The following thought-provoking series of statements ('old Kantian koan') has been attributed to the philosopher Immanuel Kant (Peltier, 2010):

I see a tiger.

I think I am in danger.

I feel afraid.

I run away.

A Question for You 8.2

What Do You Think?

Take a moment to reflect on the series of statements above. How do they relate to the concept of the 'inner game'? Capture your thoughts in your learning journal under the heading 'I see a tiger'.

Kant's series of statements provides us with an interesting way of thinking about how human behaviour occurs. 'I see a tiger' could be termed an 'activating event'. This is something that we can observe or hear. This event triggers a thought ('I think I am in danger'). The thought then leads to a feeling (in this case, fear). The feeling causes us to behave in a certain way (in this case, running away).

What is powerful for us as coaches is the chance to support clients to recognise that there are stages within this process that are easier for them to control than others. Sometimes we cannot control the activating event, and often we assume that it is the activating event that leads directly to the behaviour (based on the stimulus–response theory of behavioural psychology). It is empowering for a client to recognise that if she can change the way she thinks about an activating event, it will lead to a different set of feelings.

Please remember that this is simply a way of understanding the process that may be helpful in a coaching conversation, rather than a scientifically proven theory. There is blossoming interest in neuroscience (e.g. Brown and Brown, 2012; Brann, 2017) which may allow us to get a clearer understanding of what happens in our brains. Although these fields are in their infancy, it is hoped that new research findings will give us more sophisticated insights into the relationships between our thoughts, feelings and behaviours.

Find Out More 8.2

Neuroscience

A growing number of books explore this topic further:

Coaching the Brain: Practical Applications of Neuroscience to Coaching (O'Connor and Lages, 2019)

Neuroscience for Coaches: How to Use the Latest Insights for the Benefit of Your Clients (Brann, 2017)

The Neuroscience of Leadership Coaching: Why the Tools and Techniques of Leadership Coaching Work (Bossons et al., 2015)

Story from Practice 8.1

Training Day

Fortunately for many of us, the chance of encountering an unsupervised tiger in our everyday lives is remote. However, the series of four statements discussed above can help us to reflect on our thought processes. The case below is based on a piece of consultancy work that I undertook for a large public sector organisation.

As part of a contract that involved one-to-one executive coaching, I was asked to support a group of middle managers in a large organisation undergoing significant change. To familiarise myself with the organisation and get a sense of the proposed changes, I asked to attend a team training day to hear a presentation by the chief executive. The four people I would be coaching were in attendance, along with most of the organisation's middle and senior managers. The coaching was scheduled to take place relatively soon after the training day, so I introduced myself to each of my clients, but sat by myself so that I could concentrate on the chief executive's presentation.

The chief executive started by saying how proud she was to lead the organisation and why she had chosen to work for it. She followed with a seemingly honest appraisal of the challenges that lay ahead, suggesting that there would be difficulties and explicitly stating that the organisation would have to shed jobs to survive over the coming years. The chief executive praised the work of the change management team. I was pleased that she mentioned the important role of coaching to support key members of the team through the change process. She concluded by asserting her confidence in the organisation's

(Continued)

people and her belief that implementing the required changes would ultimately lead to a more vibrant and sustainable organisation that was even better placed to deliver to its stakeholders. In total, she spoke for about 30 minutes. There was some muted applause after which the chief executive left. The training day continued in her absence. I left shortly afterwards and then met with all the executives for their 1–1 coaching sessions within the following 2 weeks.

At the coaching sessions, I asked each client about her or his view of the presentation by the chief executive. At the time, my reason for this was that it seemed to be a good starting point for the discussion, and it was also the only experience that I had in common with my clients. I was genuinely surprised by the discrepancies in individual perceptions with relation to the presentation. Considering this using the old Kantian koan, the chief executive's input was the 'tiger', or activating event. During the coaching, each client presented me with her or his thoughts and feelings about the presentation. All four were different (although they all experienced the same event). Client 1 was very upbeat about the presentation. She told me that she was impressed with the leadership qualities of the chief executive. The client admired the 'honesty and integrity' of the chief executive as well as her ability to 'face up to reality'. The previous chief executive had always 'worn rose-tinted spectacles' and avoided confrontation. According to the client, this was one of the reasons that the organisation was facing such challenges now. The presentation had left her more motivated and committed to supporting the chief executive through the change programme, especially as the hard work of the middle managers had been recognised.

When I spoke to Client 2, it was as if he had attended a different presentation! He shared a very negative response and was reluctant to discuss the topic. He thought the speech was self-serving and cynical. 'I don't need her to tell me that she did me a favour by coming here as chief executive! I've been here long enough to know that she's only interested in her own career. She'll be long gone before this thing blows up.' He saw as 'typical' her behaviour of abandoning any real responsibility for the change programme by 'dumping it' on the middle managers of the organisation. He conceded that she was 'honest' about redundancies, but not the scale of job cuts. 'And we all know that already,' he said, dismissing the value of the information. Following the speech, he was even more convinced than before that the chief executive was good at giving presentations ('she's good at the PR') but did not really understand the business or the concerns of staff. As usual, *he* would be expected to make the difficult decisions, and, at the end of the day, it was his job and those of his team members that were at risk. He was already a member of the union and said he would be working with them to resist the proposed changes. In his view, attending the training day had been a waste of time. He would have preferred to invest his time in running the business rather than 'navel-gazing'.

You can see from Table 8.1 that the activating event was the same, and that the ultimate behaviours are very different. Using this visual representation, it becomes more evident that the intervening stages are significant. In many cases, we are not in control of the various activating events in our lives. However, what is powerful is the concept that we can choose our own responses by changing the way we think.

Table 8.1 Different responses to the same activating event

	Client 1	Client 2
'I see a tiger' Activating event	Presentation by Chief Executive	Presentation by Chief Executive
'I think I am in danger' Thoughts (cognition)	• Chief executive is being honest • Chief executive is an effective leader • Chief executive is making the right decisions • Chief executive appreciates the work we are doing	• Presentation is a cynical ploy to prepare staff for redundancies • Chief executive is good at making speeches but does not know the business • Chief executive will be on to her next job soon, and does not care about the impact of her decisions • Chief executive is abandoning responsibility by getting middle managers to deal with all the difficult decisions
'I feel afraid' Feelings (emotion)	Reassured, valued, encouraged, motivated	Angry, resentful, disengaged, fearful
'I run away' Behaviour	Engaged in training day planning Emailed chief executive to thank her	Did not engage in training day Will resist any changes to ways of working Will not attend future training days

This story may also help to highlight the difficulty (in the case of Client 2) of adopting a behavioural coaching approach to the client 'being more engaged during training days'. A simplistic use of the GROW framework to look at strategies for participating more positively at future training days would ignore the underlying thoughts and feelings of anger and resentment. Some would argue that it would be impossible (in this case) to bring about any lasting change *without* addressing the client's thoughts and emotions.

Shakespearean Interlude

William Shakespeare explored the question of how a person's perceptions can 'create' her own reality:

Hamlet: What have you, my good friends, deserv'd at the hands of Fortune, that she sends you to prison hither?

Guildenstern: Prison, my lord?

Hamlet: Denmark's a prison.

Rosencrantz: Then is the world one.

Hamlet: A goodly one, in which there are many confines, wards, and dungeons, Denmark being one o' th' worst.

Rosencrantz: We think not so, my lord.

Hamlet: Why then 'tis none to you; for there is nothing either good or bad, but thinking makes it so. To me it is a prison. (*Hamlet*, 2.2.228–237)

Hamlet's line 'there is nothing either good or bad, but thinking makes it so' eloquently and simply captures the power of the 'inner game'. According to Hamlet's own thought processes, Denmark *is* a prison. He accepts that the same place (Denmark) may *not* be a prison for Rosencrantz and Guildenstern. As coaches, we must recognise that a client's thoughts can create her reality. In other words, Rosencrantz and Guildenstern are unlikely to get anywhere by simply arguing with Hamlet about whether Denmark is a prison or not. There would be more value in understanding how Hamlet has arrived at the conclusion by supporting him to reflect on the thought process itself.

Talking about the 'Inner Game'

There are a few ways of making the 'inner game' more explicitly a focus of a coaching conversation: Sharing the old Kantian koan; following the cognitive behavioural framework; using quotes from historical figures; presenting the idea of the inner game; highlighting thinking errors; and creating performance enhancing thoughts.

1 Sharing the Old Kantian Koan

First, sharing the 'old Kantian koan' (Peltier, 2010) would allow the coach to explore the client's process from 'seeing a tiger' through to 'running away'. Once that has been discussed, attention can turn to more helpful ways of responding to the 'tiger'.

2 Adopting the Cognitive-Behavioural Framework

The coach can simply ask questions that support the client to work through their thoughts, feelings and behaviours in response to an 'activating event':

Activating Event

'Tell me more about what happened initially.'

'So, what started this off?'

'What triggered this situation?'

Thoughts

'And what did you think of that?'

'What thoughts sprang to mind when that happened?'

'What was going through your head at that moment?'

Feelings

'And how did those thoughts make you feel?'

'Tell me how that kind of thinking made you feel.'

'What sort of emotions were triggered when those thoughts were in your head?'

Behaviour

'So, what did you do?'

'What impact did your emotions have on what you did next?'

'What's the relationship between these feelings and what you did afterwards?'

When using this framework, we can encourage clients to recognise that they *are* able to change the way they perceive certain situations. We can observe that there is usually a link between what we think and how we feel – and that feelings can influence how we behave.

3 Quotes from Historical Figures

For clients who may find philosophy or drama engaging, it may be helpful to share the quote from Epictetus or the passage from *Hamlet*, allowing for a discussion about how our perceptions create our realities. From there, the discussion can turn to how the client might be able to perceive her situation differently.

4 Presenting the Idea of the 'Inner Game'

The concept of the 'inner game' can be explained. If the client recognises that her topic relates to her 'outer game', she may be more open to talking about the 'inner game' during the coaching conversation. Alternatively, if the topic is about the 'inner game', the coach and client can discuss how this affects the 'outer game'.

5 Thinking Errors

Another way of raising awareness about how a client's thinking can get in their way is to share a list of common 'thinking errors' with the client. The field of psychology has identified 'common cognitive distortions' that can impact negatively on our thinking. These thinking errors can affect us at any time but are especially likely when we are feeling challenged or stressed. While there are (unfortunately) many thinking errors, 20 that may be relevant to coaching conversations are listed below.

1 *Polarised thinking*: This refers to 'black and white' thinking. Although life is usually not this clearly delineated, people can fall into the trap of seeing things as opposites. This way of thinking necessarily limits choices. Statements such as 'I *never* win anything' and 'I am *always* the one who ends up apologising' demonstrate polarised thinking.

2 *Over-generalising*: This refers to making general or exaggerated statements based on limited information. For example, if someone encounters one person in Brussels being an inconsiderate driver, it would be over-generalising to conclude that 'Belgians are terrible drivers'. Or, if a client makes a statement about 'motivation levels in the charity sector' based on one job volunteering in a charity shop, this is another example of over-generalising.

3 *Catastrophising*: Catastrophising occurs when a person focuses unhelpfully on a mistake to such an extent that a relatively small error begins to feel like a major crisis. People who catastrophise tend to move quickly in their thinking to the 'worst case scenario' and they tend to overrate the possibility of this occurring.

4 *Personalisation*: This is about taking everything personally. If a client feels that everyone's actions are directed at her, this will lead to anxiety and defensiveness. People who get caught by this thinking error find it difficult to receive any feedback, as they are likely to take any suggestions as criticism.

5 *Blaming*: This is a relatively common thinking error involving the client blaming others completely for things that go wrong. By doing this, the client avoids acknowledging her role in a problem or difficult situation. Clients who start a coaching relationship by saying 'It's not me you should be speaking to. You should be coaching my boss' may be experiencing this thinking error.

6 *Mindreading*: This is when we think that we can tell what someone else is thinking and unreasonably believe that this guess is true (in other words, that we 'know' what may be going on in someone else's head). This can be noticed when a client says 'I know exactly how they are going to respond' or 'She hasn't said anything but I know exactly what she is thinking.'

7 *Self-criticism*: Some people believe that criticism is a good way of motivating oneself. This can lead to self-critical thoughts, and people can end up holding unreasonably high expectations for themselves. The fallacy is believing that such a view is good for us. While it can motivate for short periods of time, self-criticism is damaging in the longer term.

8 *Unchanging feelings*: This thinking error involves believing that because we feel a particular way about something, we will always feel the same way about it. An example is a young person who says 'I won't want to retire in the south of France because I get bored in quiet towns.'

9 *Halo effect*: This effect occurs when we believe that everything about a person is wonderful just because we have experienced one positive trait or aspect of her personality. The positive impression (the 'halo') influences our assessment of all that person's characteristics or behaviour.

10 *Minimising*: This is when we underplay our role in successful events or positive outcomes. People who minimise their achievements would say 'Oh, that was nothing' or 'I didn't do much', even when they had made a significant contribution.

11 *Self-serving bias*: This is when we attribute positive events to our own behaviour but negative events to external factors. In other words, when things go well, this is believed to be due to one's own efforts but when things go badly, other people or factors are blamed.

12 *Assumed similarity*: This common thinking error is based on believing that other people have similar thoughts and attitudes to ours.

13 *In-group bias*: The in-group bias is a tendency to trust and value people who are like ourselves or who are from similar cultural or social backgrounds.

14 *Positively based predictions*: This is another common error, especially in optimists. A positively based prediction is when we assume things will go well without any evidence to support this.

15 *Repeating the same behaviour and expecting different results*: Some people continue to repeat their behaviour, or do more of the same thing, while hoping for different results. For example, when repeatedly asking a child to clean her room does not work, we sometimes simply increase the level of nagging!

16 *Labelling*: This is when we attach labels to a group of people, making assumptions about how that group behave. Examples are 'IT people', 'lawyers', 'management' and so on. Labelling people can lead to us dehumanising them. For example, to suggest that 'the management should be taken out and shot' may seem like an acceptable thing to say until we consider that 'the management' is a group of human beings.

17 *Dwelling on the negative*: This denotes a tendency to focus solely on the negative, even when there is a broad range of information. For example, focusing on one negative comment on a report card when it is generally positive would suggest that we are dwelling on the negative.

18 *Emotional reasoning*: Emotional reasoning refers to situations when we take our feelings to represent facts. For example, we might believe that if we're feeling awkward, we are being awkward.

19 *Fallacy of fairness*: This relates to the unfortunately false belief that life is fair. This can cause anger or make us feel like victims. For example, if someone with lesser qualifications or less experience gets a promotion, this can seem 'unfair', and lead to demotivation or bitterness.

20 *Always being right*: This is difficult to believe! We are not always right. If you are surprised by how often you are right and everyone else is wrong, take it as a warning sign that you might be experiencing this thinking error!

Performance-Inhibiting Thoughts

'Performance-inhibiting thoughts' relate to any thinking that get in the way of what people want to achieve (Palmer and Szymanska, 2007). Palmer and Szymanska argue that the exploration of 'performance-inhibiting thoughts' (PITs) is useful in coaching contexts. This is because it focuses attention on the thoughts that are preventing the client from achieving her desired performance.

Practical Use in Coaching Sessions

A client can be asked to list her PITs following discussion with the coach. Once the client has identified her PITs, the coach can ask questions to check the accuracy of each. Once the PIT has been examined, the client is asked to create 'performance-enhancing thoughts' (PETs) for each of the PITs. This is a challenging task that can reap significant rewards. The role of the coach is to ask appropriate questions that allow the client to examine the PITs. Are they true? What can be done to prevent the PIT from getting in the way of goal attainment?

Some typical questions are:

'What is the evidence for your belief?'

'What is the impact of this way of thinking?'

'How can you create new thoughts that will support you in achieving your goals?'

What the Professional Associations Say 8.1

Cognitive-Behavioural Approach

The three professional associations (ICF, EMCC, AC) emphasise the importance of exploring the relationship between thoughts, feelings and actions. Understanding the connection between these three things is crucial for effective coaching practice, which involves fostering client growth and self-awareness. According to the ICF, the cognitive-behavioural approach facilitates the competency of **evoking awareness**. The EMCC recommends **using models and techniques** that go beyond the key coaching skills in order to facilitate insight and learning. For the AC, this would be considered an important part of **raising awareness and insight**.

Conclusion

This chapter has explored how to coach people on their thinking when adapting behaviours may not be sufficient to achieve sustainable change. The GROW framework can still be used, with coaches supporting their clients to reflect on their thinking processes using some of the approaches and tools mentioned in this chapter. It is important to remember that we should always be guided by the best interests of the client. There will be times when the change required is behavioural. In these circumstances, exploring the 'inner game' can be counterproductive. However, there will also be cases when any behavioural changes will be short-lived unless a client is willing to change the way she thinks.

See It in Practice 8.1

Ways of Thinking

Video 8.1 Exploring Different Ways of Thinking

In this clip, the coach challenges the client to think differently about the challenge that is being discussed. Notice the client's reaction to being asked about this.

Video 8.2 Asking about Ways of Thinking

Watch what happens when the coach asks if there is a different way of thinking about the client's topic. This leads to an important insight for the client.

9
Positive Bias

Having covered the skills of coaching and a conversational framework, let us now consider the importance of bringing attention to what is positive. This chapter will survey the contribution of positive psychology to the practice of coaching. We will first explore the solution-focused coaching approach and some related techniques. We will then consider the broader field of positive psychology, looking for ways of integrating it into coaching through the practice of 'positive psychology coaching' (Biswas-Diener, 2010; van Nieuwerburgh and Biswas-Diener, 2021).

Solution-Focused Coaching

This section will explore solution-focused coaching. We will consider the concept of being solution-focused and the ways of integrating it into your coaching practice.

Approach and Model

The solution-focused approach to coaching can be used as a discrete process or as part of a conversational framework. As you will discover below, the solution-focused approach can also be adopted as part of our everyday interactions.

The solution-focused coaching approach emerged from a therapeutic intervention developed in the 1960s and 1970s. At the heart of the 'brief therapy' approach were two principles considered radical at the time. First, that the purpose of therapy was not to simply clarify a difficulty or situation but to *make things better*. Second, that the therapist should accept whatever the client says, and that this should be used positively. Essentially, this thinking challenged the traditional approach to therapy by suggesting that it was not necessary to understand the history of a problem (which was the preferred method of the psychotherapeutic approach at the time). The new thinking highlighted the importance of a sharp focus on helping the client to develop new behaviours to resolve the problem instead. In its early phases, the approach was known as 'brief' therapy because it was seen to have a narrower focus. However, it is probably true to say that current interest in this approach is due to the perception that this approach can take less time.

Solution-Focused Approaches

The original 'solution-focused' model was developed by de Shazer and Berg (1995), who underscored the positive nature of the interaction. For them, the approach was based on two premises: that the future is 'created' and that small changes in the present can lead to big differences in the future. Based on this, de Shazer and Berg proposed that the focus of the intervention should rest on only one question: 'How will we know when the problem is solved?'

Using the Scaling Technique as the Framework for a Coaching Conversation

One of the preferred techniques of the solution-focused approach is called 'scaling'. It is possible to manage an entire coaching conversation using this technique, which is described below.

Following an introduction and agreement about the situation for discussion, the coach can describe a scale which has '1' on one end and '10' on the other.

Step 1: The first step is to ask the client to place the current situation on the scale, using this question (or similar): 'On a scale of 1 to 10, with 1 being the worst it could be and 10 being when the situation is resolved, where are you today?' By doing this, we are helping the client to put the situation in perspective (this counteracts the 'catastrophising' thinking error mentioned in Chapter 8). It is important that the client makes a commitment and identifies a point on the scale. If she prefers to choose a whole number or a fraction, that is OK as long as she determines a point on the scale where she considers her situation to be at that moment.

Step 2: Once the client has selected a number that represents where she is at the moment, the coach should follow it up by asking the client why she has placed it where she has. This can be done using a question such as 'What makes it a [whatever number she has chosen] and not a "1"?' This question is helpful because it helps the client to acknowledge that some things are already going well. It allows the coach to spend time listening for the existing resources of the client. The coach's role is to celebrate any number that is higher than '1' (see Story from practice 9.1). As with the GROW framework, these early steps are an opportunity to demonstrate attentive listening and empathy.

Step 3: After listening to the client explain why she placed the situation where she did, and celebrating the fact that it is not a '1', the coach moves on to the most important stage of the solution-focused approach. The coach should ask what a '9' or '10' would look like: 'What would it look/feel like if the situation were at a 9 or 10?' We ask this question to encourage the client to imagine life without the problem. As a coach, you may want to spend some time talking about this imagined future, as this is usually motivational. Ask the client to start to describe what it would be like if this situation were completely resolved. It is appropriate to spend most of the time allocated for coaching to this step. The positive emotions generated here will provide the motivation for the client to tackle the situation.

Step 4: Once the coach senses that the client is motivated by the thought of a successful outcome, the following question (or similar) is asked: 'What would make you move the situation to [a slightly higher number than originally chosen] on the scale?' In other words, the coach is asking what small steps could be taken to increase the client's assessment of the situation. So, if the client had rated the current situation as a '4', the coach would ask, 'And what would need to happen for you to rate it as a 5?' This step will seem relatively manageable, and the client should be better able to think of something to move herself towards the '5'. The coach's role at this point is to support the client to generate some practical and achievable steps that would lead to the client placing her situation slightly higher on the scale (and therefore closer to when the situation will be completely resolved). It is crucial that this comes from the client and that a specific action plan is agreed. The important factor is that the client starts to feel that she is moving towards the solution. Remember that one of the principles of this approach is that a small change in the present can lead to a big difference in the future. Additionally, a small step will feel manageable to the client, and success in achieving that small step will increase her motivation.

The coaching conversation would be concluded at this point, with a date set for the next session. Assuming that the client has achieved her small step, the process would be followed again, but this time exploring the next small step. If the client does not feel that she has achieved the small step, alternative ways of moving forward can be discussed.

Story from Practice 9.1

Scale of 1 to 10

The solution-focused coaching process identified in this chapter is not always the most appropriate for every client. I have selected an example that was particularly suited to this approach. In my experience, the solution-focused approach works best when there is a clear barrier or difficulty that the client is facing. In other words, the need for coaching will have arisen because the client is fixated on what is going *wrong* instead of focusing on what she needs to do to move forward.

The client, a first-line manager in an organisation, wanted to talk about her career development. Up to that point, due to various factors, including family commitments, this client had

(Continued)

allowed her career to 'happen to her', without being able to shape it. She felt that she was a hard worker and that this had been duly recognised by her managers. She had been promoted internally to her current role, which she had been doing now for 6 years. She felt ready to move into a more senior role but worried that her lack of confidence about interviews would let her down, and therefore did not apply for jobs that she saw advertised.

As there seemed to be a clear 'blockage' (something that was evidently getting in the way of the client achieving her aspirations), I felt that the solution-focused process would be helpful. I explained that we would be using the 'solution-focused scale' to frame our conversation. I asked her to reflect on her confidence levels about interviews and rate herself on the scale, explaining that '10' would denote that she felt incredibly confident about interviews (in other words, that the problem no longer existed), and that '1' would suggest that she had absolutely no confidence in her interview skills. After reflecting for about 10 seconds, she said '3' with some uncertainty. 'A 3?', I asked. 'Maybe a 4, actually. Am I allowed to say 3 and a half?' I replied that she could choose any number that she felt represented her current level of confidence. She settled for a '4'. Once she had made her decision, I noted that a '4' was a relatively positive assessment. I asked her what made her select '4' instead of a '1'. Although hesitant at first, she was able to explain her reasons: she had been successful at the interview for the current job, she was recently invited to be part of an interview panel for a junior member of staff and she knew that she would have very good references. Talking about these factors seemed to build her confidence, and she became less hesitant as she listed the reasons why she had selected a '4'. I concluded by commenting that she seemed to have a good foundation to build on. I then moved on to the most important part of the process: 'What would it need to be like for you to rate your confidence as a 9 or a 10?' We spent about 30 minutes of the 1-hour session on this part of the conversation. She became animated as she talked about how she would feel, what type of preparation she would have completed and how she would know each of the members of the interview panel. Most of her ideas related to feeling confident because she would be well-prepared, aware of what questions to expect and knowing the people who would be involved in the selection process. As she was talking, she realised that if she applied for a job internally, it was very likely that she *would* know everyone on the panel. Moving into the final stage, I asked the client what she could do *now* or in the near future to get her own rating of her confidence about interviews from a '4' to a '5'. Based on her assertion that 'being more prepared' would help her to feel more confident, she said that she would rate her confidence at a '5' if she had a completed, up-to-date CV and notes about some of her professional successes over the past 6 years. As she reflected on this, she said 'Actually, if I do these things, it'll probably be a 6'. She agreed to update her CV and prepare some notes about her professional successes before the next session.

Solution-Focused Coaching Techniques

We have explored how the scaling technique of the solution-focused approach could be used as a conversational framework. Some of the practices and ideas of the solution-focused approach can also be integrated into standard coaching conversations. These techniques are well suited to coaching because they draw attention to what is wanted.

Scaling

The first technique is scaling, which we have already discussed. While it can be used as a stand-alone framework for a coaching conversation, it can also feature as part of the GROW framework. For example, it can be very helpful in the Will or 'way forward' stage. A good question to ask is, 'How committed are you to the actions you have just chosen on a scale from 1 to 10?' Then the process above can be used briefly to see whether the level of commitment can be increased in some way.

As a coach, you can use some of the techniques below to support clients to move quickly towards solutions rather than getting bogged down in the 'current situation' or the 'problem'.

Exceptions to the Problem

Throughout a conversational framework, it is helpful for the coach to keep the focus and attention on how the client will know when the problem is solved. That is why it can be helpful to ask questions that aim to find exceptions to problems. So, if a client raises a recurring problem or difficulty, the coach can ask the following questions (for example):

'Always?'

'Are there times when this does not happen?'

'Can you think of a time when you were surprised by a different outcome?'

The coach can help the client by asking her to identify examples of when the problem does not seem to occur. Time, effort and energy can then be invested into understanding the circumstances for when the problem did not occur, in order to increase the frequency of the exceptions.

Asking the 'Miracle Question'

Another way of helping a client to focus on a positive future is to ask her what has become known as the 'miracle question'. The wording of the question can be adapted to suit the context.

'If a miracle happened tonight while you were sleeping and this problem completely disappeared, how would you know tomorrow morning that the miracle had happened?'

In other words, the scenario is that something inexplicable and positive has happened during the night, meaning that the problem no longer exists. However, the client does not know that this has occurred during the night. The focus of the conversation should be on how the client would find out that the problem is no longer there. The miracle question can be supplemented by asking the client what it would be like the following day:

'How would others behave?'

'How would you be behaving?'

'How would you be feeling?'

'What would be different at work?'

The reason for this is to encourage the client to start imagining life without the problem so that she can turn her attention to the solution (rather than the problem) and see the benefits of making the necessary changes.

Find Out More 9.1

Focusing on the Solution

The Solutions Focus: Transforming Change for Coaches, Leaders and Consultants (Jackson and McKergow, 2024) is a very accessible text that is ideal for coaches wishing to use this approach.

Snapshot 9.1

Being Solution-Focused All the Time

A solution-focused approach can be helpful in a stand-alone capacity or as part of your coaching practice. There are many principles of the solution-focused approach that can be incorporated into your coaching as well as everyday life. Here are some of the principles and practices that can be used in everyday life, so that we can be 'solution-focused' all the time:

- Acknowledge the difficulties that people are facing but do not prolong negative conversations about these problems.
- Minimise talk about the 'causes' of problems when speaking with colleagues or friends.
- Be curious about what people are doing to manage challenging situations.
- Avoid asking 'Why is this happening?' when people complain about something.
- Challenge thinking errors when you hear them.
- Be generous with positive feedback about the successes of others.
- Encourage others to identify small changes that can start to make a difference in their lives.

A Balanced View

After having presented the solution-focused approach so positively above, it is appropriate to acknowledge some of the criticisms that it faces. Some argue that the solution-focused approach can feel artificial and can push people too quickly towards solutions without acknowledging the difficulties that they are facing. Others predict that behavioural improvements will be short-lived because the approach seems to ignore underlying issues. Finally, some people complain that, despite its title, the solution-focused approach is essentially a problem-solving tool, continuing to consider the 'problem' the basis for discussion. In other words, although the discussion is about a 'solution', there is an implied 'problem' somewhere in the background. With awareness of these critiques, it should be possible to integrate what is most positive about the solution-focused approach into your coaching practice.

Using Positive Psychology When Coaching

Positive psychology is a relatively recent subfield of psychology that focuses attention on what is positive about human beings (rather than their deficits). Its interest in 'what makes individuals and communities flourish, rather than languish' (Boniwell and Tunariu, 2019: 2) complements the purpose of coaching. According to Dr Carol Kauffman, 'the mission of positive psychology is to develop sound theories of optimal functioning and to find empirically supported ways to improve the lives of ordinary and extraordinary people' (2006: 219). In this section, we will consider the contribution of positive psychology to coaching.

Looking for Strengths in Others

As suggested in this chapter, it is helpful for the coach to have a bias towards the positive. From this point of view, the coach could be considered a strengths-finder. This means that a coach would be listening for strengths throughout a coaching conversation, especially in the earlier stages (Goal and Reality). Doing this is helpful in building rapport and increasing the positivity and self-confidence of the client. For example, if a client is talking about how she dislikes her organisation and complains that she has been there for 15 years, it is possible to note how patient and determined she must have been to remain in an organisation that she did not like for that long.

Completing the VIA Survey

Another way of using positive psychology in coaching is to invite clients to complete the VIA Survey of Character Strengths, available at www.viacharacter.org. Clients will need to answer 96 questions, so this should be assigned for completion prior to a coaching session or as an inter-sessional task. The VIA Survey of Character Strengths will list the client's top strengths, providing a brief description of each. This allows the strengths to be the focus of a coaching conversation, with the purpose of the discussion being to see what resources the client already has, and how she can use existing strengths in more areas of her life.

Using Strengths Cards

If coaches would prefer to complete this task during the coaching conversation, it is possible to purchase 'strengths cards', which are based on the VIA Survey of Character Strengths. Each strength is presented on a card, allowing the client to read about each in more detail. Through the use of cards, it is possible for the client to identify a set of three or five top strengths. This is a very positive and interactive way of talking about strengths that involves both coach and client. A piece of research exploring the use of strengths cards during a coaching conversation suggests that the process can raise awareness and is experienced positively (Fouracres and van Nieuwerburgh, 2020).

——— Find Out More 9.2 ———

Strengths Cards

There are a number of well-designed strengths cards related to the VIA Survey that can be purchased online:

https://mindspring.uk.com/collections/our-resources/products/strength-cards

www.thepositivityinstitute.com.au/product/character-strength-cards/

Other Positive Psychological Interventions (PPIs)

Positive psychology is an area that is currently flourishing. As it continues to develop its evidence base, new interventions are being proposed. The ones suggested below are only a few of an increasingly broad range of choices, and particularly useful in the context of coaching conversations.

——— Find Out More 9.3 ———

Positive Psychology

The best and most accessible short texts on positive psychology are Christopher Peterson's *A Primer in Positive Psychology* (2006) and Ilona Boniwell's *Positive Psychology in a Nutshell: The Science of Happiness* (2012).

Three Good Things

This is a simple and effective positive psychological intervention that has been shown to have a beneficial impact on a person's subjective wellbeing. There are variations, but in essence it involves noting three positive things that happened during the day. Usually, this task is completed in the evening. The positive effect comes from taking time and intentionally reflecting on *what went well* rather than just remembering the things that did not go so well.

Activity 9.1

Positive Reflections Journal

Reflect for a few minutes. Do you tend to prioritise thinking about the things that did not go so well during the day? If so, this activity will help. Identify a section in your reflective journal to start a 'positive reflections' diary. At the end of each day, just note three things that happened which were positive. Then note what you did to make those things happen. Try it for 3 weeks. At the very least, you'll have a record of 3 weeks' worth of positive occurrences!

Despite its simplicity, there is research evidence that this method works (Boniwell and Tunariu, 2019). One way of incorporating it into coaching sessions is to ask clients to reflect on this every time you meet. The straightforward question, 'Can you tell me about three good things that have happened since we last met?' necessarily focuses attention on positive occurrences. This can lighten the mood and increase the client's enthusiasm. Another way of using this PPI is to ask the client to write down three good things about a situation that does not seem positive to her. This can be challenging, but useful. In effect, this PPI counterbalances one of the thinking errors we mentioned in Chapter 8 (dwelling on the negative). If clients find the activity useful, this PPI can be shared with them and can be used in the way described above (the positive reflections diary).

Gratitude Letter

This PPI can be shared with the client for her to use with people to whom she is grateful. Often in our busy lives we have little time to properly acknowledge or thank people around us. In some cultures there is some awkwardness associated with simply telling someone how much you appreciate them. However, there is empirical data that doing so can have a positive effect on both parties (Boniwell and Tunariu, 2019).

The PPI involves writing a letter or email that describes what a person has done for you and the positive impacts that resulted. The purpose is to express genuine gratitude, highlighting how much you appreciate the other person and the things she does. The intervention suggests that the writer should then take the letter to the person (if this is possible) and read it to her. In coaching, this intervention can be explained to the client. If appropriate and helpful, the client can start to draft the gratitude letter during the coaching session. This intervention can be effective when there has been a disagreement between the client and someone with whom she has a strong relationship.

A Question for You 9.1

How Courageous Are You?

If you're cringing at the thought of reading such a letter to someone to whom you are genuinely grateful, it's likely that you (and the other party) will get the most out of this activity. Is the relationship with the other person important to you? How will you summon the courage to tell them how much you appreciate them? Make some notes in your learning journal, and then find the time to send an email to someone, or perhaps post something on LinkedIn.

Story from Practice 9.2

Saying 'Thank You'

Having spoken to writers and recipients of gratitude letters, I know what a powerful experience this can be. I was coaching a newly qualified teacher who had just started working in the secondary school that he had attended when he was younger. He was doing a great job in school and seemed to connect well with students. The coaching topic related to his interactions with staff in the school, which I won't talk about here. However, during the conversation, the client spoke about the fact that he was inspired to become an educator because of an outstanding history teacher who still worked in the school. One of the challenges was the awkwardness of calling this person by his first name, having become so used to speaking to him more formally.

I shared the idea of the gratitude letter with the client and asked if he would be interested in drafting it during the coaching session. I could sense the positive emotion in the room as this was happening. In between coaching sessions, the client took the letter to his colleague and used this as an aide-mémoire while talking to his former teacher at a local café. There were tears both at that event and in the telling of it in the coaching session. It strengthened the bond between the two people, acknowledging the gratitude and the positive impact of the older colleague's actions. But it also allowed them to recognise that there was now a different, professional relationship which could build on this.

In the coaching session, the client was very enthusiastic about the exercise and was keen to write gratitude letters to a few other people. The greatest realisation was that the client had assumed that important people in his life somehow knew what he was thinking and how much he appreciated what they did for him. The power of having a face-to-face discussion about this was a revelation. He also acknowledged that doing this had made him feel better about his relationships with other colleagues in the school.

Best Possible Self

This PPI involves thinking and writing about yourself, imagining that you have achieved everything you want for yourself. This should be done regularly and consistently over the period of a month so that there is continuous and recurring opportunity to imagine yourself in this desired future state. The benefits can be immediate (feeling better about yourself) but can also be helpful for coaching because the client will have a clearer image about what she is working towards, and this is motivational. Again, this activity can be started during a coaching conversation.

Positive Psychology Coaching

There has been so much interest in the integration of coaching and positive psychology that a new subfield has emerged – Positive Psychology Coaching (PPC). PPC is a 'managed conversational process that supports people to achieve meaningful goals in a way that enhances their wellbeing' (van Nieuwerburgh and Biswas-Diener, 2021: 315). By integrating the latest findings from positive psychology into professional coaching practice, PPC promotes the idea that goal attainment and wellbeing should be given equal weighting when coaching. This means that coaches should support clients to achieve important goals in ways that do not damage the wellbeing of the clients or people close to them. According to leading researchers in the field, PPC focuses on strengths, rather than weaknesses; takes a holistic approach to development of a person; and works towards clients' visions of their ideal future selves (van Zyl et al., 2020).

What the Professional Associations Say 9.1

Positive Psychology

The ICF, EMCC and AC are all starting to recognise the value of positive psychology in coaching. Each of the associations offers workshops and podcasts on ways of integrating positive psychology into coaching practice. It is now likely that professional conferences on the topic of coaching include positive psychology content. Equally, positive psychology conferences often include workshops and presentations on the topic of coaching.

Broadly speaking, positive bias supports **embodying a coaching mindset** (ICF), **cultivating trust and safety** (ICF), **building the relationship** (EMCC), **using models and techniques** (EMCC), **establishing a trust-based relationship with the client** (AC) and **managing self and maintaining coaching presence** (AC).

Conclusion

In this chapter, we built on the key skills and conversational frameworks of coaching by exploring how solution-focused approaches and positive psychological interventions may enhance our practice. As we will discuss in Chapters 12 and 13, these approaches inform the necessary 'coaching way of being'. As Boniwell and Tunariu point out, 'coaching and positive psychology are natural allies in sharing an explicit concern with the enhancement of optimal functioning and well-being, arguing for performance improvement, finding what is right with the person and working on enhancing it' (2019: 244).

See It in Practice 9.1

Positive Bias

Video 9.1 Starting with Strengths

In this clip, the coach asks the client whether it is OK to start with 'what is already good'. Notice the client's reaction and reflect on the impact that this question has on the conversation.

Video 9.2 Using the Scaling Technique

Watch how the coach sets out the scaling technique. It is important to set out what '1' and '10' stand for. Pay attention the client's response and the relevance of the number that is selected.

Part IV
Tools and Techniques

10
Body Language and Emotional Intelligence

Human beings are inherently social creatures. We express ourselves not only through words but also through the rich and subtle language of the body. Our gestures, facial expressions and body posture reveal volumes about our thoughts and emotions. This chapter delves into how your coaching can be more effective through a better awareness of non-verbal cues. Being able to decipher body langage will enhance your emotional intelligence by allowing you to be more aware of your own feelings and better attuned to the emotions of others.

The Role of Body Language in Coaching

Body language is an important consideration for coaches. To put it simply, it is a source of additional information during coaching conversations. We will explore body language from two perspectives: noticing the body language of our clients and being aware of the messages that we send to our clients through our own body language.

We have already established that the coach has many responsibilities during a coaching conversation. The coach should be noticing, listening, playing back, asking powerful questions and facilitating a conversational framework. In addition, it is helpful for the coach to be alert for as much relevant information as possible. As we noted when discussing the skill of noticing, information is everywhere in a coaching conversation. This includes what is spoken (and not), what happens between the coach and the client, what each person is wearing, what each is thinking or feeling, amongst many other factors. Body language is a rich source of additional information for a coach.

A client's body language can provide the coach with useful information before, during and after a coaching conversation. As coaches, we should avoid being overly confident about what certain body language signals indicate. Body language provides *supplementary* information which may give the coach clues about what the client *might* be feeling or thinking. Such information should be used with caution, and only in conjunction with supporting data to minimise inaccurate assumptions. Tables 10.1, 10.2 and 10.3 list some commonly seen gestures and body postures with an indication of what each *may* suggest. We should note that these are not scientifically proven or verifiable.

Table 10.1   Body language clues: Posture

Body posture	Possible meanings
Leaning forward	Anticipation, excitement
	Engaged in topic
	Eagerness to leave
Leaning backward	Comfortable
	Does not want to talk about topic being discussed
	Repulsed, disgusted
Sitting upright	Reserved
	Confident
	Uncomfortable
Stooped shoulders	Dejected
	Deflated
	Feeling hopeless

Table 10.2   Body language clues: Hands

Hands	Possible meanings
Fists clenched	Nervous
	Angry
Drumming fingers	Irritated
	Impatient
Hands clasped	Comfortable
	Wishing for something
Hands in steeple shape	Feeling superior
	Thinking deeply
Biting fingernails	Anxious
	Impatient
Hand on chin	Thinking
	Bored
Rubbing chin	Thinking
	Evaluating
Hand in front of mouth	Concealing something
	Does not believe what she has just said
Finger in front of mouth	Thinking that she should not speak
	Thinking of something that cannot be discussed
Head leaning on hand	Bored
	Demotivated
Hand on forehead	Worried
	Embarrassed or ashamed
Finger on temple	Instructing self to think
	Trying to remember something

Hands	Possible meanings
Scratching head	Confused
	Embarrassed
Touching nose	Has said something she does not believe
	Has an itchy nose
Stroking head	Self-comforting
	Rewarding self
Playing with hair	Self-comforting
	Feeling awkward
Touching eyebrows	Trying to hide
	Embarrassed
Playing with fringe	Trying to hide
	Embarrassed
Clutching armrest of chair	Feeling anxious
	Angry
Rubbing hands together	Anticipation
	Savouring a future moment

Table 10.3 Body language clues: Arms and legs

Arms	Possible meanings
Crossed	Defensive
	Feeling protective about topic
Linked behind head	Feeling superior
	Aggressive
Dangling behind chair	Disengaged
	Tired
Stroking shoulder	Self-comforting
	Rewarding self
Stroking forearms	Self-comforting
	Relaxed
Legs	**Possible meanings**
Crossed	Defensive
	Uncomfortable about topic
Feet twisted around each other	Anxious
	Uncomfortable about topic
Stroking thighs	Self-comforting
	Relaxed
Feet swinging	Playful
	Feeling dependent
Legs bouncing up and down	Anxious
	Impatient
Legs stretched out to the front	Feeling comfortable
	Playful

As the coaching conversation progresses, the coach can be alert for changes to body language and notice the level of engagement or discomfort of the client. This is partly to ensure that appropriate questions are asked, but also so that any observations can be fed back to the client to raise her self-awareness.

———————— Find Out More 10.1 ————————

Body Language

One of the best books on the topic is *The Definitive Book of Body Language* (Pease and Pease, 2017). It provides a comprehensive guide to understanding non-verbal signals and gestures. The book offers readers valuable insights into how body language can influence communication and relationships.

Facial Expressions

The facial expressions of the client may provide further information about what may be happening beneath the surface. Facial expressions can provide a link to the 'inner game' (see Chapter 8) of the client. Even when people attempt to hide their true thoughts and feelings, an observant coach can notice 'micro expressions' which are almost impossible to suppress.

———————— Find Out More 10.2 ————————

Facial Expressions

If you are interested in studying facial expressions, Professor Paul Ekman is the world's leading authority in this area. To start your exploration, go to paulekman.com.

How to Use Body Language in Coaching

As stated previously, body language can provide us with *hints* about what might be happening for our clients. Coaches must be careful not to draw conclusions based on body language alone. For example, it has been suggested that touching one's nose could imply that someone is lying. Equally, the client might have an itchy nose!

One useful way of using body language is to play back aspects of what you notice to the client. Often clients are not aware of their own body language and therefore may benefit from having this information. For example, a coach could notice that a client is much more animated when talking about one of her options. In this case, the coach could say, 'When you were talking about the idea of setting up your own business, you sat forward and spoke more quickly. Did you notice that?' An opposite example would be if a client declared that she was enthusiastic about a certain course of action and her body language did not convey the same impression. A coach could challenge the client by saying, 'You've said that you are committed to this course of action, even using the word "enthusiastic", but I noticed that you were sitting back in your chair and you were not very animated when you were describing it.'

The client's body language can also be used to inform the way in which the coach manages the session. You may, for example, want to take notes about certain examples of positive or negative body language in order to return to particular topics later, or avoid them. For example, if talking about communication within her organisational team seems to completely demotivate the client, it may be preferable at times to avoid the topic. Conversely, if you have noted that talking about the topic of being promoted seems to give the client energy, you may want to bring this up just before the end of the session.

Activity 10.1

Watching People

This activity will take an hour of your time but may also pass as a pleasant extended coffee break. Go to a café on your own, taking your learning journal with you. Once you have ordered your drink, sit at a table and watch the people around you. Try to do this discreetly! Look for the body language signals mentioned in this chapter, jotting them down when you see them. What facial expressions do you notice? Are people sitting still, or fidgeting? If two people are sitting together, how matched is their body language? Are their facial expressions aligned? When capturing what you notice, include commentary about the hints that they are providing. (If you're in France when you do this, you don't need to be discreet about it. People-watching is a national pastime!)

Cultural Specificity

If you need a good excuse for a holiday, try to convince yourself that you need to go on a short break to somewhere that has a culture different from your own so that you can observe body language. There is no doubt that the extent to which we use our bodies and facial expressions to convey our thoughts and feelings varies depending on many social and cultural factors. As coaches, we need to be sensitive to this. People from some cultures use their hands when talking much more than others. This does not necessarily mean that they are unusually excited. Equally, when people in some cultures speak loudly to one another, we must not assume that they are being aggressive. Eye contact also varies significantly between cultures. It is appropriate in some cultures to maintain eye contact for relatively long periods of time, while in others eye contact should be brief or even avoided. Such avoidance should not necessarily be taken to suggest shyness or disengagement. Views about the importance of 'personal space' vary across societies, with some more sensitive about this than others. Another important variable is the acceptability of physical touching between strangers. As I have discussed elsewhere, intercultural sensitivity is essential when coaching in order to reduce misunderstanding and to ensure mutual respect and appreciation (van Nieuwerburgh, 2017).

Coach's Body Language

The first part of this chapter has considered the body language of the client. Let us now turn our attention to the body language of the coach. Initially, coaches should become aware of their own body language. What messages does your body give out, and what, if anything, is your face saying without your knowledge? As coaches, our communications are at the heart of the coaching process. Each question, each time we summarise, each silence, each frown and each nod carries significance. For this reason, coaches need to manage various forms of communication with their clients. We should avoid discrepancies between what we say verbally and the messages we give through our facial expressions or body language.

Remember that your client may also be the proud owner of this book and may also have access to this chapter which lists various body language signals. Your client may be noting your every move! For this reason, it is helpful to develop a neutral stance for use during coaching conversations. Open body language is helpful when creating relationships or listening actively. When you are learning to coach, it is natural to feel a bit nervous, so it helps to minimise the visual signs of anxiety. For example, make sure that you are not fidgeting, playing with a pen or biting your fingernails. This kind of anxious behaviour is contagious, and it can affect the client's level of comfort with the session.

Matching and Mismatching

As one of two people in the coaching room, what you do has a profound impact on the session. Of course, the same applies the other way round – what the client does profoundly impacts the session too. However, it is the coach who is facilitating the conversation and supporting the client to find ways to achieve more of her potential. To aid this, it is useful to occasionally be intentional about the use of body language.

During the early stages of the coaching conversation, matching your body language to that of the client is one way of building rapport. The more that the person we are talking to behaves like we do, the more comfortable we are, and the stronger the relationship. So, for example, if the client has her arms crossed, the coach may choose to do the same. Or if the client is leaning forward when speaking, the coach can lean in too. Novice coaches often worry that this will be too obvious. Of course, it is helpful to do this discreetly, but this happens naturally when two people are connected well to one another. A client is unlikely to feel that there is something strange going on if both of you have your arms crossed.

Matching is useful in the early stages, especially in the Reality stage when the coach should do most of the listening. Loosely matching the client's body language will allow her to feel more relaxed and listened to. Take time to notice how the body language changes based on what the client is talking about. By consciously being aware of body language, the coach will be better able to gather important data about what irritates the client, motivates her or de-energises her.

The intentional use of body language in coaching also includes *mismatching*. While the primary concern in the first two stages of the GROW framework is to build rapport and strengthen the relationship, the final two stages should be about passing responsibility on to the client and helping her to be motivated about what she is going to do. For this reason, it may be helpful at times to mismatch body language. If the client seems demotivated and lacking in energy during the Options phase, introducing some liveliness into the coaching session by using more hand gestures, leaning forward or speaking more loudly can change the dynamic. Because of the early mirroring, the client is likely to follow the coach's lead and become more animated. However, sometimes the reverse may be the case. If the client is very excitable, switching from one possibility to another during the latter stages of a coaching conversation, it may help to bring energy levels down by speaking slowly, putting your hands in your lap and sitting back slightly, allowing for more silences during the conversation. Again, if handled well, this will slow the pace of the conversation and allow the client to consider her options in a measured way.

———————— Reflect on Practice 10.1 ————————

Record Yourself Coaching

One of the best ways of enhancing your coaching practice is to record yourself coaching others. If this is a daunting prospect, all the more reason for doing it! All you need is permission from the client to video record the session.

When recording a coaching session, be aware that you may need a bit longer than usual to get relaxed, so perhaps spend a bit more time on small talk. Once you get into the coaching, it is sometimes possible to forget that the session is being recorded. It may be helpful to start by recording a 30-minute coaching session. The client should be asked to bring a *real* topic to the session. When you have finished the session, make a note in your learning journal about what you think you did particularly well. You may want to wait a day or two before watching the recording. When you do watch it, start by looking for evidence of your strengths (what you thought you did very well). Add any comments to your original notes. When watching the recording for a second time, stop to think about alternatives to the questions you asked. How might you have done things differently? Finally, watch the video for a third time. This time watch it with no sound. Observe only the body language (both your body language and the client's body language). What do you notice? Who was working harder? How similar is the body language? What differences are there?

Emotional Intelligence

Another source of information comes from our emotions and those of the client. For this reason, coaches should have relatively high levels of emotional intelligence. Only a very brief definition of emotional intelligence will be provided here. Readers who are interested in further enhancing their emotional intelligence are invited to explore the concept further.

Find Out More 10.3

Emotional Intelligence

Daniel Goleman is the person most associated with the concept of emotional intelligence. He popularised the phrase 'emotional intelligence' and his books remain the most accessible and informative on the subject (particularly Goleman, 1996).

The leading writers on the topic of emotional intelligence are John Mayer and Peter Salovey (who developed the concept) and Daniel Goleman (who adapted and popularised it). Salovey and Mayer defined emotional intelligence as 'the ability to monitor one's own and others' feelings and emotions, to discriminate among them and to use this information to guide one's thinking and actions' (1990: 189). For the purposes of coaching, it is best understood as the ability to understand our own feelings, notice the emotions of others and, importantly, change our behaviour based on this information. Emotional intelligence is not *simply* being able to understand our own feelings and those of other people. Unless we change our behaviour as a result of this understanding, we cannot say that we are being emotionally intelligent.

Tears

Tears should not be avoided in the coaching space. Both coach and client are human beings with emotions. Strong emotions are acceptable in coaching conversations. If you, as the coach, have created the right conditions, the coaching space will feel like a place where it is OK to cry. Tears can signify trust, relief, pain and sadness (amongst other normal human emotions). For most coaches, the challenge comes not from the fact that the client is crying, but because the coach feels awkward and does not know what to do. As always, our focus must be on the client and her best interests. If the client has chosen to show her emotions by crying, this is a good thing. It is an indication that you are talking about the *right* thing. Every coach will develop her own way of managing tears in the coaching space. In the 'Story from practice' below I have provided some of the techniques that I use, not as a guide but so that you can feel more prepared for tears.

Allowing and welcoming authentic emotions during coaching conversations is part of creating a safe, reflective environment for meaningful conversations.

———— Story from Practice 10.1 ————

Tissues and Tears

Whenever I meet a coaching client face to face, I always provide tissues (not just when I think the client is likely to cry during a session!). If a client looks like she is on the verge of tears, I ask whether she would like to carry on with the conversation. This gives the client an important set of choices. Some continue, knowing the tears will come. Some want to compose themselves and try to control the tears. Some will stop the conversation and talk about something else. Some will leave the room. Every one of these choices should be made to feel legitimate and welcome in the coaching relationship.

When the client is crying, I give time and space for this. I do not apply pressure by asking if the client is 'OK'. I do not promise that 'things will be alright'. I do not extend a hand or give the client a hug. I do not cry with the client. All I do is maintain a quiet, respectful space where crying is OK. When the emotions seem to have subsided, I give the responsibility of restarting the session (or not) to the client by saying, 'Just let me know when and if you'd like to continue with our coaching conversation.'

———— What the Professional Associations Say 10.1 ————

Body Language and Emotional Intelligence

All three professional associations emphasise the importance of non-verbal communication and emotional intelligence. Having an understanding of body language and being emotionally intelligent will allow you to demonstrate the competencies of **cultivating trust and safety** (ICF), **establishing a trust-based relationship with the client** (AC), **building the relationship** (EMCC), **communicating effectively** (AC) and **listening actively** (ICF).

Conclusion

In this chapter, we have considered the important roles of body language, facial expressions and emotional intelligence during coaching conversations. Coaches can enhance their effectiveness by becoming aware of their own body language while monitoring the body language of their clients. At the same time, coaches need to notice their own emotions and the emotions of the client, ensuring that the coach's behaviours respond appropriately and with empathy to those of the client.

See It in Practice 10.1

Body Language

Video 10.1 Matching Body Language

Watch this clip, paying special attention to the idea of 'rhythm'. Keep an eye out for movement and facial expressions. Notice the increasing energy of the client as the conversation progresses.

11

Inspiring Creativity

This chapter covers the use of activities and tools during coaching conversations. Experienced coaches and satisfied clients often highlight this type of activity as a source of key insights during coaching conversations. It could be argued that the use of such activities differentiates coaching from other one-to-one conversational interventions. Creative activities also keep things fresh for both coaches and clients.

New thinking is required during coaching sessions, especially during the Options stage of the GROW framework. In a sense, the Options stage is meant to be a dynamo for new ideas. Creativity is often required to overcome challenges or circumvent barriers. Many people come to coaching because they want to discover new and innovative ways of making progress towards their goals. In this chapter, we will look at ways of inspiring creativity during coaching sessions through conversational techniques, pen-and-paper tasks and active participation.

Coaching sessions can be made more engaging by involving the client in conversational, drawing or practical activities. It is useful for the coach to have a toolkit of activities ready to inspire creativity.

——— A Question for You 11.1 ———

How Engaged Are You?

I have tried to be as engaging as possible in writing this book. You will have noticed that I have provided activities throughout the book, posed questions directly to you, offered snapshots of information, shared stories from practice and included videos of real coaching sessions. How have these supported your interest and engagement?

Each of the activities presented in this chapter can be adapted to suit the style of the coach and the needs of the client. There is no 'correct way' of applying these interventions. The main consideration is how helpful they are to clients. Coaches may feel that they are taking a risk by introducing some of these activities, but in the worst case, it is easy enough to try something else. There is nothing wrong with abandoning an activity if it is not meeting the needs of the client.

Coaching is appropriately understood as a type of conversation. As a result, it is to be expected that many people assume that talking is all that happens within a coaching conversation. However, my own experience and that of other coaches and former students is that creative activities can sometimes be the key to unlocking a person's potential, the trigger for 'A-ha!' moments and a way to encourage clients to see things differently. Below are a few examples that I have used during coaching conversations. They are intended to whet your appetite – and you can explore or design many other approaches.

Find Out More 11.1

Creativity in Coaching

If you would like to embrace creativity in your coaching practice, there is an excellent book available. Written by Jen Gash, *Coaching Creativity: Transforming Your Practice* (2017) will delve into this topic and provide you with practical ideas and frameworks.

Creative Activities

Three Wishes

Share an image of a magic lamp and ask your client to imagine that a genie has offered her three wishes relating to the current situation. What would she ask for? At this stage, clients often seek clarification: 'Any wish?' or 'Do the wishes need to be realistic?' The purpose of the activity is to generate thoughts that are not restricted by what is perceived to be 'realistic', so the client should be encouraged to set aside any conceptions about what is or is not possible for this activity. The only constraint is that there are only three wishes available.

As the wishes are chosen, ask the client to make a note of these. Once all three wishes have been identified, the client is invited to move on to the evaluation stage. The client is asked to evaluate two things. First, to what extent are some elements of each wish already in place? Second, can she now think of a few small steps to move closer to at least one of the wishes?

When It Can Be Helpful: Three Wishes

The 'three wishes' activity works particularly well in the following situations:

- When the client cannot think positively about the future during the Goal stage. Some clients find it difficult to get beyond what they want to *avoid*. For example, 'I know that I cannot work within this department any longer.'
- When the client says that she is unable to formulate many ideas during the Options stage.

Crystal Ball

Share the image of a crystal ball, inviting the client to attempt to see into her own future. This may be a very short activity, depending on the openness of the client to this type of activity. The question to ask is: 'If you look into the crystal ball and imagine that you can see elements of your future, what are they?' Encourage the client to say what she thinks she sees, even if it is 'fuzzy'. Do not push her to be specific. The intention is to discover what the client *wants* to see in her future. Analysis and evaluation are not part of this activity. Using this activity can make it easier to identify some goals and subgoals relating to the client's glimpses into her future.

When It Can Be Helpful: Crystal Ball

This activity is helpful during the Goal stage, especially if the client is not clear about her goals.

Practical Tip

If the client is finding it difficult to 'see' anything in the crystal ball, a useful follow-up question can be, 'What would you *like* to see in your future?'

If You Did Know the Answer

If we, as coaches, create ideal thinking environments, clients often start to ask seemingly rhetorical questions while they are exploring their topics (e.g. 'I know what I want to achieve, but I don't know how others would react to these changes. Will they support me or are they going to dislike the choices I have made?'). Each question posed by the client provides an opportunity for the coach. The question is often a probing one, demonstrating that the client is beginning to reflect more deeply about her situation. At this point, coaches can ask, 'And what is the answer to that question?' or 'I'm guessing that you don't know the answer to that question right now, but what do you *think* it might be?' This may lead to further exploration, or a more defensive response, 'I don't know the answer.' Although this may seem challenging, it is worth pursuing by asking, 'If you *did* know the answer, what would it be?' This question can lead to surprising insights.

When It Can Be Helpful: If You Did Know the Answer

This can be used at any point during a coaching conversation. It works best when the client asks a seemingly rhetorical question of herself.

Story from Practice 11.1

What if You Knew the Answer?

One of my clients was contemplating the possibility of being transferred to another country. In a reflective mood, she said, 'I do think it's a great opportunity. These things don't come up very often. I would need to be based in our office in Singapore for at least 3 years. It will be great for my career – there is an immediate promotion on the cards and the experience I would gain means that I would be in line for a VP [Vice President] position by the time the project has been delivered. The only thing is that I don't know how my family would react if I told them that I was thinking of moving to Singapore!' After a short pause I said, 'I know you have just said that you don't know how your family would react … but what do you *think* would happen if you suggested this?' There was another short pause where she looked upwards and reflected. 'Well, actually I think that it wouldn't be a complete surprise to them. They know that the company I work for has offices all over the world. I have been out to our office in Dubai quite regularly. And now that I think about it, they have been supportive about every other career-related decision that I've made. That's really helpful. Thanks for the question!'

Random Object

This activity encourages playfulness and creativity. Ask your client to pick any object that is within reaching distance. Once she has selected the object, ask the client to consider her coaching topic using the object. Present this as a challenge. For example, 'How can you bring this object into our discussion about the current situation?'

When It Can Be Helpful: Random Object

This activity is most useful when the coaching session feels 'stuck' and a new way of approaching the topic is required.

Story from Practice 11.2

Referee's Whistle

During the third coaching session, we felt stuck. The goal had been identified in the first session, and some ways forward decided. In the second session, we had focused on progress and the question of how motivated the client was to make the changes. We talked about whether the self-selected goal of the client was important enough for him to invest significant energy towards making it happen. The client came to the third session frustrated. He had not been able to carry out the tasks that he had identified for himself at the previous session. 'I don't know why I cannot stick to simple commitments that I made to myself. I could make excuses, but in reality, I should have been able to do this!' We decided to explore what was stopping him from delivering on commitments that he made to himself. During the conversation, he concluded that he often 'procrastinated', putting off difficult tasks and uncomfortable conversations for as long as possible. He realised that this was a pattern that kept repeating itself. And what frustrated him the most was that he could tell that he was doing it again in relation to the coaching. In this situation, he *knew* that procrastination was something he wanted to address, but the risk was that he would put off tackling this issue because it was difficult to change.

At this point, I asked how the client would feel about engaging in a creative activity. He agreed. 'Looking around the room you're in, can you find the most unusual object that we can use for our coaching?' The client glanced round the room. 'My kids are off school this week,' he said. 'They are always leaving toys round the house. I found something!' He became more animated immediately. The change from frustration to curiosity was very noticeable. He showed me a shiny silver whistle.

Coach: 'How does this item relate to the situation you've been talking about?'
           There was a lengthy silence.

Client: 'I don't know. I don't think it has anything to do with it.'
           I allowed the client more thinking time.

Coach: 'What does it make you think of?'

Client: 'It makes me think of a football referee.'

Coach: 'And how does that relate to the challenge you're grappling with?'

Client: 'Well, I guess that a referee has to be decisive. In fact, even when he makes a mistake, a referee doesn't change his mind. He'll stick with his original decision. He can't be seen to change his mind. But it must be tough for him to see later, on TV, that he's made a howler [obvious mistake]. Having said that, though, I can understand why he doesn't change his mind. It would undermine his credibility, wouldn't it?'

Coach: 'Yes, you're right. I guess a referee needs to stick with decisions that had been made.'

Client: 'The players give him grief, and that is even though they know that he won't change his decision. If they thought he might change his mind, that would be even worse.'

Coach: 'Is there anything about this idea that could be helpful in your situation?'

Client: 'Well, the idea of sticking to one's decision isn't a world away from following through on commitments, I guess. The way to overcome procrastination is to

(Continued)

stick to my own decision to do something.'

He looked at the whistle for a few moments.

Client: 'I think that the idea of sticking to a decision, no matter what happens, even if it's the wrong decision, is relevant. I need to take a page out of a referee's book.'

This exploration led to a decision to commit to only one thing at a time, and follow through on it, no matter what. The client decided to test his ability to stick to his commitments by setting himself one important task between coaching sessions. Gradually, he was able to change his own view that he was a 'procrastinator'. This had a positive effect on the client and supported him to make progress towards his goal.

Friendly Advice

Although this is a very simple technique, it can have a significant impact. If the client is finding it difficult to generate options, ask her what advice she would give to somebody else (e.g. sister, friend, colleague) in the same situation. The question can be phrased like this: 'If a good friend of yours was in a very similar situation, and came to you for help, what advice would you give them?' This technique can overcome some of the negative 'inner game' talk that the client may be experiencing. By sidestepping any internal dialogue which is insisting that the client is 'stuck' or 'does not know the answer', she is liberated to think about the situation in another context.

When It Can Be Helpful: Friendly Advice

This activity is most effective when the client says that she does not know what to do. For this reason, it is often used during the Options stage.

Storyboard

The coach can introduce this activity by explaining how a storyboard is used to prepare for marketing campaigns or as part of film-making. A storyboard looks like a cartoon strip, with each frame containing a drawing. Storyboards are chronological, showing a series of events one frame at a time. For the purposes of this activity, six or eight frames are usually sufficient.

The first step is to ask the client to draw a representation of the current situation in the first frame. The current situation will have been discussed in the Reality stage of the GROW framework. With this and all other drawing activities it will be important to reassure the client about the perceived quality of their artwork. The drawings or sketches need to be meaningful to the client and should not be evaluated in any other context.

Once the drawing of the current situation is completed, the coach should ask the client to explain its significance. The coach can ask questions or share observations about how the current situation has been represented. The next stage is for the client to complete the final frame by drawing a visual representation of her goal (which will have been identified in the Goal stage). Allow the client as long as is needed to complete her drawing. Once she has finished, ask her to share it with you, providing time for the client to explain the significance of the drawing. Ask the client to elaborate if necessary, as it is important that the client describes the desired future state as vibrantly as possible.

At this point, the client will have the desired future state in the final frame and an image of the current situation in the first frame. Now they are given some time to sketch in the missing frames, capturing the types of things that should happen to get from the first frame to the last frame. This could be completed on sticky notes. For each blank frame, the client can sketch the missing step on a sticky note, before placing each one in order. Using sticky notes allows the client to rearrange the order of events if necessary. The process of sketching and drawing the intervening frames can be done during the coaching session or completed at home, in between sessions.

When It Can Be Helpful: Storyboard

This activity can be helpful during the Options stage, supporting the client to consider the steps necessary to move closer to her goal. It is also an engaging way of thinking about what needs to happen next. The comic strip format is well known, and therefore it can seem easier to complete the missing frames.

Drawing the Metaphor

If the client uses an interesting or rich analogy, simile or metaphor, pause and ask her to draw it out on a piece of paper or tablet-based drawing application. It is helpful to explain that exploring metaphors can be fruitful during coaching conversations. Often, drawing the metaphor can lead to additional insights. Once the drawing is complete, ask the client to share it with you. Once you have both seen the drawing, discuss various options and possibilities. The coach should ask questions about the drawing from a position of curiosity. The purpose of this activity is to allow the client to explore her thinking much more deeply and freely than she normally would. In my experience, talking about the metaphor is often easier than discussing the issue that it represents.

When It Can Be Helpful: Drawing the Metaphor

Drawing the metaphor is most helpful during the Reality phase. The process of drawing it allows both coach and client to comment and ask questions about the metaphor, thus increasing awareness about the situation and broadening the client's perspectives.

─────────── **Story from Practice 11.3** ───────────

Being at Sea

In a coaching session with a teacher who had been offered a job at a different school, the client made a comment about feeling that she was 'all at sea'. Taking the new job would have required her to relocate to a town some distance away and the client was feeling uncertain about the implications her move would have on the school, her students and her family. Because the client was finding it difficult to express her feelings, I asked her what she thought of drawing the metaphor she had just used so that we could explore it further. I volunteered that I thought it might be helpful. As we both felt a bit 'stuck' in the conversation (she wanted to accept the job but was not prepared to 'let people down'), she was glad to take a break from talking. The tension eased as she stood up to get a piece of paper.

'What should I draw?' she asked.

'Anything you like. How about starting with being "all at sea"?' Although she claimed that she was 'not good at drawing', she drew a raft, bobbing on the ocean. As she drew, she explained what she was doing. 'It's a raft, not a boat. It feels flimsy, bobbing very lightly on the ocean.' As she held it up for me to see, she changed her mind about the ocean, drawing larger waves around the raft. 'There are waves, but the raft can manage these.' 'What about you? Where are you in this picture?' I asked. She drew herself on the raft, standing right in the middle. She gave herself a cartoon face with a straight line for a mouth. 'What is that facial expression?' I asked. 'It's determination,' she said. She then drew some sharks (just the fins), not around the raft but further in the distance.

Coach: 'Tell me about the sharks.'

Client: 'These sharks are preventing me from venturing out any further. I think they'll knock me off the raft.'

Coach: 'And where are you going?'

The client drew a tiny island in the distance with a castle on it. She drew a flag on top.

Client: 'I need to get there.'

Coach: 'What's it like there?'

She smiled as she talked about what it was like on the island with the castle and I could see her eyes shine.

Coach: 'So, you're on a raft. The raft can manage the rough seas that it is in, but there are sharks just beyond, and you're worried that they may flip the raft over. But there's an island in the distance with a castle that you seem determined to get to. What are your options?'

Client: 'I guess I could just brave it out and go through. But I don't feel well protected. And I know the sharks will do their best to stop me. They don't want me to reach the castle. And there's something else that I haven't drawn.'

The client now drew another island. There were people on the island, waving. It was sunny, and the sea was calm.

Coach: 'Why are they waving?'

Client: 'Some are wishing me well. Others are waving me back to the island. That's the real problem … not the sharks. I'm closer to the shore of this island.' She pointed at the one with the people waving. 'This island is comfortable, it's warm. People want me to stay here because they like me. And I like it, too.' She became emotional and was quiet for a few minutes. 'If I go any further on this raft, I might not be able to get back to them.' She seemed to finish her story.

Coach: 'Sticking with the metaphor for a bit longer, what options can you think of?'

Client: 'Well, I can just stay here (pointing at raft) and wait for better weather …'

Coach: 'Anything else?'

Client: 'I could wait for the sharks to get bored and go somewhere else.'

Coach: 'Assuming that you're on the raft, what else could you do?'

Client: 'I could attempt the crossing, but I don't have any supplies or any protection. I guess I could try to get more supplies? Or I could wait for a passing ship to escort me. Or I could go back …. But the island is very comfortable. I'm afraid that if I go back to the island, I will never have the courage to set off again, especially if I turn back now. But I guess that I have seen the island and the castle now. I know it's there, because I can see it from here (pointing at the raft). I couldn't see it from here' (pointing at the 'home' island). She became more animated at this point. 'Yes! I can go back to the island and build a better raft, with more supplies. Actually, I *should* go back and build a boat so that even if the sharks wanted to stop me, they wouldn't be able to. And most people on the island *do* want me to get across to Castle Island, so they will be there to help me! Rather than risk everything now, I will get back to shore, take some time to enjoy being on the island and build the boat at the same time. And I will be more useful *on* the island rather than bobbing around on the ocean in between islands. Now that I have seen Castle Island, I won't change my mind about making the journey.' She seemed relieved and ended her story with a laugh: 'And I'll be packing a harpoon!'

Having drawn being 'all at sea', we then returned to the action planning stage. She would not accept the job now but wanted to commit to another year at her current school. However, she decided to undertake new tasks and get involved in school-wide challenges that would strengthen her CV. She identified an appropriate time for relocating that would cause minimum disruption to her partner and children, and therefore knew when she should start applying for senior roles that she was interested in. According to the client, 'I didn't realise until I drew it, but the real issue wasn't the sharks at all!'

Mind Map

The use of mind maps (Buzan, 2002) has become relatively widespread, both in business and in educational settings. It is often a good way to engage a client. Mind-mapping involves drawing a spider diagram of a person's thinking. The client can note or draw a small representation of the goal in the centre of the piece of paper or tablet. Then the client can draw a line from this to the first option that comes to mind. Once this is written down, any further thoughts that emerge as a result of this can be represented as offshoots of this option (and so on). Once this option has been explored fully, the client should go back to the central goal and consider a second option (and so on). What is powerful about this method is that people are usually drawn to using the whole page and therefore tend to generate more creative ideas to fill the areas that look relatively empty. Of course, this activity can be undertaken without a coach present, so the coach should add value by asking questions and providing positive feedback about the completion of the task. When the client is satisfied with the drawing, the coach should ask her to summarise the key options that have been identified.

When It Can Be Helpful: Mind Map

Mind-mapping is especially useful in the Options phase of the coaching process. This activity is best used with clients who are aware of the technique. This activity can be assigned to clients prior to the first meeting. Clients can be asked to draw a mind map of their topic to bring along with them as a starting point for discussion.

Building Blocks

In this activity, a client is asked to spend 10 minutes with the building blocks to represent the current situation she is facing. It can be helpful to include characters or figurines that can be used to represent people involved in the situation. Allow the client to work on this herself for at least 10 minutes before commenting or getting involved. Unless the client requests more time, wrap up the activity punctually and then ask her how helpful the activity was. If she has found it unhelpful, the coach can ask whether the task provided any insights. If the answer is still 'no', it is probably not worth pursuing it any further.

However, if the client does comment positively about the activity, first ask what the client learned about herself while playing with the building blocks. (It's OK to use the word 'playing'!) Ask the client to use that learning to think about what options arise from looking at her creation. If the activity resonates with the client, it is possible that she will use her creation as she talks about her options, moving characters, figurines and building blocks around to explore different possibilities.

In this activity, ensure that the client is the only person handling the building blocks. It is one way of allowing the client to take full ownership of her situation and any options that might be generated.

When It Can Be Helpful: Building Blocks

This activity is helpful during the Options stage, especially if the client feels that she has very few choices. It can also lead to insights when trying to make sense of the client's current situation.

Find Out More

LEGO SERIOUS PLAY®

In 1996, the world-famous toy company LEGO designed a strategy for professionals to bring creativity into their work. Most readers of this book will already be familiar with LEGO. If you would like to know more about the SERIOUS PLAY® approach, you can download a free resource by searching online for the LEGO® Serious Play® Open Source PDF Guide.

Role-Play

Many clients (and coaches) may find the idea of role-play daunting, so it is better to present this idea when you have established a reasonably strong relationship with the client. The first step is for the coach to offer to take the role of the other party. This is especially useful if the client would like to consider different ways of approaching an issue or topic with the other person. Again, it is important for both coach and client to get into their roles, using personal pronouns and trying to represent their characters as realistically as possible. This stage of the process is useful because it builds the confidence of the client (she is playing herself and knows what this feels like). Even more importantly, it will give the client an opportunity to correct your portrayal of the other party (e.g. 'My line manager is always positive and optimistic. He wouldn't have highlighted the risks in that way'). By having this role-play and the following discussion, the client is likely to get a better sense of the nature of their relationship.

The crucial second step of this activity involves a role reversal. This can be managed very smoothly if the client points out that you, as the coach, are not representing the other person accurately. In this case, you can suggest that she takes on the role of the other party, with you (the coach) taking on the role of the client (while she plays the other party). By requiring the client to put herself in the place of the other person, the activity can lead to insights about the other person's motives, thoughts and point of view.

When It Can Be Helpful: Role-Play

Role-play is helpful when the topic of the coaching conversation revolves around a professional relationship at work that is getting in the way of the client's goals and aspirations. In the Reality phase, role-play can aid a deeper understanding of challenging relationships. In the Options phase, different ways of approaching a situation can be tested. In the Will phase, role-play can be used very effectively to 'rehearse' what the client has decided to do to prepare her for forthcoming conversations.

Story from Practice 11.4

Acting It Out

In a conversation with a middle leader in a small start-up organisation, the client finally decided to confront her manager about the lack of clarity about whether she was required to work on weekends. This had been frustrating the client for a few months. She worked, albeit reluctantly, on some weekends when she was given substantial pieces of work with short deadlines. At the Will stage, the client concluded that her only option was to be 'open and honest' about this with her direct line manager. As we had not had much time to talk through the implications of this, I suggested that we could act it out. The client was enthusiastic about the activity, so I explained that we could rehearse the interaction with myself taking on the role of her manager. As agreed, she left the room. She knocked on the door and popped her head round the door. 'Hello, Layla,' she said. I responded kindly, asking her to come in. At this point, the client said, 'This is the difficult bit! How can I suddenly start talking about my issue with Saturdays? It won't feel right.' Although the activity was brief, it helped the client realise that she was not ready to do what she had thought would be her next step. As a result of this, she identified a different plan which felt more appropriate to her.

Walk and Talk

When the topic of conversation relates to someone feeling 'stuck' or 'trapped', we should question the logic of confining them in a room for 90 minutes to talk about it! Of course, there are many times when sitting in a room for over an hour can provide a moment of insight. In other cases, it may be worth considering taking the coaching outdoors.

It is possible, and sometimes powerful, to have a coaching conversation when walking. There is an interesting human dynamic when two people walk next to one another that requires some type of connection. As with every coaching conversation, it will be necessary to contract before the coaching starts. There will be more distractions, and, as a coach, it may be helpful to acknowledge this. There are also some risks to confidentiality that should be considered.

For the walk and talk approach to be effective, a relatively quiet or relaxing environment is beneficial. Perhaps an art gallery, a museum, a park or even a large garden would provide an appropriate environment. Apart from the fact that the coaching takes place outdoors, the rest of the process can be the same, perhaps finishing off at a café or a park bench to agree a way forward.

When It Can Be Helpful: Walk and Talk

This approach can be helpful if the topic is relatively demotivating or when the client is frustrated because she feels 'stuck'. It can also be used for a particular stage of the coaching process. For example, 'walking and talking' may be a good way to establish the current state of play (Reality stage) or think of new ways of approaching a topic (Options stage).

Snapshot 11.1

Tips for Using These Activities

- Build your own confidence and belief in the use of activities by trying these out with clients.
- Remember that the post-activity discussion is an important part of the process. In other words, exploring what the client learned through the activity is as valuable as the activity itself.
- Choose the activities intentionally based on what is most helpful for the client. The choice of activity should be led by the desired outcome.
- Match the activity with the client's learning style if you are building rapport and strengthening your relationship.
- Mismatch the activity with the client's learning style to challenge her and gain new insights.

What the Professional Associations Say 11.1

Creativity

All three professional associations advocate the use of creativity during coaching. They see it as an important part of supporting clients to explore new perspectives and solutions. Coaches should be skilled in creating environments in which clients can think 'outside the box'. The ICF focuses on the role of creativity in **evoking awareness** and **facilitating client growth**. The EMCC sees it as an important part of **enabling insight and learning** and advocates for the **use of models and techniques** to do so. The AC promotes creativity as a way of **raising awareness and insight**.

Conclusion

Creativity leads to new thinking. Because it invites people to 'do things differently', creativity is an important part of the coaching process. Otherwise, coaching itself can run the risk of falling into a rut. For a client, knowing that she will be speaking to her coach for a fixed time, in the same place, every month for 6 months can become too comfortable.

As you will hopefully be thinking by now, perhaps this applies to the coach as well. A coach should be fresh, curious and interested. It is normal to be anxious in the beginning, in the same way a person might feel nervous when learning how to ride a motorcycle. It will feel a bit 'clunky'. But after a while, if you like riding, you will start to look forward to getting on the motorcycle. You'll enjoy the ride. And if, after you've learned to ride, you find that you do not enjoy motorcycling, then you would probably look for something else to do. Coaching is the same.

Part V
Coaching Way of Being

12
Being Human

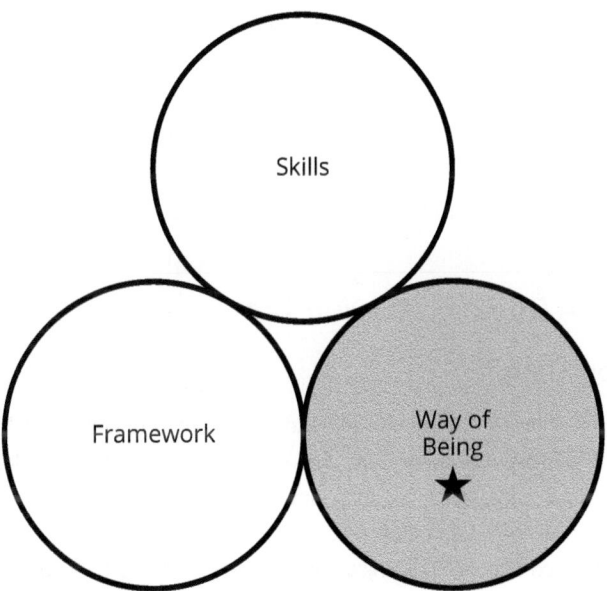

Figure 12.1 The three elements of effective coaching

By now, I hope you are feeling more confident about your coaching skills. As you practise coaching, I believe that this sense of confidence will increase. In addition, you
understand how to use a conversational framework to facilitate coaching conversations.
As mentioned in the previous chapter, like learning to ride a motorcycle, it may feel a
bit uncomfortable at first but you will soon be able to glide through a coaching conversation, and many of your questions will emerge naturally. Practising the coaching skills
will make you more fluent at asking the right kinds of questions. You will be better able
to play things back, listen attentively and notice what is happening during coaching
sessions. As outlined in Chapter 2, there are three elements to effective coaching. The
skills and a conversational framework are two of them. The third element relates to what
I describe as a 'coaching way of being'. Many would say that this underpinning philosophy is impossible to 'teach' in a book or on a course. While this may be true, I believe
it can be learned through coaching and effective reflective practice. Developing a 'coaching way of being' is a lifelong journey. Although I am evidently biased, I would add that

it is a worthwhile endeavour. In this chapter, I will describe the coach's 'way of being' before proposing some attributes that you may wish to work towards.

Way of Being

The phrase 'way of being' in relation to one-to-one relationships was coined by the influential humanistic psychologist Dr Carl Rogers (1980). He founded the 'person-centred approach' and his principles continue to influence coaching and counselling practice today. The field of coaching is heavily indebted to the work of Rogers and the human potential movement.

Rogers based his thinking on two foundational premises. First, he proposed that people are their own best experts. In other words, people know themselves better than others can. Second, he believed that people are self-actualising. This means that people are naturally drawn towards achieving their full potential, rather like plants growing towards the light.

A Question for You 12.1

What Do You Think?

What do you think of these two premises? Take a moment to reflect on each. What thoughts and feelings do you experience as you consider them? First, the idea that people know themselves and their contexts better than anyone else. Second, that people are naturally drawn towards achieving more of their potential. These ideas are central to Rogers' philosophy and to the practice of coaching. Enjoy capturing your reflections in your learning journal.

These two premises led Rogers to suggest that the role of a counsellor is to simply create the conditions in which a person can be allowed to self-actualise. He famously outlined the 'necessary and sufficient conditions' for a successful counselling relationship:

- Two persons are in psychological contact.
- The client is in a state of incongruence.
- The counsellor is congruent in the relationship.
- The counsellor experiences unconditional positive regard for the client.
- The counsellor experiences an empathetic understanding of the client's internal frame of reference and endeavours to communicate this experience to the client.
- This communication is achieved to a minimal degree. (Adapted from Rogers, 1957: 95)

Bearing in mind that Rogers developed this set of necessary and sufficient conditions for counselling relationships (he used the word 'therapist' instead of 'counsellor' in the bullet points above) rather than coaching relationships, which are relevant and appropriate for us as coaches? Below, I propose a list of similar conditions for coaching:

1   There is a good working relationship between the coach and the client.
2   The client desires change.
3   The coach is authentic in her interactions with the client.
4   The coach demonstrates positive regard for the client.
5   The coach is empathetic, and this should be obvious to the client.

Point 4 may need some clarification. The phrase 'the coach demonstrates positive regard for the client' means that the coach should respect the client and view her positively (as a human being) regardless of what she might say or do during the coaching conversation. Rogers had stipulated that the coach should have 'unconditional positive regard', which is a much higher bar. To understand the near impossibility of unconditional positive regard for most of us, it is sufficient to note that the opposite would be *conditional* positive regard, meaning that a client would be given respect and viewed positively (as a human being) as long as she spoke and behaved in a way that met with the approval of the coach. Coaches should aim for for the highest level of positive regard possible in their situation. It is worth reflecting at this point how much positive regard in our societies is *conditional*. In other words, the way we treat people is often related to how they interact with us. In real, everyday coaching practice, we are talking about ensuring that we provide positive regard with minimal conditions.

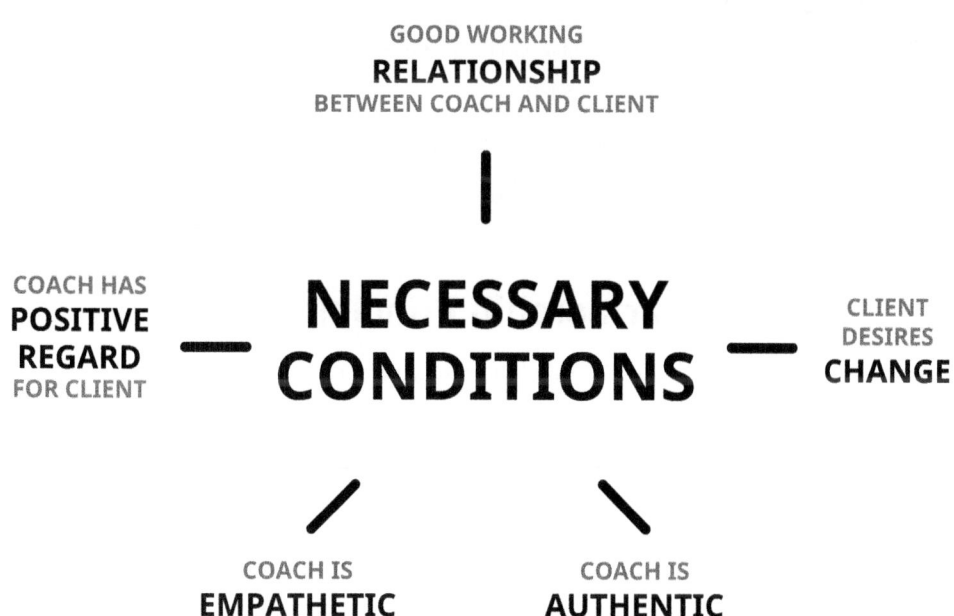

Figure 12.2   The necessary conditions for effective coaching practice

Based on Rogers' necessary and sufficient conditions for therapeutic change, it is proposed that the five revised 'conditions' listed above may be necessary for successful coaching to take place. There is currently debate about whether Rogers' conditions, by themselves, are *sufficient* for change to occur. In my view, when translated into a coaching context, the conditions are *necessary* but may not be sufficient. To put it another way, the conditions are necessary, but other things need to happen as well. I have argued that three elements are needed:

- A conversational framework facilitated by the coach.
- A set of conversational skills.
- A 'coaching way of being' (including the five revised conditions listed here).

Review Your Practice 12.1

The Necessary Conditions for Effective Coaching Practice

I invested time and energy to develop a good relationship between myself and the client. ☐

I assessed the motivation of the client and ascertained that she wanted to make a change. ☐

I remained authentic during the coaching conversation and in every interaction with the client. ☐

I maintained a high level of positive regard for the client throughout the coaching conversation. ☐

I listened carefully and demonstrated empathy through my words, facial expressions and body language. ☐

Partnership Principles

Rogers spent a lifetime explaining and elaborating the notion, and it is difficult to convey the exact sense of what is meant by 'way of being' in summary. Below we will consider seven 'partnership principles' that can guide your practice as a coach.

Find Out More 12.1

The Way of Being

A Way of Being (1980) is the title of Carl Rogers' seminal book which is central to the humanistic approach. It has deeply influenced the field of psychology and is foundational to modern coaching practices. If you would like to undertand the concept of 'way of being' at a deeper level, I recommend reading this book when you have quality time for learning and reflection.

A leading educationalist and coach, Dr Jim Knight, proposes that every coaching inter-action should be underpinned by a set of 'partnership principles' (2011). The principles are equality, choice, dialogue, praxis, voice, reciprocity and reflection. Each is explained below, with a brief description of the principle and a consideration of how this might inform effective coaching practice.

Equality

For us as coaches, the word 'partnership' denotes a relationship between equals. Each partner's thoughts, beliefs and feelings are held to be valuable while recognising that each person is different. At the heart of this notion of equality is a clear commitment to respect one another. In an equal relationship based on mutual respect, one partner will not impose her will on another.

Implications for Practice

Ensure that you create a sense of partnership and equality in all interactions with the client. As a coach, you must see the client as being of equal value (and demonstrate this to her). When decisions need to be made, they should be discussed between both parties. If you are meeting in person, ensure that you are doing so in a neutral space, or that you alternate between meeting in a place that is convenient for the client and then a place that is convenient for the coach. Seemingly trivial details like the arrangement or selection of chairs should demonstrate the principle of equality. Both chairs should be identical or similar. The moment that one party sits on a leather chair and the other is perched on a stool, the principle of equality has been contravened. This concept of equality also applies to the responsibility of both parties. There is a shared responsibility for a successful coaching session.

Choice

Choice is a critical factor in the type of relationship we are talking about. Both parties should feel that they have genuine choices. In coaching, one person cannot make deci-sions for the other. The coach must respect the autonomy of the client, and this means that the client must make her own choices.

Implications for Practice

When coaching, the fact that the client makes her own choices should be made explicit. For example, coming to coaching should be a choice. It should never be imposed. Whenever possible, the client should feel that she has a choice about who her coach is. When agreeing the coaching contract, both parties should be clear that they are able to withdraw from the coaching relationship if it is not working. To make this a *real* choice, it should be possible to withdraw without giving any reason. This principle also means that the client can choose any way forward that she thinks is appropriate at the end of the session. This includes the freedom to make 'bad' choices. Many coaches are concerned about allowing the client to make the 'wrong' choice. There is no such thing. By the end of the conversation, the client will have considered a broad range of options and will have had time to think through the consequences. Therefore, her choice of next step should be respected. For the client, having choices makes her feel more autonomous.

Dialogue

Although I suggested earlier that a coach should only be speaking for about 20% of the time, the nature of a coaching conversation is a dialogue. This means that both parties are engaged in the conversation, and both recognise that they are learning together as they explore ideas. According to Knight, 'Dialogue is talking with the goal of digging deeper and exploring ideas together' (2011: 38).

Implications for Practice

As coaching is a dialogue between equals, it is important that issues are considered together. It is entirely appropriate (and helpful in many cases) if both parties are exploring a situation about which neither person has expert knowledge. This creates a genuine dialogue between two people. Everything that the client says should be considered carefully, and the coach must not reject, ignore or belittle any statement. At the heart of the concept of dialogue is listening respectfully to what the other person has to say. Dialogue requires both parties to fully 'hear' what the other person has said before intervening or presenting their own views. The coach should avoid interrupting as far as possible. This means that they should not be planning the next question or activity while the client is speaking. Such an approach may lead to short silences when the client has finished sharing her thoughts. And that is OK. It demonstrates that you were listening to her and thinking about what was said.

Praxis

Coaching is powerful because of its focus on the application of learning in the *real world*. In other words, coaching is not a theoretical exercise even though much of the time can be spent talking about ideas. According to Knight, clients should have 'opportunities to think about how to apply new ideas to their real-life practices' (2011: 43).

Implications for Practice

Praxis is the application of learning into practice. In other words, it is a way of turning knowledge into action. Both the coach and the client have a shared responsibility to ensure that the coaching conversation results in a change in the client's behaviour or performance. For the coach, this means ensuring that practical next steps are considered in the final part of a coaching session. The start of subsequent coaching sessions can be initiated by reviewing what the client has *done* differently since the previous meeting. The focus on the implications of the coaching discussion on the lived experience of the client makes the conversation more meaningful. Questions such as, 'How will this play out in your workplace?', 'What are the consequences for the way in which you interact with your colleagues?' or 'If you were to proceed with this option, how would this impact on your project?' will help to highlight the relationship between the coaching discussion and the 'real world'.

Voice

This principle reminds us that both parties in the relationship should be able to express their points of view honestly. It is important that the client feels comfortable expressing her thoughts and aspirations. 'If partners are equal, if they choose what they do and do not do, they should be free to say what they think, and their opinions should count' (Knight, 2011: 34).

Implications for Practice

Coaches should encourage their clients to voice their thoughts and emotions. In some situations, a client will be voicing her concerns or aspirations for the first time, and this voice needs to be encouraged and nurtured. This is why coaches remain non-judgemental, being open to whatever the client may say. Any judgement or criticism from the coach is likely to lead to the client 'losing' her voice. She may start to censor her thoughts if she fears a judgemental response. For coaching to be successful, clients should be able to provide honest feedback about the coach and the coaching relationship. A coach's genuine openness to feedback encourages the client to share her thoughts and feelings more openly.

Reciprocity

The principle of reciprocity posits that both parties should benefit from a coaching conversation. This means that both coach and client enter into a coaching conversation expecting to learn from each other and develop as a result. Knight puts it this way:

'Reciprocity is the belief that each learning interaction is an opportunity for everyone to learn' (2011: 44).

Implications for Practice

In practice, both coach and client should emerge from a coaching session feeling better, in some way, from the interaction. This approach enhances the sense of equality. As the title of this chapter suggests, the 'coaching way of being' is essentially about bringing our 'human-ness' to the fore. As human beings, we learn through interaction. We are social animals. So, as a coach, it is important to see each coaching conversation as an opportunity to learn. The primary purpose of the client is to learn more about herself, the situation that she is in and what she might achieve. But it is also a learning experience for the coach who can learn about herself, the way in which humans engage with challenges and opportunities, and about the coaching process. A practical way of capturing this is to note down at least one thing that you learned after each coaching conversation.

Reflection

The appropriate 'way of being' for coaches should encourage reflection, both for the coach and the client. Through her behaviour and by applying the principles, a coach can create a valuable thinking space for her clients.

Implications for Practice

As you will soon discover, we, as coaches, do genuinely learn during our coaching. Working together, the coach and the client are responsible for creating the conditions in which throughtful reflection and valuable learning can take place. The right environment leads to learning about ourselves and learning about others. Through the process, we develop our own coaching way of being.

── Reflect on Your Practice 12.1 ──

Coaching Logs

One of the most helpful ways to develop your own 'coaching way of being' is to capture your reflections in your learning journal. This will reinforce the principle of reciprocity, because you will be acknowledging that you are learning from each coaching session. The best form of professional development for coaches is reflective practice. This will be discussed in Chapter 16.

For now, use your learning journal to capture your thoughts and feelings before, during and after coaching sessions. These notes can take the form of a journal entry or simply a list of bullet points. If it is helpful for you to have a consistent layout for your reflections, you can adopt the structure below:

Date:

Purpose of coaching session:

Personal reflections:

My learning:

What I will do differently:

Remember to completely anonymise the entries. Mark the date of your journal entry, but not the date of the coaching session. Also ensure that you do not use any names or provide any information that could identify the client. It is possible that your learning journal could get lost or hacked into. To ensure the confidentiality of your coaching conversations, write in your journal in such a way as not to jeopardise anonymity even if the coaching logs were to be compromised.

Story from Practice 12.1

Not Wanting to Be There

When learning to become a coach, one of my fears was to be confronted by a client who was not willing to be coached. I now find such situations a much richer learning experience for both the coach and the client. When reflecting on a challenging coaching conversation, I was able to see how the partnership principles helped to create the right conditions for a successful outcome. The story below is taken from my own learning journal, with details changed for the purposes of protecting the anonymity of the client. The notes in square brackets are taken directly from my original handwritten notes.

Journal Entry

I had travelled for an hour to get to the client's place of work. There was parking nearby, but this was underground and seemed to be designed for very small cars! It was difficult to get from the car park to the city centre office building and I had to ask for directions. [I arrived for the coaching session a bit frazzled. In future, I will allow an extra 15 minutes. A quick coffee somewhere nearby would have settled my nerves.]

(Continued)

I arrived at the office a few minutes early, but the secretary kept me waiting for another 10 minutes. When I met the client I wasn't sure whether I should apologise for lateness. I did anyway while noting that I *had* arrived on time. [This may have come across as defensive and was not a good way to start our interaction.]

We both looked very formal and we walked to a small room with comfortable seating and some chairs. The client was civil but not friendly. The client sat down on one of the sofas and gestured for me to sit on a chair. He did not offer any drinks. [Another reason it would have been helpful to arrive 15 minutes early for a coffee!] I said I would prefer to sit on the sofa opposite to where he was sitting. There was a low table between us, but this did not feel like a barrier.

Before I had a chance to talk about contracting, the client announced: 'Before we start, there's something that I would like to tell you. I don't believe in this coaching bull-shit. I am here because my line manager has instructed me to be here. I think it's a waste of my time, and you have one hour, not longer.' [I felt myself becoming defensive. Some anxiety set in. Even an hour seemed like a very long time!] So, before contracting, we had a brief chat about the situation. I played back to the client that he seemed angry about being in the coaching session, and I said that it seemed like we both felt obliged to be in the room – he had been told to attend a coaching session, and I had been paid to deliver it. I asked whether he and I could agree something that would make best use of the time that we 'had' to spend together. We agreed to talk for an hour, rather than the 90-minute session that I had been contracted to deliver. I said that we could decide whether to continue the coaching sessions at the end of our time together. When my client said that his manager would not be happy if he rejected any further sessions, I said that I would be willing to write to the manager myself, saying that *I* did not see the value in any further sessions.

I could see a change in attitude in the client. We reframed the coaching session as a 'pre-coaching chat', which was simply a two-way conversation about whether there would be any benefit from carrying on with the coaching assignment. [If I am honest, there was also a change in me. There was less pressure on both of us, and the worst-case scenario seemed to be that the client would want to drop out. At this stage, I would have been quite comfortable with that outcome!] Despite this, I did go through the contracting, especially highlighting confidentiality and the fact that I would not divulge any of the conversation to the line manager. At the end of the entire process (if we did decide to continue), I said that I would be providing a summary of the topics discussed and my simple assessment of whether the sessions were useful or not. I promised to show this to the client before sending it to his line manager.

To start the pre-coaching chat, I said that he could speak about anything he liked, and that we did not need to talk about the issue for which he had been 'sent' to be coached. Again, there was a positive response. 'What shall we talk about then?' he asked. 'Anything you like,' I replied. I asked him whether he would like to tell me a bit about why he was so set against the idea of coaching.

We could have spent 2 hours talking, but we stopped after an hour, as this was part of our amended agreement. Just before the end of our 60 minutes, I reminded the client of our initial conversation. I said that we had agreed that we would make a joint decision about future sessions. I reiterated that I would be pleased to pursue any of the routes available. We could both report back to the line manager saying that we found no value in the coaching conversations, he could talk to the line manager himself and withdraw from the process, or we could agree to meet again. The only stipulation was that the next conversation would be a more traditional coaching conversation, and that we would need to work on the client's goals (as this one had been almost entirely about how the client felt about coaching and what had led to the current situation). Although it was grudging, the client said that he now thought there might be some value in coaching, checking that he would be able to set the agenda for the next coaching session.

Reflecting on the Session

In the face of obvious resistance to coaching, I felt that trying to pursue a traditional coaching conversation would have been futile. Rather than focus on the topic (which was implied by the line manager), I chose to focus on seeing if we could build a relationship.

I was genuine in the coaching session by saying that both of us felt compelled to be there, and that neither of us was looking forward to the session. It was a bit of a risk to say that I did not want to be there either, but in the moment it was true. I had arrived a bit frazzled, I did not have a cup of coffee and I was faced with a defensive client who seemed determined that the coaching session would fail. However, I did not judge the client and, importantly, I resisted an early instinct to put up my own defences and barriers. Throughout the process, I maintained positive regard for the client.

That honesty, though, changed the dynamic. It seemed like the barriers came down, and both of us were talking to each other like human beings. I was surprised at how quickly we built a relationship, and I was able to empathise genuinely with the client who explained why he was angry.

At the end of the conversation, I thought that we had built a relationship but I was not sure whether further coaching sessions would be of value, and was prepared to support either decision from the client. At the same time, while I thought we spent our first hour together effectively building a relationship, I was clear that if we chose to pursue the coaching, future sessions would have to focus on the client's performance in the workplace (which is what I had been contracted to deliver). So when the client said, 'Yeah, I guess we could continue with the sessions,' I asked whether he thought that further sessions would be helpful to him in relation to his performance at work. He replied that he was prepared to give it a go.

As it happens, this series of coaching conversations was very successful despite the rocky start – both for the client and for me as the coach. I learned so much about how people respond to negative pressure and the importance of the relationship in coaching. Even more remarkably, that coaching conversation and the way in which the client made decisions about his own future, influenced decisions that I took about my own professional future.

Towards a 'Coaching Way of Being'

I hope that this book is encouraging you to be self-reflective and more self-aware. This chapter has considered the 'necessary conditions' for effective coaching, and we have also grappled with the concept of the 'coaching way of being' by looking at Jim Knight's partnership principles (2011).

Below, I will outline some ideal attributes for coaches based on a loose understanding of Rogers' 'way of being' (1980) and my own experiences of being coached and coaching others. Each represents a lifelong journey of development. These attributes can be considered aspirational goals for coaches. Self-awareness is important as you consider each point. You may already possess some of these attributes, others may require a lifetime of learning and development. We must be honest and humble when deciding whether to invest time in any of the points below.

The Most Effective Coaches Are Humble

Humility is an important attribute for a coach. The term has been defined as 'the noble choice to forgo your status, deploy your resources or use your influence for the good of others before yourself' (Dickson, 2011: 24). There are three ways that humility supports effective coaching. First, status games have no place in the coaching arena because they imply the superiority of one person over another. Without humility, it is difficult to enter into equal relationships. Second, humility allows a person to see herself as a constant learner. This supports coaches to engage meaningfully in reflection, leading to more impactful practice. Third, humility allows coaches to recognise that they do not know what is best for their clients. This means that coaches can genuinely embrace the idea that their clients are best placed to identify the most appropriate ways forward.

The Most Effective Coaches Are Confident in Their Ability as Coaches

It may sound odd to include both humility and confidence as helpful attributes for coaches. However, they both apply. In this context, we are referring to the coach's confidence in their ability to be an effective thinking partner (Kline, 1999). In other words, coaches need to be confident in their coaching abilities. Such confidence can be sensed by the client. Any self-doubt on the part of the coach can be contagious. In my experience, the best way of increasing confidence is through regular practice followed by thoughtful reflection.

The Most Effective Coaches Care about People

Most coaches are driven by a desire to make things better for people. At the same time, many people make a living as professional coaches. Whatever the case, 'making things better for people' should be the primary driver, not financial gain. Coaching is a very *human* way of interacting.

Reflect on Your Practice 12.2

Showing You Care

There is no doubt that clients are more likely to be open, honest and vulnerable if they believe that their coaches care about them. How can coaches demonstrate that they genuinely care about their clients and the topics that they bring to coaching conversations? This is likely to vary based on personalities, cultures and circumstances. Take a moment to note down three practical things that you can do or say that will tell a client that you care about them.

The Most Effective Coaches Believe that Their Clients Will Achieve More of Their Potential

The belief of the coach is an integral part of the self-belief of the client. Research has shown that a person's positive expectation about another person's abilities can become a self-fulfilling prophecy (Rosenthal and Jacobson, 1966, 1968). It can be helpful if coaches are hopeful and optimistic, as this will influence their evaluation of their clients' chances of success.

The Most Effective Coaches Treat Others with Respect

Feeling respected is one of the non-negotiables of trusting relationships. To build long-term, successful professional relationships, coaches must respect their clients and be able to demonstrate this respect rapidly and consistently. Human beings are quick to sense the absence of respect. If people feel that they are not being respected, nothing else matters. My sincere hope is that increased awareness of the power of coaching will lead to greater respect in conversations and interactions between people.

The Most Effective Coaches Have Integrity

Clients must trust their coaches for them to be open and honest about their feelings, thoughts, aspirations and fears. Trust is built as clients start to recognise that their coaches always operate with integrity. In other words, we want clients to believe that their coaches do not have any hidden agendas. The primary motivator of the coach should be the client's best interests.

The Most Effective Coaches Demonstrate Intercultural Sensitivity

Our world is culturally diverse. Therefore, coaches should be able to demonstrate intercultural sensitivity. This should not be limited to situations in which there is a perceived 'difference' but should apply to every coaching conversation. Intercultural sensitivity means accepting the client's cultural views and social norms without judgement.

Snapshot 12.1

Intercultural Sensitivity in Practice

These are some practical tips for ensuring intercultural sensitivity during coaching conversations:

- Coaches should be clear about the purpose of coaching.
- Coaches should follow a clear conversational framework.
- Coaches should explicitly commit to the principle of non-directivity.
- Coaches should respect the role of the client as primary decision-maker.
- Coaches should occasionally check the health of the coaching relationship.
- Coaches should demonstrate appropriate curiosity about the client.
- Coaches should take an interest in the client's cultural milieu (if this is relevant).
- Coaches should maintain a respectful attitude to the self-identified cultural group of the client.
- Coaches should avoid making assumptions about the client's cultural group or groups.
- Coaches should not allow cultural stereotypes to influence their perceptions of the client.
- Coaches should avoid discriminatory language.
- Coaches should not make humorous comments or otherwise belittle the client's self-identified cultural group.
- Coaches should avoid ethnocentric tendencies to impose their cultural values onto others

(van Nieuwerburgh, 2017)

Review Your Practice 12.2

The Coaching Way of Being

I did not play status games.   ☐

I demonstrated humility throughout the coaching conversation.   ☐

Through my knowledge of a conversational framework and the use of coaching skills, I demonstrated confidence in my ability to coach. ☐

I maintained a strong interest in the client, as a person, demonstrating my commitment to 'making things better for people'. ☐

Throughout the coaching conversation, I maintained my belief that the client could achieve more of her potential, despite any challenges or difficulties that she might be facing. ☐

I ensured that I always behaved and interacted in a way that demonstrated a high level of respect for the client. ☐

I behaved with integrity in relation to the coaching contract, my code of ethics and the client, only acting in ways that were in her best interests. ☐

I accepted, without judgement, the client's cultural views and social norms, even if this challenged some of my own personal beliefs and values. ☐

A Question for You 12.2

What Do You Notice?

Now that we have had the opportunity to present you with all three elements of effective coaching practice, it may be a good time to watch the full-length coaching session in Video 7.1 again. As you watch the video, please notice the following things:

How did the coach demonstrate humility during this conversation?

What did the coach do that showed confidence in his ability to coach?

How did the coach demonstrate a strong interest in the client and their success?

How does the coach demonstrate belief in the client?

How does the coach demonstrate respect for the client?

Did the coach behave with integrity throughout the conversation?

Was the coach able to accept the client's cultural views and social norms without judgement?

As you watch the video clip, use these questions to inform the notes that you take in your learning journal.

What the Professional Associations Say 12.1

Coaching Way of Being

The three professional associations use different language to refer to the coaching way of being. One of the ICF competencies is **embodying a coaching mindset**. This is defined as 'develops and maintains a mindset that is open, curious, flexible and client focused'. Another dimension of the coaching way of being is captured in the ICF competency **maintaining presence**. It is described as being 'fully conscious and present with the client, employing a style that is open, flexible, grounded and confident'. The EMCC incorporates these ideas in their competency of **understanding self**. This is understood as demonstrating 'awareness of own values, beliefs and behaviours' and recognising 'how these affect their role/s and practice, using this self-awareness to manage their effectiveness in meeting the client's … needs as applicable'. The AC captures these ideas in their competency of **managing self and maintaining coaching presence**.

Conclusion

In this chapter, we have carefully considered some of the key principles and attributes of effective coaches. As I hope you will have seen, they are based on the humanistic principles of Carl Rogers. The 'coaching way of being' is the most 'human' part of coaching, so the ideas are fluid and will vary depending on the nature of the coach and each coaching conversation. Essentially, coaching is a humanising activity for both coach and client. To be a coach is to be respectful of others and embrace the most positive aspects of being human.

13
Inspiring Others

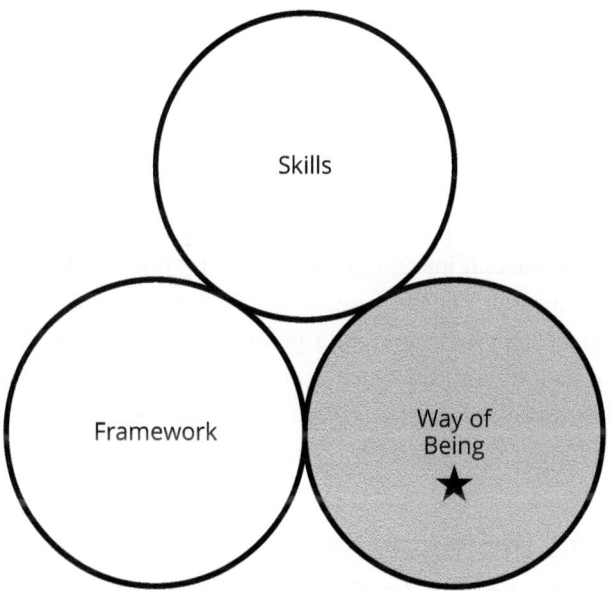

Figure 13.1 The three elements of effective coaching practice

Many clients report that they have been 'inspired' to overcome challenges, pursue their dreams and achieve their ambitions through coaching. Sometimes this inspiration is a result of the coaching relationship (enhanced by the coach's 'way of being') and a series of coaching conversations. In other situations, the inspiration emerges from an 'A-ha!' moment, which can take place within or in between coaching sessions. In this chapter, we will explore the curious phenomenon that we call the 'A-ha!' moment.

'A-Ha!' Moments

The 'A-ha!' moment refers to a sudden realisation or recognition that can have a lasting effect. It is the moment when a person 'gets it'. For some, it is a life-changing experience. If you have had an 'A-ha!' moment, you will immediately know what we are talking about. Coaches and educators are often motivated by the idea of creating 'A-ha!' moments in their clients and students. Importantly for coaches and clients, 'A-ha!' moments provide evidence of fresh insights and new perspectives.

Through my own experience, I have come to believe that there are a few common themes that seem to recur in discussions about 'A-ha!' moments. These are:

- A sense of connection.
- Sharper clarity.
- A positive sensation.
- A feeling of excitement.
- Increased confidence.

'A-ha!' moments usually involve the linking of disparate thoughts. Clients have reported that it can feel like a 'fog lifting', 'a light bulb coming on', 'the moment the clouds part and the sun shines through' or a 'fireworks display lighting up the darkness'. These descriptions align well with research into the phenomenon by Erik de Haan and his colleagues (2010). Participants in the research study described some critical moments in coaching with phrases such as 'lightbulb', 'a tipping point' or 'moment of realisation'. This study demonstrated that critical moments (such as the 'A-ha!' moment) can lead to clients making significant changes (de Haan et al., 2010).

How to Increase the Likelihood of 'A-Ha!' Moments in Coaching Sessions

There are two interesting paradoxes concerning 'A-ha!' moments in coaching. First, although many coaches would recognise the critical importance of these moments, very little is said about them, and even less has been written about 'A-ha!' moments in coaching. So, in this chapter, let us address this topic so that we can consider how we might be able to make 'A-ha!' moments more likely during our coaching sessions. Here, we should pause to reflect on the second paradox: the more actively you pursue an 'A-ha!' moment, the more elusive it becomes. So rather than chasing 'A-ha!' moments, it is more helpful for coaches to focus on creating the right conditions for them to take place.

— A Question for You 13.1 —

What 'A-Ha!' Moments Have You Experienced?

Make some notes in your learning journal about when you have experienced 'A-ha!' moments. How did it come about? What was the context? What factors led to your 'A-ha!' moment?

Creating the Right Context

While remaining mindful that pushing too hard for an 'A-ha!' moment may be counter-productive, let us focus on how coaches can create the conditions in which such moments might emerge. First, the coach should ensure that the 'necessary conditions for coaching' exist. We explored these in Chapter 12. Second, the coach should invest in developing a strong, trusting relationship. Research has shown that such relationships are key determinants of coaching success (de Haan, 2008b). In the early stages of a coaching relationship, it is important to prioritise the relationship above anything else. Without that strong foundation, the coaching is less likely to succeed, and the chances of an 'A-ha!' moment are diminished. Third, discomfort is often a feature of effective coaching conversations. De Haan's research has found that there is usually some discomfort before a critical moment in coaching conversations (2008b). This means that if you have a tendency to avoid uncomfortable situations in coaching, you may be minimising the chances of 'A-ha!' moments occurring.

Story from Practice 13.1

Piggy in the Middle

I was coaching a middle manager in a large educational organisation. She was frustrated because her staff were not supporting her during a challenging period of change. This was despite all the efforts she made to represent their views and champion the cause of her team. She explained the situation:

> 'I feel like I'm "piggy in the middle". Management have been clear with me about what changes they would like to see. They're frustrated by the slow progress that my team is making. But this is because I have been consulting with people in my team throughout the process. I take the messages from our management group to my own team and present the new initiative in a positive way. When my team (sometimes rightly) is dissatisfied with some element of the proposals, I represent this strongly to the management group. I don't know what more I can do. When I go to the management group, they see me as a troublemaker. When I speak with my team, they are resistant and unfriendly. They cannot see that I am working for their benefit.'

After exploring the discrepancy between her view of what she was doing and the response she was getting from her team, the client realised something. She stopped talking and looked down. I could see tears welling up in her eyes. 'They don't trust me,' she said. It was uncomfortable, and I was tempted to relieve this discomfort by suggesting that there might be other reasons for their behaviour. Instead, I waited. She wiped away the tears and looked up again.

(Continued)

'It makes sense now. I can understand why they are behaving this way. They think that I am trying to manipulate the situation – that I have already agreed to the proposals and I am just manipulating them towards my way of thinking. All they see is that I am away talking to senior managers at least once a week. They don't know what happens there.'

Having realised why her team were behaving that way helped the client to develop a new strategy. The client was determined and upbeat. What had been a mystery now seemed clear. It allowed her to turn her attention to finding a way to rebuild trust with her team.

'A-ha!' moments occur when a person has new thoughts or connects previously disparate ideas. For this to happen, the coaching conversation is likely to enter uncharted territory. There will be times when both the coach and the client will not know what to do or think. As a coach, you must be able to resist the temptation to return to safe ground by taking control of the situation or by telling the client what to do. Uncertainty during coaching conversations is a sure indication that you are entering fertile new ground – a place in which 'A-ha!' moments are more likely. It is also liberating for the coach to start to feel that 'not knowing' is acceptable. By feeling this way, we demonstrate to the client that it is OK for her not to know either.

In a research paper, de Haan notes that critical moments sometimes follow silences (2008a). Silences often precede new thoughts, because a moment of quiet can be an indication that the client is thinking. As we have seen previously, the use of silences is appropriate in coaching. It allows for quality thinking and it puts the responsibility for new ideas where it should be – with the client.

Finally, there are times when focusing too hard on a difficulty or barrier can heighten the feeling of being 'stuck'. Sometimes it is helpful to 'zoom out' or talk about something on the periphery of the client's topic. This can reduce frustration and allow for creative thoughts to emerge. Our minds can continue to think through an issue even when we are not focused on it. This explains why we sometimes wake up with the solution to something that may have been troubling us when we went to bed.

So, to create the right context for 'A-ha!' moments to occur, we should:

- provide the necessary conditions for coaching;
- invest in the relationship between coach and client;
- accept that discomfort is a necessary part of the coaching process;
- be comfortable with the unknown during coaching conversations;
- use silences to encourage new thinking;
- reduce feelings of being stuck by refocusing on peripheral topics.

Encouraging Creativity

In addition to creating the right context, we must also encourage creativity during the coaching conversation. First, a coach can encourage creativity by using the activities described in Chapter 11. Although this may sound counterintuitive, it is often better to invite a client to undertake activities that do not match her learning style. There may be a little bit of 'nudging' out of comfort zones required. Remember, it is likely that the client will already have tried her preferred problem-solving techniques before seeking a coach. When discussing possible options, the coach is advised not accept the first one or two options that a client presents. More often than not, these will be options that have been considered and tried before. Although it may feel irritating to the client, it is a good idea to push the client by continuing to ask, 'What else could you do?' Often, if the client can answer this question straight away, she is not presenting a new idea. Finally, you need to hold your nerve and believe that the client will come up with the best solution or way forward in relation to the topic. We must not 'give up' on our clients. The moment we provide a client with a solution or a way forward, there is an implied suggestion that we do not think she would be able to come up with a solution for herself.

So, to encourage creativity during a coaching conversation, we should:

- use creative activities;
- invite the client to engage with an activity that does not match her preferred learning style;
- encourage the client to generate more than one or two options;
- believe in the ability of the client to identify her own way forward.

If you embrace the ideas above, creating the right context for the client and encouraging her to be creative, she is much more likely to experience an 'A-ha!' moment that can have a significant and lasting impact on her life.

Find Out More 13.1

Eureka!

An excellent book entitled *The Eureka Factor: Aha Moments, Creative Insights and the Brain* (Kounios and Beeman, 2016) provides an engaging and enlightening guide to intuitive flashes and inspiration.

Using a 'Coaching Approach'

As you practise coaching, you will improve your skills, broaden your range of questions and develop a 'coaching way of being'. If you do this, I am confident that you will make a difference to the people you coach. People interested in this topic often talk about the idea of a 'coaching approach' which can take place beyond the scope of coaching conversations. Leaders in organisations are sometimes described as adopting a coaching approach when managing their teams, leading change and developing corporate cultures. Some educators report that they use a coaching approach with their classes or groups of students. Similarly, health professionals adopt a coaching approach when they empower their patients to take responsibility for their health and wellbeing.

A coaching approach alludes to the possibility of using coaching skills and techniques without necessarily having one-to-one conversations. Based on the three elements model presented in Chapter 2, the coaching approach can be understood as the 'skills' and 'way of being' elements, without the use of a formal coaching framework. Essentially, we are talking about using some of the skills and approaches that we employ as coaches in other contexts and situations.

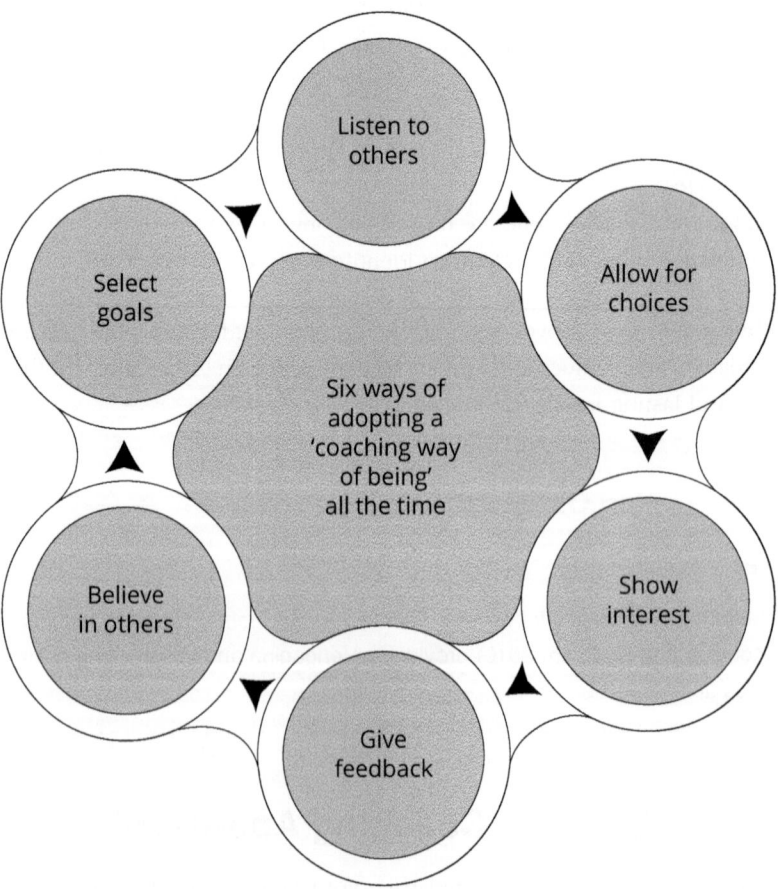

Figure 13.2 Adopting a 'coaching way of being'

There are six things that you can start to do every day, based on the skills and 'coaching way of being' that you are developing:

- Listen to others.
- Allow for choices.
- Show an interest in others.
- Provide helpful feedback.
- Believe in others.
- Encourage others to identify meaningful goals.

Listen to Others

First, it is possible to be a 'radical listener' (van Nieuwerburgh and Biswas-Diener, 2025) in everyday conversations, at home and in the workplace. If you are a parent, you may have been guilty of what might be called 'half-listening' to your children, especially if you are preoccupied with work-related matters or in the middle of doing something else. This can be changed straight away, by providing quality listening time to children or family members when they have something to say. Even if this is not possible, it is preferable to postpone the conversation until you are able to give others your full attention. At work, if you have gone into a conversation 'knowing' what the other party will say, you will have made it more difficult for yourself to genuinely listen. There may also be times when you reject what a colleague will say, even before she has started talking! Every interaction is an opportunity to build connection. Radical listening is respectful and it can build and repair relationships.

Find Out More 13.2

Becoming a Radical Listener

If you want to spend more time learning about listening in ways that value others, please read *Radical Listening* (van Nieuwerburgh and Biswas-Diener, 2025). Radical listening is a way of building relationships and connecting powerfully with others. The book provides practical skills and strategies for enhancing your listening.

Activity 13.1

Increasing Airtime

Next time a family member, close friend or important colleague talks to you, try to implement the 80:20 rule. Allow the speaker 80% of the airtime. After the experiment, pause to reflect on what was different. Make some notes in your learning journal.

Allow for Choices

Second, allow people choices. We know that it is essential for clients to feel that they have choices. Researchers Deci and Ryan have found this to be necessary for human flourishing (1985). According to self-determination theory (SDT), human beings require three things to flourish:

- Feeling autonomous.
- Having positive human relationships.
- Knowing how well they are doing.

The feeling of autonomy is at the core of SDT. Through your behaviours, you can help others feel autonomous. This can apply at home or in the workplace. The feeling of autonomy is not dependent on unlimited freedom or a total lack of constraints. On the contrary, it is possible for autonomy to exist within a clear set of rules and boundaries. For example, for employees, whether they respond to customer inquiries helpfully should not be negotiable. However, the way that the individual staff member responds can be left as a choice for the employee. This has the additional benefit of allowing the employee to respond resourcefully to situations that they encounter. Parents may reasonably expect their child to study for upcoming exams, but how and when this is done could be left to the child. Forcing someone to do something and stipulating exactly how and when it must be done is likely to engender resistance. When this is done to professionals, it is likely to be perceived as disrespectful. It is preferable, when using a coaching approach, to agree and be explicit about a desired outcome, and then allow the person the autonomy to achieve it in a way that suits her. Choices can be created even when there is little flexibility. A parent could insist that a child wears a jacket before going out in the cold. Even then, the child could be presented with a choice of jackets.

Show an Interest in Others

Another element of SDT is the need for 'relatedness'. As stated earlier, human beings are social animals. We need differing levels of social interaction to feel positive about ourselves. So, at work, it is helpful to show an interest in others as human beings rather than simply as professional colleagues. A small thing such as remembering a person's name can be very meaningful to an employee. When people encounter personal difficulties, a compassionate and empathic response is always appreciated. In times of personal distress, human kindness is most powerfully felt. In some societies, grief is perceived as awkward, and people worry that they 'won't know what to say'. However, this can be interpreted as indifference. A clumsy show of compassion is better than none. At work, remembering to ask about things that our colleagues are doing outside the workplace can provide evidence of interest in them as human beings.

Provide Helpful Feedback

In coaching conversations, it may be easier to provide honest feedback to the client. This is because the relationship is explicitly about supporting the client to achieve her goals and the coach's intentions are usually obvious. Outside the coaching space, the provision of feedback is still valuable. First, be generous with positive feedback. If someone does something well, or shows a positive side to her personality, let her know. Tell people what you admire about them. We sometimes hold back from doing this, worrying that people might assume that we are being patronising. Again, it is the intention that matters. If you are being genuine and authentic about your feedback, it will usually be taken positively. And if you notice that something is holding a person back – perhaps the way she responds to emails, or how she dresses for certain work functions – think about whether that person would benefit from the information that you have. Remember, giving this type of feedback outside a coaching conversation carries greater risk. If it is not explicitly requested, this would fall under the category of 'unsolicited advice'. Before sharing constructive feedback, make sure the person has asked for your perspective. Think about whether she is likely to be open to receiving this feedback from *you*. Be explicit about the reason that you are providing the feedback, tentative in the way you deliver it and clear that you are simply sharing your personal perspective. In my own experience, it has become clear that unsolicited advice is hardly ever welcome, so make sure that any constructive feedback is requested before sharing it!.

Believe in Others

Believing in potential is one of the foundations of the 'coaching way of being'. Seminal research referenced earlier demonstrated how teachers' positive expectations could determine increases in pupils' IQ scores (Rosenthal and Jacobson, 1966). Called the 'self-fulfilling prophecy', Rosenthal and Jacobson showed that holding high expectations of others can lead to enhanced performance. There are many ways of doing this. For example, being enthusiastic about other people's plans suggests that you believe that they will become a reality. In certain circumstances, this can be stated explicitly: 'I think you'll be brilliant' or 'I can see you being successful at that'. Believing in the potential of others will lead to more patience as people find their own solutions.

Encourage Others to Identify Meaningful Goals

The pursuit of meaningful goals can lead to longer-lasting feelings of subjective wellbeing than achieving goals that are less meaningful (Boniwell and Tunariu, 2019). Sometimes, asking a person about their intention can encourage reflection about meaningful goals. For this reason, it can be helpful to ask people to reflect on their goals, encouraging them to articulate what they are trying to achieve.

When you adopt a coaching approach, you will have a more positive impact on those around you. To wrap up this chapter, let us return to an activity that you completed at the very beginning of this book.

Reflect on Your Practice 13.2

Noticing What Has Changed

In Chapter 2, I asked you to assess your level of confidence about coaching. It would be helpful if you did this again, without referring to the earlier activity. Take a moment to reflect on your current levels of confidence about coaching and make some notes in your learning journal.

At this moment, how confident are you about your ability to coach? Draw a line with a '1' on one end and a '10' on the other. On this scale, select a number that represents your current level of confidence. Below the line, write down some of your thoughts about why you selected that number. For example, if you picked '8', what makes it '8' and not '1'?

Now look back at the earlier activity. Do you remember what you scored yourself initially? How has this changed?

What the Professional Associations Say 13.1

'A-Ha!' Moments

All the professional associations recognise the importance of supporting clients to gain new insights and perspectives so that they can make progress. The ICF highlight the importance of **evoking awareness** and **facilitating client growth**. The EMCC advocate the **use of models and techniques** to **enable insight and learning**. The AC emphasises the role of coaches in **raising awareness and insight** for clients.

Conclusion

In this chapter, we have reflected on how we can increase the chances for our clients to experience 'A-ha!' moments. We also explored how we could adopt a coaching approach in other areas of our lives. Ultimately, the coaching way of being is highly transferable. Hopefully, you will find many ways and opportunities to use the coaching way of being in your interactions with others.

Part VI
Next Steps

14
Coaching in Context

This chapter explores the nuances and variations of coaching in different contexts and for varying purposes. In the early days of the coaching profession, it was assumed that the use of coaching would be consistent and similar across sectors and professions. Given the premise that coaches did not need to be experts in the client's professional field, this was an understandable assumption. This led to the view that any coach could coach any person. However, as the profession of coaching has matured, it has become clear that there are some variations between professional contexts.

In this chapter, you will have a chance to consider the implications of coaching in a range of professional contexts. After a broad overview of the topic, the use of coaching in education and health settings will be considered as examples of unique professional contexts. You will then have an opportunity to reflect on the different purposes of coaching. Traditional executive coaching focuses on behavioural change and performance improvement. The emerging subfield of Positive Psychology Coaching brings wellbeing into the heart of coaching conversations while there is increasing interest in coaching models that support clients to achieve greater balance and alignment. Let's start with reflecting on what this means for you.

A Question for You 14.1

What Is Your Context?

Please consider which professional contexts you will be coaching in.

Who are the clients that you would most like to work with?

Which professional contexts are most appealing to you?

Take a few moments to capture your thoughts in your learning journal.

Differences and Similarities

In *Coaching in Professional Contexts* (2016), I explored the application of coaching across various sectors. As an edited book, it included chapters on the use of coaching in financial services, local government, professional services, healthcare and education. Practising coaches in each of these sectors contributed chapters. The project brought to light that there *were* some differences across professional contexts ranging from levels of formality to the focus on performance (see Snapshot 14.1). This is important to consider when preparing to coach in various professional contexts. If you would like to get a better sense of what to expect, the best source of information will be people who already coach in the sector.

Snapshot 14.1

Differences across Professional Contexts

- Some organisations value and respect hierarchy more than others.
- Common topics of interest of clients vary across contexts.
- Some contexts prioritise measuring return on investment (ROI) more than others.
- The 'value' of coaching is assessed differently.
- Staff career paths and trajectories vary.
- The wellbeing of staff is given more attention in some contexts.
- The extent to which coaching is used to support performance management varies.

When we consider these differences, it becomes apparent that they are likely to have an impact on how coaching initiatives are designed and implemented. That is why it is important for you to be thinking in advance about the professional contexts in which you would like to work.

Those who maintain that coaching should be the same regardless of context will be pleased to note that *Coaching in Professional Contexts* also identified areas of consistency and similarity right across the professional contexts that were considered. These are also important for you to know (see Snapshot 14.2).

Snapshot 14.2

Similarities across Professional Contexts

- People want to work with coaches who understand them and their profession.
- Senior leaders prefer to be coached by external executive coaches.
- Middle leaders and other staff are often coached by internal coaches.
- There is broad agreement that coaches need relevant, high-quality training.
- There is a preference for accredited professional coaches.
- Most people recognise that there is no 'one-size-fits-all' approach to coaching.
- There is a continuing interest in the concept of 'coaching cultures'.

Evidently, there is some consistency across professional contexts. And yet, as we have discussed, there are subtle differences too. We will delve into two professional contexts (education and health) as examples of how adaptations and contextual understanding can be helpful.

Coaching in Education

There has been significant interest in the application of coaching in educational settings. Coaching in education varies from other contexts in that the driving motivation is better outcomes for learners (van Nieuwerburgh, 2012). For example, the Global Framework for Coaching in Education (van Nieuwerburgh et al., 2019; see Figure 14.1) identifies four areas in which coaching is being used: to support leaders; to support teachers; to support students; and to support parents. At the heart of the model is 'student success and wellbeing', making it explicit that the desired outcome of all coaching initiatives is greater success and wellbeing for students. It is worth noting that the success and wellbeing of all stakeholders is important in this framework. Many educators argue that the wellbeing of leaders, teachers and parents is *necessary* so that they are better able to support the wellbeing of students. The reason for highlighting *student* success and wellbeing is to remind practitioners of the ultimate purpose of coaching in education.

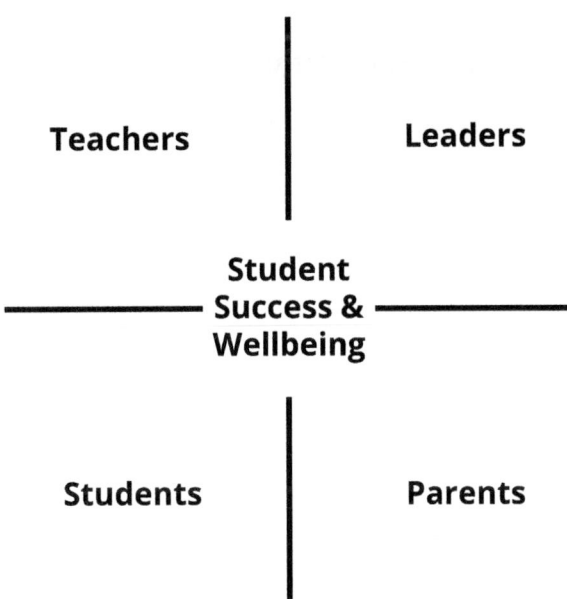

Figure 14.1 Global Framework for Coaching in Education

In educational settings, there are two broad approaches to coaching: the facilitative and the dialogical. The dialogical and facilitative approaches to coaching fall under the broader umbrella of 'partnering'. These two partnering approaches are important in education as an alternative to a directive way of interacting (which we call a 'telling' approach, see Figure 14.2). With the skills and understanding that you have developed in this book, you are well prepared to adopt either or both partnering approaches.

	Partnering	vs	Telling
Type of Interaction	Facilitative	Dialogical	Directive
Choice?	Yes	Yes	No
Sharing of Information?	No	Yes	Yes

Figure 14.2   Telling vs partnering approaches

The Facilitative Approach

The facilitative approach to coaching in education involves supporting people to achieve more of their potential by creating ideal environments for them to do their best thinking. When you are a facilitative coach, you partner with your client to support her to identify the best way forward for herself. You do not tell people what to do, and you do not share information or advise your clients. The starting point for facilitative coaching is that the client is resourceful and competent. In other words, the coach believes that the client has everything that she needs in order to make progress. From this perspective, the client is the expert – she knows herself better than anyone else, and she is the person who is in the situation.

The Dialogical Approach

Another way of partnering is to take the dialogical approach to coaching. Instructional Coaching is a methodology designed to support the professional learning and development of educators (Knight, 2022). As you can see in Figure 14.2, dialogical coaches do share information, but they do not tell the client what to do. For a coach to adopt a dialogical approach, she needs to have relevant professional experiences and knowledge. So, for example, there are Instructional Coaches for mathematics and for literacy. An Instructional Coach for literacy would be familiar with best practice and strategies for teaching literacy. She would still need to deploy her coaching skills, facilitate a conversational process and demonstrate a coaching way of being. One difference is that in the Options stage of the GROW model the coach would share strategies about teaching practices or other information that is relevant for her client. In this case, both the coach and the client are experts, and the coach's role is to share helpful and relevant information. Importantly, the coach does not advise the client or tell her what to do. A dialogical coach simply shares information and then defers to the client. It is the client who is the decision-maker.

Find Out More 14.1

Coaching in Education

If you would like to learn more about the facilitative and dialogical approaches to coaching in education, visit www.instructionalcoaching.com. There are many free resources available on the website.

Coaching for Health and Wellbeing

Interest in the use of coaching to support health and wellbeing has surged since the Covid pandemic. This has led to new coaching roles being created to support health and wellbeing. As with education, there are two ways of partnering to support the health and wellbeing of people in addition to the ever-present directive (or prescriptive) approach. Bearing in mind that this is still an emerging field of practice, I have tentatively separated out 'coaching for wellbeing' and 'coaching for health'.

Coaching for Wellbeing

Coaching for wellbeing is a conversational intervention designed to boost a person's subjective wellbeing and improve her overall satisfaction with life. Some examples of coaching for wellbeing are conversations about achieving greater work–life balance, wanting to be more engaged at work, finding ways to reduce stress, increasing moments of joy in one's life and trying to improve relationships to reduce feelings of loneliness. The facilitative approach is best suited for coaching for wellbeing. The role of the coach is to create an ideal environment in which the client can do her best thinking. It is the client who is the expert, and she generates all the ideas and identifies a positive way forward for herself. This means that the coach does not have to be an expert in any wellbeing strategies. The coach's main contribution is to create a safe, respectful environment for the client to engage in reflection and commit to positive action.

Health Coaching

Health coaching is different. It takes a dialogical approach because clients often need access to expert knowledge to improve their health. In other words, it would be unhelpful if a health coach who specialises in nutrition did *not* share information about food choices with her client. This is now a significant area of interest and there are increasing demands for coaches in health systems all over the world.

Snapshot 14.3

Ethical Practice and Health Coaching

This is an area where there is risk of harm to clients if coaches *without* a health background work with people who require the support of health professionals. For example, a facilitative coach should not try to work with a client to manage an eating disorder. Such clients should be referred to trained professionals or specialist health coaches.

Adopting a dialogical approach means that health coaches continue to respect and encourage the autonomy and independence of their clients whilst also sharing relevant evidence-based or research-informed strategies or practices. For this to be considered health *coaching*, the intervention must remain non-prescriptive. In other words, although the health coach shares information, she does not *tell* her client what to do. The purpose of health coaching is to allow the client to take personal responsibility and feel a sense of ownership of her own health goals.

Positive Health Coaching

Positive Health Coaching (PHC) is an example of a dialogical approach to improving the health of clients (van Nieuwerburgh and Knight, 2024). PHC combines three essential components – positive psychology, coaching psychology and lifestyle medicine. It aims to enhance an individual's overall health by leveraging strengths, focusing on what is working and encouraging healthy behaviours and positive lifestyle changes. Through PHC, patients and clients take personal responsibility for their own wellbeing and work to achieve holistic, self-selected health goals. PHC is a recognised intervention within health settings and research is under way to study its efficacy and impact (e.g. Loughnane et al., 2025).

The PHC conversational framework is designed to support clients to take personal responsibility for making informed choices and implementing actions in relation to their health and wellbeing (see Figure 14.3). The first step of the framework is 'discovery'. In this phase, the coach listens to the client talk about her current levels of health and wellbeing. During this part of the conversation, the coach will ask about the client's attitude to her own wellbeing. The purpose of this is to raise the client's awareness about the level of responsibility that she is willing to take. The second step is to ask about the client's 'desired outcome'. The coach is aiming to elicit the overarching aspiration of the client, rather than a narrow health-related goal. For example, 'I would like to lose weight' is a narrower health-related goal. 'I would like to feel healthy'; 'I want to have more energy for my family'; and 'I want to live healthier for longer' are examples of overarching aspirations. In these first two steps, the coach maintains a facilitative stance. In the 'pathways' stage, the coach invites the client to generate ideas about how she can move closer to her desired outcome. At this point, it is helpful for the coach to assess how well informed the client is about possible pathways. This will clarify if the client requires further support and guidance from an appropriate specialist. Once the client has shared her ideas, the coach can add to the suggested pathways by sharing strategies, practical ideas and research-informed interventions that might be helpful to the client. The client then evaluates the pathways that have been put forward (including those identified by herself) and selects the one she believes will be most appropriate. Once the client has selected a pathway, the coach and client work together to consider how it would play out in the client's specific context. Together, they discuss whether it would be necessary to make some adaptations to the selected pathway to increase the chances of success. In the final phase

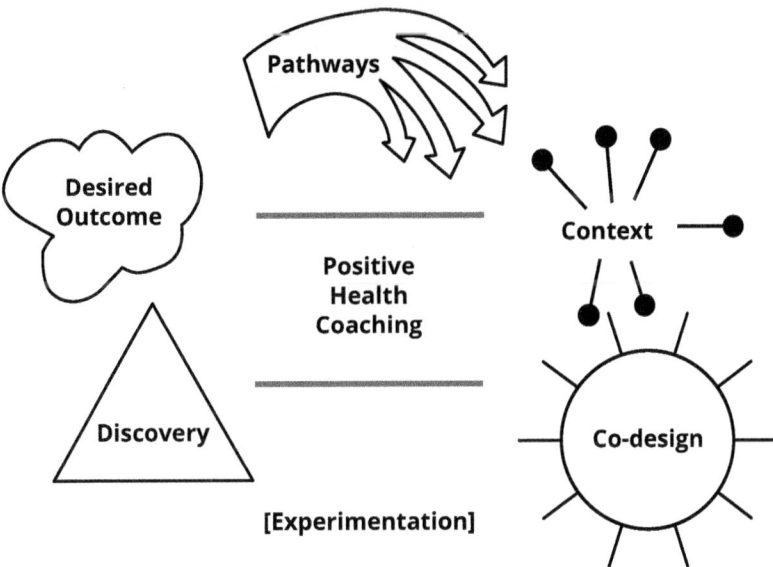

Figure 14.3 Positive Health Coaching framework

of the conversation, the coach and client co-design an experiment that the client is willing to put into practice after the session. The word 'experiment' emphasises that the client will be trying out something new to see how it works. The experiment may also include identifying barriers and facilitators to change—and will increase the client's awareness of her own levels of readiness and intrinsic motivation. If it moves the client closer to her desired outcome, then the positive health coach can support the client in future sessions to embed the practice. If it has not worked as planned, the positive health coach will work with the client to consider what learning she can take from the experiment. This learning will inform further coaching conversations.

Find Out More 14.2

Positive Health Coaching

To find out more about the field of positive health and the role of coaching to support health and wellbeing, visit the website of the Centre for Positive Health Sciences of RCSI University of Medicine and Health Sciences: www.rcsi.com/dublin/about/faculty-of-medicine-and-health-sciences/centre-for-positive-health-sciences

---

The Different Purposes of Coaching

We will now turn our attention to the different purposes of coaching. Most traditional approaches to coaching are explicitly about changing behaviours, usually with the aim of getting people to achieve more, do better or become more efficient. Below, we will explore the relationship between performance and wellbeing and the idea that sometimes, coaching can be used to support people to do *less*.

A Question for You 14.2

What Has Drawn You to Coaching?

In your mind, what is the primary purpose of coaching?

What do you want most for your clients?

Take a few moments to capture your reflections in your learning journal.

Positive Psychology Coaching

Positive psychology coaching (PPC) has already been mentioned in Chapter 9. It stands out due to its dual focus on success and wellbeing. Unlike traditional executive coaching, which aims to enhance performance or drive behavioural change, PPC integrates well-being into every conversation. This idea is typically introduced during the contracting phase where the coach expresses a commitment to helping the client achieve meaningful goals while also considering the client's own wellbeing and the wellbeing of those around her.

PPC has gained popularity due its positive attitude towards sustainable success. Although the coaching skills, conversational framework and coaching way of being are the same as those discussed earlier in this book, the distinct emphasis on fostering wellbeing is what sets it apart. This unique focus has made PPC an invaluable tool for personal and professional development in the increasingly busy world we live in.

Coaching for Alignment

The original purpose of coaching was to enhance performance. In fact, the focus on performance has been a consistent theme throughout the professional history of executive coaching. Recently, however, the narrow focus on performance has been called into question. Many people are realising that there are times when it is more important to support people achieve greater balance in their lives. In these cases, a framework such as the Coaching for Alignment model (van Nieuwerburgh and Allaho, 2020) may be helpful. Coaching for Alignment aims to support clients to become more aligned with their values and purpose. Another aspect of this relates to aligning a person's desires and wishes with their everyday behaviours and interactions.

A Question for You 14.3

How Aligned Do You Feel?

Take a moment to reflect on how your everyday behaviours and interactions are aligned to your own personal values. Are there times in your life when you have felt more aligned or less aligned than now? Take a moment to capture these thoughts in your learning journal.

Coaching for Alignment (see Figure 14.4) is distinct from traditional forms of coaching as it focuses on achieving balance and alignment rather than pushing for increased performance or greater productivity. It helps clients align their personal goals with their values, principles and the ecosystem around them. The process begins with the 'discovery' phase where the coach and client explore current successes and strengths. This is followed by the 'intention' phase which focuses on a client's positive intentions rather than specific targets. Next, the 'pathways' phase explores various ways to achieve these intentions. The 'alignment wheel' then ensures that these pathways align with a client's important relationships, values and ecosystem. Finally, the 'effort' phase identifies the necessary actions to progress along the client's chosen pathway. This framework supports clients to find balance and alignment in their lives, making it ideal for those seeking deeper fulfilment in their personal and professional lives. This approach ultimately aims for harmonious alignment of a person's work relationships and values, setting it apart from performance-centric coaching models.

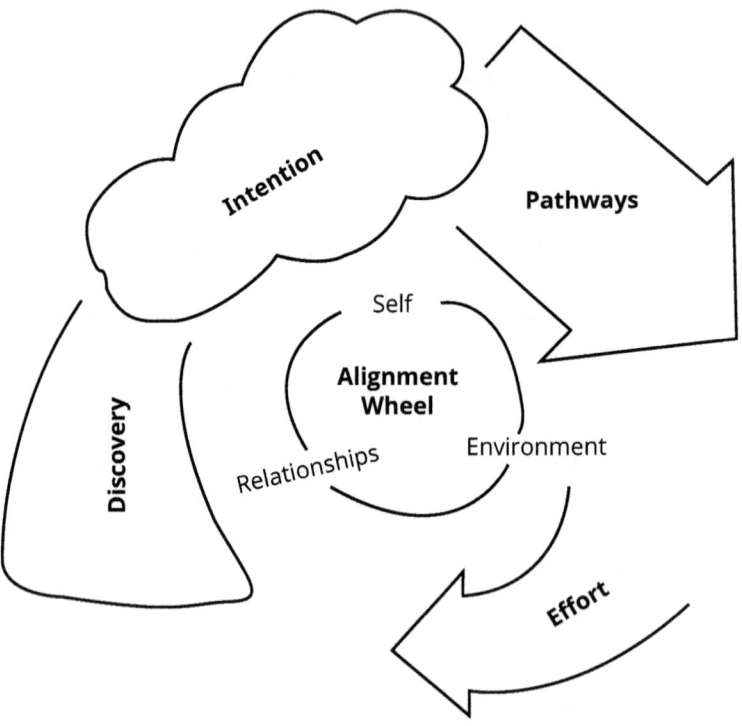

Figure 14.4   Coaching for Alignment model

— What the Professional Associations Say 14.1 —

Professional Contexts

All the professional associations recognise that an organisation's environment can influence coaching outcomes. While agreeing that the foundational coaching skills presented in this book are universal, the ICF, EMCC and AC would propose that coaches should adapt their approach to suit their professional environments. For the ICF, part of the competency of **establishing and maintaining agreements** includes partnering with relevant stakeholders. The EMCC reference the importance of considering organisational objectives in their competency of **managing the contract**. The AC has additional competencies for executive coaches that include **working within the organisational context** and **working in partnership with the organisation**.

Conclusion

In this chapter, we have considered how the application of coaching may vary depending on the professional context or purpose of coaching. However, the foundational aspects remain the same. Effective coaches should be competent in coaching skills; they must be comfortable facilitating a conversational framework; and they need to embrace a coaching way of being. These are the things that are at the heart of every coaching interaction, regardless of context or situation.

15
Reflecting on Practice

As we reach the final chapter of this book, you should be feeling more confident about your ability to coach. I hope that the notion of 'becoming' a coach rather than learning *how* to coach is resonating with you. Together, we have considered the skills of coaching, some conversational frameworks, activities and tools that you can integrate into your practice, a 'coaching way of being' and the various contexts and purposes of coaching. In this chapter, we return to something that has been implicit throughout the book: the need to be ethical and operate with integrity as a coach.

If you embrace what you have learned so far and choose to become a coach, you will, at times, be faced with 'ethical dilemmas' during your coaching conversations. We will start by discussing 'ethics' before outlining how we can prepare to coach with ethics and integrity. The chapter will conclude by proposing ways of developing and maintaining your professional coaching practice.

Ethics

What are 'ethics'? The Oxford Dictionary (www.oxforddictionaries.com) defines 'ethics' as 'moral principles that govern a person's behaviour or the conducting of an activity'. For our purposes, we can understand ethics as a set of principles and values that guide and underpin coaching practice. Words such as 'good', 'bad', 'right' and 'wrong' are used when discussing ethics. Our focus here is on making the 'right' decisions during coaching conversations. As we will discover together, this is not as straightforward as we might wish. The decision relating to the 'right' thing to do in a coaching conversation is dependent on numerous factors and will vary between coaches, situations and contexts.

Let us begin by considering some foundational ethical principles. In a survey of the codes of ethics of a range of related professions, Brennan and Wildflower (2010) noted that there was broad consistency:

1 Do not cause harm to others.
2 Act in ways that promote the welfare of others.
3 Know the limits of your competence and work within these.
4 Respect the interests of the client.
5 Respect the law.

What Is the Situation with Ethical Codes of Conduct for Coaches?

A Question for You 15.1

Which Code of Ethics?

Go online and download the Global Code of Ethics and the ICF's Code of Ethics. Scan through each of the documents and decide which one you will be adopting. Once you have chosen your preferred code of ethics, read through each of the commitments, ensuring that you are willing and able to adhere to them.

If you plan to coach professionally, I recommend that you select a professional association and apply to become a member. While the content in this book is aligned with the competencies of the ICF, the EMCC and the AC, there are other professional associations that you may wish to consider. Select the best one for you based on which will provide the most support for you in your chosen location. First, being a member of such an association will build your professional credibility. Second, these associations can be useful sources of information and networking opportunities. Third, they can provide you with links to coaching supervisors, group supervision sessions, podcasts, webinars, training opportunities and other professional services for coaches. Most importantly, you will become a member of a supportive community of like-minded professionals.

Ethical Moments of Choice

As a coach, you will inevitably encounter 'ethical moments of choice' as part of your practice. In the coaching profession, these are usually referred to as 'ethical dilemmas' but this phrase can be limiting. The word 'dilemma' suggests that these moments are always negative and implies that there may be only two ways to engage with them. By determining something to be an 'ethical dilemma', we are approaching a critically important moment in a coaching conversation from a negative position. I prefer to use the phrase 'moment of choice', which I have adopted from Allard de Jong (2010). We shall use the term 'ethical moments of choice' to refer to instances when a coach is faced with an ethical question and must decide how to respond to it.

Stories from Practice 15.1

Ethical Moments of Choice

You may be curious about the kind of 'ethical moments of choice' that may arise during coaching conversations. A few genuine examples taken from supervisory conversations are listed below.

- *The client seeks to exceed the agreed number of coaching sessions*: The initial agreement between the coach and the client was for five sessions. In the last 15 minutes of the fifth session, the client requests 'some more coaching' because she feels that there is still some 'unfinished business'.
- *The coach is offered additional work in a client's organisation*: The initial agreement between the coach and the client was for six coaching sessions to support the executive's leadership style. The client is so impressed with the coach that she now offers additional work delivering in-house training to staff in her organisation.
- *The coach develops a physical attraction to the client*: The coaching sessions are progressing well. Initially the coach notices that she looks forward to meeting the client more than normal. At one point during a coaching conversation, she realises that her feelings towards the client are affected by a physical attraction.
- *The client claims that she is being bullied*: The client had requested coaching to discuss her relationship with colleagues at work. As this issue is explored, the client uses the word 'bullying' to describe how she is treated by a senior manager in the organisation.
- *The coach cannot accept the moral position of the client*: The coaching topic is about returning to work after maternity leave. During the third coaching session, the client makes a decision related to family planning that the coach cannot accept from a religious point of view.
- *The client contravenes the principle of equal opportunity*: The coach has been employed to support the client to implement a restructuring programme. During a coaching conversation, the client discloses that she will ignore her organisation's recruitment process when offering a position to a colleague whose job is at risk.

Although it is easier to read about an ethical moment of choice here than engage with it during a coaching conversation, I hope that you found some of these scenarios challenging. Each is an ethical moment of choice for the coach. Here, you are reading about ethical moments of choice without any pressure to respond to them straight away. As a reader, you have time to think about these carefully and none of your principles or values is being directly tested. In coaching conversations, we do not have the luxury of this kind of thinking time as the ethical moments of choice are usually unexpected. As a coach, you would need to make an in-the-moment decision about how to respond. The section below proposes how to prepare for these ethical moments of choice.

1 Refer Back to Your Coaching Contract

In Chapter 7, the necessity of coaching contracts was emphasised. Contracting should precede any coaching assignment. At a minimum, a coaching contract must include a shared understanding of what coaching entails, an explicit reference to the importance of confidentiality (including any exceptions), a mention of what will happen if the client divulges any information about illegal activity and what action will be taken if the coach feels that the discussion is moving towards an area which is outside her area of competence. Good practice would suggest that a conversation about the contract should be comprehensive before the first session and then revisited briefly at the start of every coaching conversation. When faced with an ethical moment of choice, the first point of reflection should be 'What have we agreed in the coaching contract that relates to this situation?'. The necessity of a coaching contract cannot be over-emphasised. It forms the backbone of a shared understanding of the coaching relationship and is critically important when ethical moments of choice are encountered.

2 Identify a Code of Ethics

As I have noted above, it is essential to adopt a code of ethics. This is an important element of being prepared for ethical moments of choice. A necessary point of reflection is 'What does my code of ethics tell me about this situation?'. It is good practice to keep a copy of the code of ethics with you. Some coaches share their code of ethics with their clients.

3 Reflect on Your Own Principles

Alongside the code of ethics, coaches should reflect on their own deeply held principles and values. These are personal to you. Each of us has values and a set of principles but few of us spend much time reviewing these. Doing so provides us with a moral compass that can guide us through our lives. When coaching, our client's principles and values are also important. There may sometimes be a tension between the client's values and yours. For this reason, decisions about ethical moments of choice should be taken after considering different elements (contract, code of ethics, our own principles and previous experiences).

A Question for You 15.2

What Are Your Deeply Held Beliefs?

Allocate about 30 minutes for this activity. In your learning journal, write down your deeply held beliefs and principles about what is right and what is wrong. This is a valuable activity. It is possible that some of the principles and values contradict one another. If this is the case, it is OK. However, I would invite you to regard this list as tentative. Once completed, this page of 'principles and values' can be used when reflecting on your coaching practice or during supervisory conversations.

4 Undertake Reflective Practice

As suggested throughout this book, coaches develop their craft through practice and reflection. Based on the premise that we learn during every coaching session, it makes sense to capture this learning and think about how we can use any new information to enhance our coaching practice. There are essentially two practical ways of ensuring effective reflective practice: keeping a coaching journal and undertaking regular supervisory conversations.

Snapshot 15.1

Responding to Ethical Moments of Choice

1   Refer back to the *coaching contract*. What has been agreed with the client? Is there any reference to this situation?
2   Think about the *code of ethics* that you have adopted. What guidance can the code of ethics provide in this instance?
3   Consider your own deeply held *principles and values*. What should you do, based on your principles?
4   Take advantage of your *reflective practice*. Have you been in this type of situation before? How was this managed previously?

Supervisory Conversations

There is currently much discussion about the need for coaching supervision. According to the leading writers in this field (Hawkins and Smith, 2013), supervision is 'the process by which a coach, with the help of a supervisor, can attend to understanding better both the client system and themselves as part of the client–coach system, and, by so doing, transform their work and develop their craft' (p. 20). According to Hawkins and Smith, coaching supervision has three clear functions:

- *Developmental*: To develop the skills, understanding and capacities of the coach.
- *Resourcing*: To attend to the emotions and wellbeing of the coach.
- *Qualitative*: To ensure the quality of the coaching and adherence to ethical standards.

The last point is what makes coaching supervision different from peer coaching. Coaching supervision has an evaluative, 'quality assurance' function, and the supervisor has a responsibility to the profession of coaching. Coaching supervisors tend to be experienced coaches or counsellors.

There is no doubt that coaches benefit from effective reflective practice with more experienced colleagues as they continue to develop their practice. Different ways of accessing coaching supervision are listed below.

- *One-to-one supervision with a coach supervisor*: This is the most traditional way of accessing coaching supervision. The coach and her supervisor meet regularly to talk about the coach's practice. Supervision sessions can last between one and two hours. The conversation focuses on the coach and her experiences, successes and challenges when coaching. This method is usually the most costly form of coaching supervision. Increasingly, telephone or online coaching supervision is available and may be a cost-effective alternative.
- *Group supervision facilitated by a coach supervisor*: This approach is growing in popularity within the field of coaching. In this way of working, a small number coaches attend regular supervision sessions with a coach supervisor. These sessions are of varying length, depending on the number of coaches involved. The focus of the conversation remains on the experiences, success and challenges of the participating coaches (supervisees). Not every coach will necessarily have the chance to share her own experiences at every session. However, there are opportunities for learning from one another's experiences. Group supervision is usually more cost-effective than one-to-one supervision.
- *Facilitated peer supervision in groups*: Some groups of coaches have developed internally managed peer supervision groups. In this format, every member of the group adopts the position of peer supervisor. One member of the group takes the role of facilitator and manages the coaching supervision process so that everyone involved has a chance to support the coach (supervisee) as she shares her experiences with the group. Again, participants can support one another and learn from other coaches' experiences. All members of the facilitated peer supervision group would require an understanding of the coaching supervision process.
- *Supervisory conversations with an experienced coach*: Less formal, but still helpful, are agreed supervisory conversations organised on an ad hoc basis with an experienced coach. As needed, the coach will contact the more experienced coach if there are coaching-related topics that she would like to discuss.
- *Peer supervision*: Some coaches have arranged peer supervision in pairs, working with a coach with whom they have a good relationship. Peer supervision can take place regularly, with coaches taking turns to bring topics to the conversation or splitting the time equally so that both parties can receive supervisory support. Both coaches require some training in coaching supervision.

Snapshot 15.2

What Level of Coaching Supervision Is Required?

To some extent, this is a personal decision. Every coach must create structured opportunities to reflect on her practice. Table 15.1 is only a recommendation. Different approaches will suit different coaches.

Table 15.1 Suggested ways of accessing supervision

Role	Supervisory arrangements
People who coach professionally and frequently	One-to-one supervision with a coach supervisor
People who coach professionally but infrequently	One-to-one supervision with a coach supervisor or group supervision facilitated by a coach supervisor
People learning how to coach	Group supervision facilitated by a coach supervisor or facilitated peer supervision in groups
People working in organisations who coach others as a secondary role	Group supervision facilitated by a coach supervisor or facilitated peer supervision in groups
People who manage others using a 'coaching approach'	Peer supervision if needed
People with significant experience of coaching who coach infrequently	Supervision arrangements may include any of the suggested options

---

Snapshot 15.3

Topics for Supervisory Conversations

Good practice would suggest that it is helpful for coaches to take at least 15 minutes of reflection time prior to a coaching session and a similar amount of time at the end of a coaching session. Supervision exists to support the coach to explore or resolve any questions, concerns or doubts that emerge from coaching. So, if there is something niggling away at your mind following a coaching session, this is the best indication that this topic should be taken to a supervisory conversation. Resolving this type of concern in a timely way is an important part of the coach's wellbeing and represents good professional practice.

A Question for You 15.3

How Will You Ensure that You Are an Ethical Coach?

Write at least one paragraph in your learning journal explaining how you will ensure that you practise ethically and professionally as a coach.

Find Out More 15.1

Effective Reflective Practice

For a practical and easily-implementable approach to reflective practice, consult *Your Essential Guide to Effective Reflective Practice*, written by myself and David Love (2025). We wrote this book specifically to demystify the process and propose a way of capturing your learning and demonstrating your engagement with reflective practice.

Developing Ethical Maturity

Ethical maturity is developed through reflective practice and coaching experience. It has been proposed that ethical maturity can be 'enhanced by engaging in regular supervision in which hypothetical testing of dilemmas can be utilised, by recurrent ethical thinking, engaging in activities associated with coach training and pursuing wider continual professional development' (Duffy and Passmore, 2010). Based on the discussion in this chapter, I would like to propose the virtuous cycle of ethical maturity. Following this cycle will provide a structured process for developing your ethical maturity as a coach.

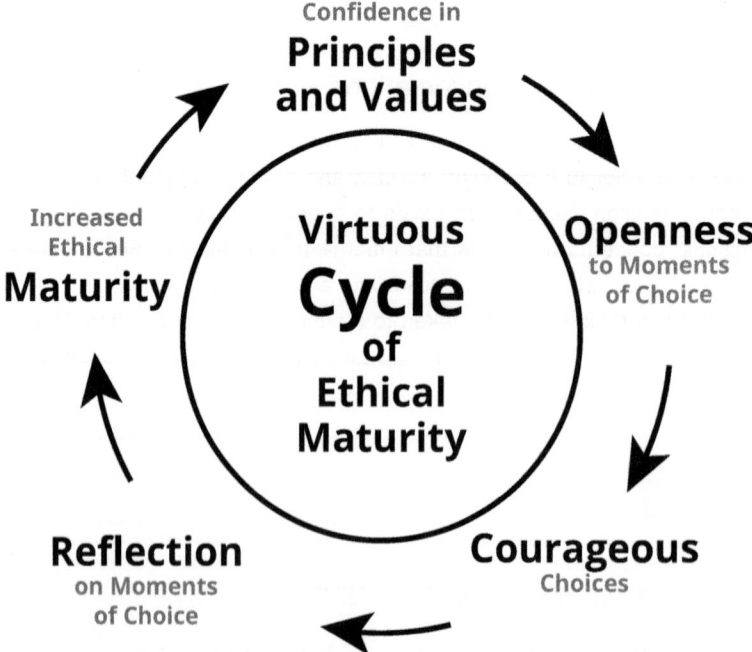

Figure 15.1 Virtuous cycle of ethical maturity

Reflect on the principles and values that you noted in your learning journal earlier in this chapter. Building your confidence in these (alongside effective contracting and adherence to an ethical code) will allow you to approach ethical moments of choice with a more positive and open attitude. If you respond with such an attitude, you are likely to make courageous choices. In other words, you will not avoid or ignore the ethical moment of choice. You will be able to see it as a critical moment in the coaching conversation and address it in a way that respects the client and is ethically justifiable. Your courageous choices should be reflected upon and discussed during supervision. This will allow you (and others) to celebrate and learn from ethical moments of choice and therefore develop your ethical maturity. Increased ethical maturity will build confidence in your principles and values. And the virtuous cycle continues!

Continuing Professional Development of Coaches

As we approach the end of this part of your learning journey, you will need to start considering how to continue to develop yourself professionally. Due to the current interest in coaching, there are many coach training providers. These range from very short courses provided by commercial training organisations, in-house coach training programmes delivered within large corporations, to postgraduate coaching programmes at universities.

It is now possible to study for Master's degrees in coaching at university and even to complete professional doctorates or PhDs on the topic. Each coach is best placed to identify what will be most helpful for her own professional development. For some, a certificate or university qualification will provide credibility and an endorsement of their skills. Others will be interested in broadening their 'toolkit' of approaches and techniques by attending short courses and seminars on specialist topics such as cognitive-behavioural therapy, neuroscience, mindfulness or the use of psychometrics.

Find Out More 15.2

Advanced Practice

Advanced Coaching Practice: Inspiring Change in Others, written by myself and my good colleague David Love (2019), will be a good follow-up text once you have had some experience of coaching. The book supports readers to become more comfortable with the 'tensions' of coaching practice.

┌─────────────── **What the Professional Associations Say 15.1** ───────────────┐

Coaching Supervision and Ethics

Recognising that coaches, clients and the profession of coaching all benefit from coaches engaging in reflective practice, the three professional associations (ICF, EMCC and AC) are unanimous in promoting and recommending coaching supervision. The ICF 'supports Coaching Supervision for professional coach practitioners as part of their portfolio of continuing professional development (CPD) activities designed to keep them fit for purpose'. According to the EMCC, 'the purpose of supervision is to enhance the wellbeing, and develop the practice of coaches … of all levels of experience. Supervision is considered a powerful vehicle for deep learning: its benefits extend beyond the supervisee and include their clients and sponsoring organisations.' The AC expects its coaches to 'regularly seek consultative support, typically from a qualified and experienced coaching supervisor'.

The first ICF competency is **demonstrating ethical practice**, while the EMCC expects coaches to **commit to self-development** and **evaluation** of the effectiveness of their practice. The AC also has **meeting ethical, legal and professional guidelines** as their first competency and calls for coaches to **undertake continuous coach development**.

└──┘

Conclusion

I hope that this text has provided you with a foundation for your practice and a burning curiosity about human beings and a desire to continually develop as a coach. If you have not done so already, you may want to find a coach for yourself. If you believe that coaching is beneficial and potentially life-changing, you should have a coach too!

┌─────────────────── **A Question for You 15.4** ───────────────────┐

What Is the Most Important Thing You Have Learned?

Now that you have read through the entire book, it is a good time to reflect on your learning journey so far. Take a moment to look through your learning journal. If you were to select one piece of personal learning that you would highlight above any other, what would it be? Capture it in a sentence and jot it down under the heading 'most important thing I have learned'.

└──┘

If you are still a little bit anxious about coaching others, this is wonderful news. This anxiety is something that should be kept alive and part of your coaching practice. Being anxious about a coaching session is an indication that you want to get it right for your client. A reasonable level of anxiety also allows us to remain humble, interested and present during coaching conversations. The challenge is to get just the right level of anxiety! And the best way to get the balance right is to coach, coach and coach.

As you become more experienced, you will notice that you are starting to automatically and naturally integrate the three elements of coaching. The skills will start to feel natural, the conversational framework will dissolve into the background and your 'coaching way of being' will infuse and enhance your relationships. As we close off our relationship (as author and reader), I would like to leave you with a drawing that I created for you (see Figure 15.2). My intention was to convey the beauty, complexity and humanity of the coaching way of being. Once you have become the confident and effective coach that you would like to be, you will be able to identify your own personalised path towards further development, learning and fulfilment. Finally, I am grateful to you for being such a committed learner. The world needs coaches like you. Thank you for allowing me to accompany you on your journey for a short while.

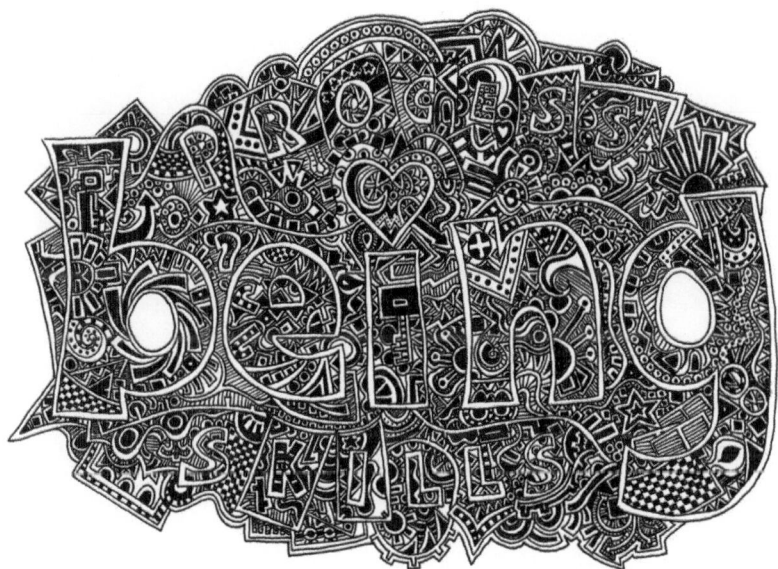

Figure 15.2 Author's drawing of the 'coaching way of being'

References

Alexander, G. (2010) 'Behavioural coaching – the GROW model', in J. Passmore (ed.), *Excellence in Coaching: The Industry Guide*, 2nd edn. London: Kogan Page. pp. 83–93.

Alexander, G. and Renshaw, B. (2005) *Supercoaching: The Missing Ingredient for High Performance*. London: Random House.

Banyard, P., Dillon, G., Norman, C. and Winder, B. (eds) (2019) *Essential Psychology*, 3rd edn. London: Sage.

Biswas-Diener, R. (2010) *Practicing Positive Psychology Coaching: Assessment, Activities, and Strategies for Success*. Hoboken, NJ: Wiley.

Boniwell, I. (2012) *Positive Psychology in a Nutshell: The Science of Happiness*, 3rd edn. Maidenhead: Open University Press.

Boniwell, I. and Tunariu, A. (2019) *Positive Psychology: Theory, Research and Applications*, 2nd edn. London: Open University Press.

Bossons, P., Riddell, P. and Sartain, D. (2015) *The Neuroscience of Leadership Coaching: Why the Tools and Techniques of Leadership Coaching Work*. London: Bloomsbury.

Brann, A. (2017) *Neuroscience for Coaches: How to Use the Latest Insights for the Benefit of Your Clients*, 2nd edn. London: Kogan Page.

Brennan, D. and Wildflower, L. (2010) 'Ethics in coaching', in E. Cox, T. Bachkirova and D. Clutterbuck (eds), *The Complete Handbook of Coaching*. London: Sage. pp. 369–80.

Bresser, F. and Wilson, C. (2010) 'What is coaching?', in J. Passmore (ed.), *Excellence in Coaching: The Industry Guide*, 2nd edn. London: Kogan Page. pp. 9–26.

Brock, V.G. (2012) *Sourcebook of Coaching History*. Self-published.

Brown, P. and Brown, V. (2012) *Neuropsychology for Coaches: Understanding the Basics*. Maidenhead: Open University Press.

Buzan, T. (2002) *How to Mind Map*. London: Thorsons.

Campbell, J. (2016) 'Framework for Practitioners 2: The GROWTH Model', in C. van Nieuwerburgh (ed.), *Coaching in Professional Contexts*. London: Sage. pp. 235–9.

Cox, E., Bachkirova, T. and Clutterbuck, D. (eds) (2023) *The Complete Handbook of Coaching*, 2nd edn. London: Sage.

Deci, E.L. and Ryan, R.M. (1985) *Intrinsic Motivation and Self-Determination in Human Behaviour*. New York: Plenum.

Deci, E.L. and Ryan, R.M. (eds) (2002) *Handbook of Self-Determination Research*. Rochester, NY: University of Rochester Press.

de Haan, E. (2008a) 'I struggle and emerge: critical moments of experienced coaches', *Consulting Psychology Journal: Practice and Research*, 60 (1): 106–31.

de Haan, E. (2008b) *Relational Coaching: Journeys towards Mastering One-to-One Learning*. Chichester: Wiley.

de Haan, E., Bertie, C., Day, A. and Sills, C. (2010) 'Critical moments of clients and coaches: a direct-comparison study', *International Coaching Psychology Review*, 5 (2): 109–28.

de Jong, A. (2010) 'Coaching ethics: integrity in the moment of choice', in J. Passmore (ed.), *Excellence in Coaching: The Industry Guide*, 2nd edn. London: Kogan Page. pp. 204–14.

de Shazer, S. and Berg, I.K. (1995) 'The brief therapy tradition', in J. Weakland and W. Ray (eds), *Propagations: Thirty Years of Influence from the Mental Research Institute*. Binghamton, NY: Haworth Press. pp. 249–52.

Dickson, J. (2011) *Humilitas: A Lost Key to Life, Love, and Leadership*. Grand Rapids, MI: Zondervan.

Downey, M. (2003) *Effective Coaching: Lessons from the Coach's Coach*, 2nd edn. London: Texere.

Duffy, M. and Passmore, J. (2010) 'Ethics in coaching: an ethical decision making framework for coaching psychologists', *International Coaching Psychology Review*, 5 (2): 140–51.

Fouracres, A. and van Nieuwerburgh, C. (2020) 'The lived experience of self-identifying character strengths through coaching: an interpretative phenomenological analysis', *International Journal of Evidence Based Coaching and Mentoring*, 18 (1): 43–56.

Gallwey, W.T. (1974) *The Inner Game of Tennis*. New York: Random House.

Garvey, R., Stokes, P. and Megginson, D. (2009) *Coaching and Mentoring: Theory and Practice*. London: Sage.

Gash, J. (2017) *Coaching Creativity: Transforming Your Practice*. Abingdon: Routledge.

Goleman, D. (1996) *Emotional Intelligence: Why It Matters More than IQ*. New York: Bantam.

Grant, A.M. (2003) 'The impact of life coaching on goal attainment, metacognition, and mental health', *Social Behavior and Personality*, 31 (3): 253–64.

Grant, A.M. (2012) 'An integrated model of goal-focused coaching: an evidence-based framework for teaching and practice', *International Coaching Psychology Review*, 7 (2): 146–65.

Grencavage, L. and Norcross, J. (1990) 'Where are the commonalities among the therapeutic common factors?', *Professional Psychology: Research and Practice*, 21 (5): 372–8.

Hall, L. (2013) *Mindful Coaching: How Mindfulness Can Transform Coaching Practice*. London: Kogan Page.

Hawkins, P. and Smith, N. (2013) *Coaching, Mentoring and Organizational Consultancy: Supervision, Skills and Development*, 2nd edn. London: McGraw–Hill.

Iyengar, S. (2010) *The Art of Choosing*. New York: Twelve Books.

Jackson, P. and McKergow, M. (2024) *The Solutions Focus: Transforming Change for Coaches, Leaders and Consultants*, 3rd edn. London: Nicholas Brealey.

Kahneman, D. (2011) *Thinking Fast and Slow*. New York: Farrar, Straus & Giroux.

Kashdan, T. (2010) *Curious? Discover the Missing Ingredient to a Fulfilling Life*. New York: Harper.

Kauffman, C. (2006) 'Positive psychology: the science at the heart of coaching', in D.R. Stober and A.M. Grant (eds), *Evidence Based Coaching Handbook: Putting Best Practices to Work for Your Clients*. Hoboken, NJ: John Wiley. pp. 219–53.

Kline, N. (1999) *Time to Think: Listening to Ignite the Human Mind*. London: Cassell.

Knight, J. (2011) *Unmistakable Impact: A Partnership Approach for Dramatically Improving Instruction*. Thousand Oaks, CA: Corwin.

Knight, J. (2022) *The Definitive Guide to Instructional Coaching: Seven Factors for Success*. Alexandria, VA: ACSD.

Kounios, J. and Beeman, M. (2016) *The Eureka Factor: Aha Moments, Creative Insight, and the Brain*. London: Windmill.

Locke, E.A. (1996) 'Motivation through conscious goal setting', *Applied and Preventative Psychology*, 5 (2): 117–24.

Locke, E.A. and Latham, G.P. (2002) 'Building a practically useful theory of goal setting and task motivation', *American Psychologist*, 57 (9): 705–17.

Loughnane, C., O'Donovan, R., Duggan, A. and Dunne, P. (2025) 'Learning through reflection: A team's reflection on a digital, text-based positive health coaching intervention for healthcare professionals', *International Journal of Evidence Based Coaching and Mentoring*, 23 (1): 371–383.

McKenna, D.D. and Davis, S.L. (2009) 'Hidden in plain sight: the active ingredients of executive coaching', *Industrial and Organizational Psychology*, 2 (3): 244–60.

Neenan, M. (2009) 'Using Socratic questioning in coaching', *Journal of Rational-Emotive and Cognitive-Behavior Therapy*, 27 (4): 249–64.

O'Connor, J. and Lages, A. (2019) *Coaching the Brain: Practical Applications of Neuroscience to Coaching*. London: Routledge.

Palmer, S. and Szymanska, K. (2007) 'Cognitive behavioural coaching: an integrative approach', in S. Palmer and A. Whybrow (eds), *Handbook of Coaching Psychology: A Guide for Practitioners*. London: Routledge. pp. 86–117.

Passmore, J. (2007) 'Behavioural coaching', in S. Palmer and A. Whybrow (eds), *Handbook of Coaching Psychology: A Guide for Practitioners*. London: Routledge. pp. 73–85.

Passmore, J. (ed.) (2010) *Excellence in Coaching: The Industry Guide*, 2nd edn. London: Kogan Page.

Passmore, J. (ed.) (2012) *Psychometrics in Coaching: Using Psychological and Psychometric Tools for Development*, 2nd edn. London: Kogan Page.

Pease, A. and Pease, B. (2017) *The Definitive Book of Body Language*. London: Orion.

Peltier, B. (2010) *The Psychology of Executive Coaching: Theory and Application*, 2nd edn. London: Routledge.

Peterson, C. (2006) *A Primer in Positive Psychology*. Oxford: Oxford University Press.

Rogers, C.R. (1957) 'The necessary and sufficient conditions of therapeutic personality change', *Journal of Consulting Psychology*, 21 (2): 95–103.

Rogers, C.R. (1980) *A Way of Being*. Boston, MA: Houghton Mifflin.

Rosenthal, R. and Jacobson, L. (1966) 'Teachers' expectancies: determinants of pupils' IQ gains', *Psychological Reports*, 19: 115–18.

Rosenthal, R. and Jacobson, L. (1968) *Pygmalion in the Classroom: Teacher Expectation and Pupils' Intellectual Development*. Norwalk, CT: Crown House.

Salovey, P. and Mayer, J. (1990) 'Emotional intelligence', *Imagination, Cognition, and Personality*, 9 (3): 185–211.

Schwartz, B. (2004) *The Paradox of Choice: Why More Is Less*. New York: Harper Perennial.

Thaler, R. and Sunstein, C. (2008) *Nudge: Improving Decisions about Health, Wealth, and Happiness*. New Haven, CT: Yale University Press.

van Nieuwerburgh, C. (ed.) (2012) *Coaching in Education: Getting Better Results for Students, Educators, and Parents*. London: Karnac.

van Nieuwerburgh, C. (ed.) (2016) *Coaching in Professional Contexts*. London: Sage.

van Nieuwerburgh, C. (2017) 'Interculturally-sensitive coaching', in T. Bachkirova, G. Spence and D. Drake (eds), *The SAGE Handbook of Coaching*. London: Sage. pp. 439–52.

van Nieuwerburgh, C. and Allaho, R. (2020) White Paper: Coaching for alignment: supporting people to live their values. https://coachonamotorcycle.com/wp-content/uploads/2025/02/Coaching-for-Alignment-White-Paper.pdf (accessed 28 February 2025).

van Nieuwerburgh, C. and Biswas-Diener, R. (2021) 'Positive psychology approaches to coaching', in J. Passmore (ed.), *The Coaches' Handbook: The Complete Practitioner Guide for Professional Coaches*. London: Routledge. pp. 314–21.

van Nieuwerburgh, C. and Biswas-Diener, R. (2025) *Radical Listening: The Art of True Connection*. Oakland, CA: Berrett Koehler.

van Nieuwerburgh, C. and Knight, J. (2024) 'Positive health coaching: adopting a dialogical approach to health and wellbeing', in J. Burke, I. Boniwell, B. Frates, L.S. Lianov and C.A. O'Boyle (eds), *Routledge International Handbook of Positive Health Sciences: Positive Psychology and Lifestyle Medicine Research, Theory and Practice*. London: Routledge. pp. 220–36.

van Nieuwerburgh, C., Knight, J. and Campbell, J. (2019) 'Coaching in education', in S. English, J.M. Sabatine and P. Brownell (eds), *Professional Coaching: Principles and Practice*. New York: Springer. pp. 411–26.

van Nieuwerburgh, C. and Love, D. (2019) *Advanced Coaching Practice: Inspiring Change in Others*. London: Sage.

van Nieuwerburgh, C. and Love, D. (2025) *Your Essential Guide to Effective Reflective Practice*. London: Sage.

van Zyl, L., Roll L., Stander M. and Richter, S. (2020) 'Positive psychological coaching definitions and models: a systematic literature review', *Frontiers in Psychiatry*, 11: 793.

Whitmore, J. (1992) *Coaching for Performance: A Practical Guide to Growing Your Own Skills*. London: Nicholas Brealey.

Whitmore, J. (2009) *Coaching for Performance: GROWing Human Potential and Purpose: The Principles and Practice of Coaching and Leadership*, 4th edn. London: Nicholas Brealey.

Wildflower, L. (2013) *The Hidden History of Coaching*. Maidenhead: Open University Press.

Willis, P. (2005) *EMCC Competency Research Project: Phase 2*. Watford: European Mentoring and Coaching Council.

Zimbardo, P. and Boyd, J. (1999) 'Putting time in perspective: a valid, reliable individual-difference metric', *The Journal of Personality and Social Psychology*, 77: 1271–88.

Index

Page numbers in *italics* refer to figures and tables.